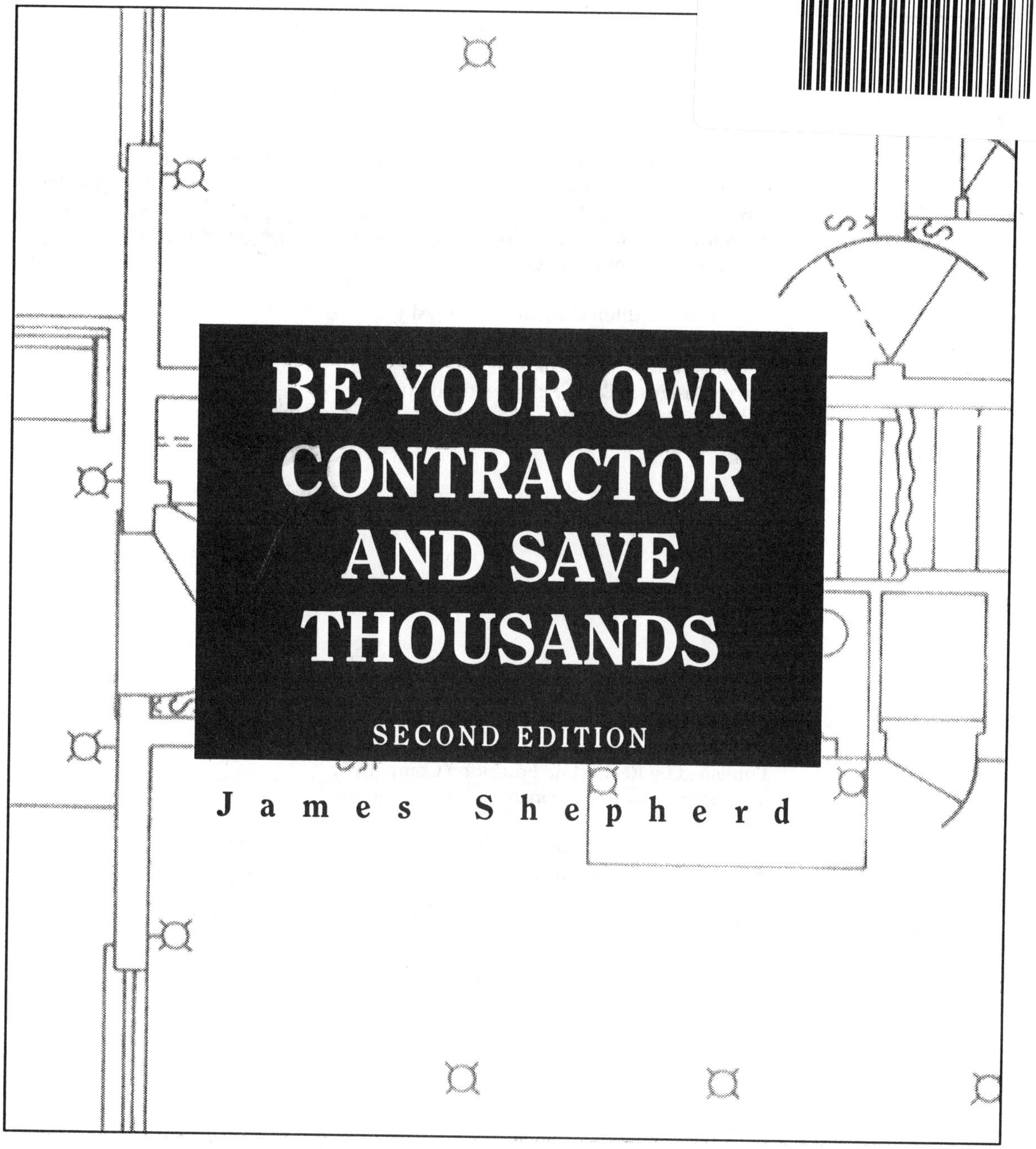

BE YOUR OWN CONTRACTOR AND SAVE THOUSANDS

SECOND EDITION

James Shepherd

This publication is designed to provide accurate and authoritative information in regard to the subject matter covered. It is sold with the understanding that the publisher is not engaged in rendering legal, accounting or other professional service. If legal advice or other expert assistance is required, the services of a competent professional person should be sought.

Acquisitions Editor: Christine E. Litavsky
Managing Editor: Jack Kiburz
Interior Design: Lucy Jenkins
Cover Design: S. Laird Jenkins Corporation

Published by Real Estate Education Company®,
a division of Dearborn Financial Publishing, Inc.®

Printed in the United States of America

98 10 9 8 7 6 5 4 3 2

Library of Congress Cataloging-in-Publication Data

Shepherd, James. M.
Be your own contractor and save thousands / James M. Shepherd.—
2nd ed.
p. cm.
Rev. ed. of: Be your own contractor! Chicago : Dearborn Financial, 1993.
Includes index.
ISBN 0-7931-1731-3 (paper)
1. House construction. 2. Contractors. I. Shepherd, James M.
Be your own contractor! II. Title.
TH4811.S47 1996
690'.837—dc20 95-50805
CIP

Real Estate Education Company books are available at special quantity discounts to use as premiums and sales promotions, or for use in corporate training programs. For more information, please call the Special Sales Manager at 800-621-9621, ext. 4384, or write to Dearborn Financial Publishing, Inc., 155 N. Wacker Drive, Chicago, IL 60606-1719.

Contents

Preface

Be Your Own Contractor and Save Thousands has been written to teach you how to manage the building of your home, save money and finish with a high-quality house.

By being your own general contractor you can save the money paid to the professional general contractor for his services. This service payment can consist of the professional general contractor marking up the cost for labor and material by about **20 percent.** Thus, if you take on the job of general contractor, a house bid at $50,000 from a general contractor could be built for about $40,000, a house bid at $100,000 could be built for $80,000 and so forth.

You can make sure your finished house will be of high quality by following the principles of selecting the best materials and equipment within the limits of your pocketbook and by supervising installation according to the advice contained in this book.

This book will *not* show you how to lay bricks or frame a house. It is intended that the owner subcontract all the labor to trained and experienced trade contractors while he or she oversees the building as general contractor.

If you prefer to use a professional general contractor, this book will be most useful in teaching you how to understand what you're going to get in the completed house. Misunderstanding is usually caused by incomplete specifications prepared by the general contractor or by lack of knowledge on the part of the owner as to what the specifications mean, or both.

If your goal is to expand the living space of an existing house, this book also discusses the special techniques for a job of this type.

Others who can benefit from this book are

- *REALTORS®*, so they can recognize the quality of the home they are selling and be able to offer sound advice as to its best features and how to correct the poor ones;
- *sellers of building supplies*, so they can give sound advice on which product is the best for each stage of construction;

- *bank officials,* who are engaged in monitoring construction loans so they can inspect the progress of the construction with confidence that the job is being done properly; and
- *young contractors* just starting in the business, who will find the information in this book very helpful and very difficult to locate in any other single source.

CHAPTER 1

Understanding Your Options

There are two methods of contracting for the homeowner to consider before building a new home. The first choice is to select a general contractor to manage the entire job. The second choice is for the homeowner to take on the job of general contractor and supervise construction using subcontractors (carpenters, masons, electricians, plumbers, etc.) to do the actual work.

USING A PROFESSIONAL GENERAL CONTRACTOR

If you decide to work with a professional general contractor, it is important that you get involved with the selection of the following:

- Placing the house on the lot (Chapter 5)
- The framing system (Chapter 7)
- Doors and windows (Chapter 8)
- Exterior finishes (Chapter 9)
- Heating and cooling systems (Chapter 15)
- Plumbing fixtures (Chapter 16)
- Interior finishes (Chapter 18)
- Cabinets (Chapter 19)
- Flooring (Chapter 20)
- Painting and decorating (Chapter 21)
- Finishing touches (Chapter 22)

ACTING AS GENERAL CONTRACTOR YOURSELF

If you decide to be your own general contractor, this book provides information for you to do the job with a potential savings of 15 to 20 percent of the total cost of the house. General contracting, however, will require spending a lot of your time in organizing subcontractors, ordering materials and checking actual work by almost daily visits to the site. Each chapter includes a section describing how to compute the costs that enable you to completely determine the total house cost before any construction begins. Appendix B illustrates this costing process.

PLANNING TO SAVE MONEY

There are two ways to reduce the cost of your house. One is to use cheaper materials, and the other is to build a smaller house. The use of cheaper materials is the least desirable of the two. You will end up with a product that will deteriorate faster, require more maintenance, and give you less comfort and satisfaction. By cutting corners with bargain materials of any kind, you are inviting problems that may be very expensive to correct. For example, poor framing lumber will cause warping in the floors, ceilings and walls. Poor-quality windows and doors will result in higher fuel costs.

The much better choice is to build less house. Choose a smaller house or temporarily omit certain aspects of the construction that can be finished later when your financial position improves. Leave part of the house unfinished, or plan to expand the house in the future and include the basics in your present plan to accommodate the expansion. For example, pour the footings for a planned later expansion along with the footings for the current house. Then cover the footings to be used later with soil and grass. This also reduces labor cost.

MANAGING THE CONSTRUCTION

If you are going to be your own general contractor, you must know how to check the work to see that it is being done properly and how to schedule the work at a pace that ensures completion. Each chapter in this book contains suggestions on how to avoid problems by thorough and detailed planning and thus how to prevent delays in construction and potential increases in cost.

On the other hand, do not *overmanage.* All trade contractors must be allowed to go ahead with the work they have contracted to perform without undue interference from the owner/general contractor. Naturally, if they are not performing the job according to the plans and specifications, it is your responsibility to step in and get the job straightened out. Be careful, however, not to take the time of the trade contractors and their crews unnecessarily by failure to have material on-site in the proper quantities or by too many questions to satisfy your curiosity.

It is good practice to always work directly with the contractor rather than one of his or her crew. Another caution is to ensure that all of the preliminary work has been completed *before* scheduling a trade contractor to begin his job. Failure to check this measure in many cases will justify extra payment to the trade contractor for lost time.

Appendix C contains an overall schedule for the entire construction task. Here you will find the sequence of the various jobs with explanatory notes regarding materials and other essential information.

AVOIDING DIRECT HIRE

If you are to be the general contractor, do not get involved in the direct hire of labor or with payment on an hourly basis. Once you establish yourself as the employer, you will need to keep a score of records to handle the deductions for withholding federal and state income taxes, deductions for and matching social security, workmans' compensation insurance payments and other items. In addition, payment for labor on an hourly basis tends to drag out the job unless proper, close supervision is available. *Your job is much easier if you work solely on a contract basis with the trade contractors being the employers of labor.*

CONSERVING ENERGY

With the cost of fuel today and the indications that prices will continue to rise, the efficient application of energy-saving principles to your house construction becomes increasingly important.

Although energy is discussed throughout the book the most significant aspects are covered in the following: Chapter 12, Air Infiltration; Chapter 13, Energy-Saving Insulation Options; Chapter 14, Heating with Sunshine (Solar Energy); Chapter 15, Heating and Cooling Considerations.

The objective of these chapters is to assist you in the application of energy conservation measures and in the selection of the best heating and cooling systems to fit the requirements in your environment. Before you make any selections, study these chapters thoroughly.

■ DOING IT YOURSELF

You may feel inclined to do some of the work yourself for the self-satisfaction of having built your own house, at least in part, or to save money. There is certainly nothing wrong with this approach. However, consider the following:

- Do you have the necessary skills to do a creditable job?
- Do you have the time to do the job?
- Will doing it yourself hold up other work and perhaps cost you more money in the long run?
- Will your work make it difficult to pin down responsibility should something go wrong?

If you can give yourself satisfactory answers to these questions, then by all means go ahead and do the job. Whatever your choice, this book will make the experience of building a house easier to manage.

Read the book from cover to cover to get an overall working picture of its contents. Then go back over it again at a slower pace, studying in detail those areas that pertain to building your house before you make your major decisions. This procedure can save distress and make building your own home a satisfying experience.

■ CHAPTER 2 ■

Beginning with Plans and Preliminaries

■ THE HOUSE BUILDING JOURNEY BEGINS WITH ONE OF TWO STEPS

There are generally two ways to begin building your house. Either select a lot you like and then decide on a house plan that fits that particular lot, or select a house plan and pick a lot to suit it. Whichever you choose, the matching of the house plan and lot is very important.

Choose a House Style To Fit Your Lifestyle

The most common styles of houses are the rancher, two story or colonial, story and a half, split level and split foyer (see Figure 2.1).

- The *rancher* consists of only one level although it may have a basement.
- The *two story* or *colonial* consists of two above-ground floors with each floor about the same size. It may also have a basement.
- *The story and a half* also has two floors, but the second floor is built within the roof and is thus less spacious than the first floor. Light to the second floor can be provided by separate dormer windows or a shed dormer of several windows together as one unit. The shed dormer is usually in the rear of the house.
- The *split level* has three different levels of floors with intervals of about four feet between, rather than the usual eight feet.
- The *split foyer* is similar to the two-story house except that the main entry is split between the elevations of the two floors. The bottom floor is usually partially underground.

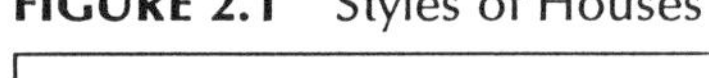
FIGURE 2.1 Styles of Houses

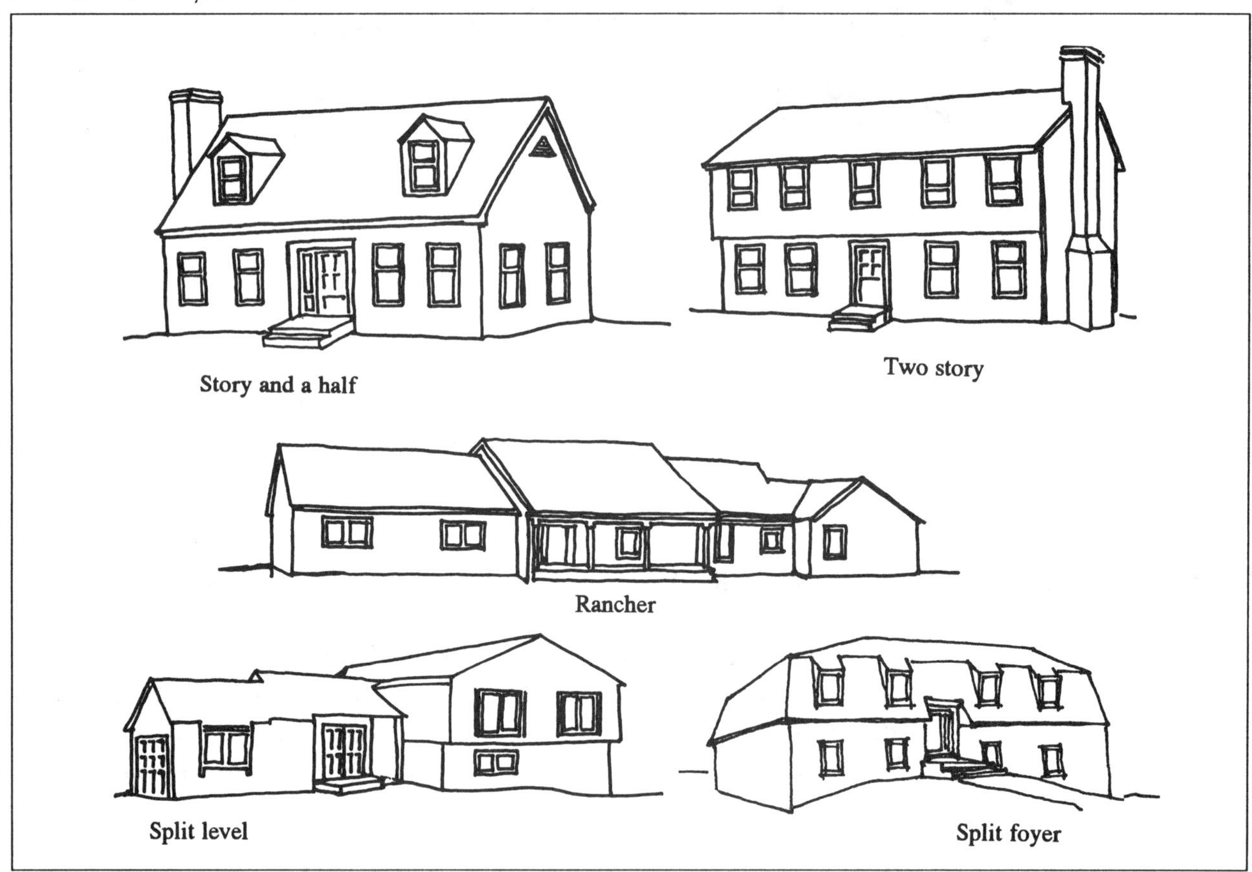

Matching the House Style to the Lot

Most styles of houses will fit most lots, but there are pitfalls that should be avoided. Do not match a rancher to a lot with a substantial forward slope. Ranchers look best if they appear to be hugging the ground, but a forward-sloping lot portrays an exaggerated foundation in the front that detracts from the low look of the rancher. If you have no choice, this problem can be minimized by planting the proper shrubbery. Help from a good landscaper is useful.

Rancher, two-story, and story-and-a-half houses are ideally suited for flat lots. They can also be attractive on lots that slope to the sides or rear, particularly if the plans include a walkout from a lower living area. This is also a way of economically increasing the size of the living space, since the lower level is an extension of the foundation (see Figure 2.2).

Split levels are ideally suited for side-sloping lots, and split foyers are best placed on rear-sloping lots (see Figure 2.3).

FIGURE 2.2 Rancher with Basement

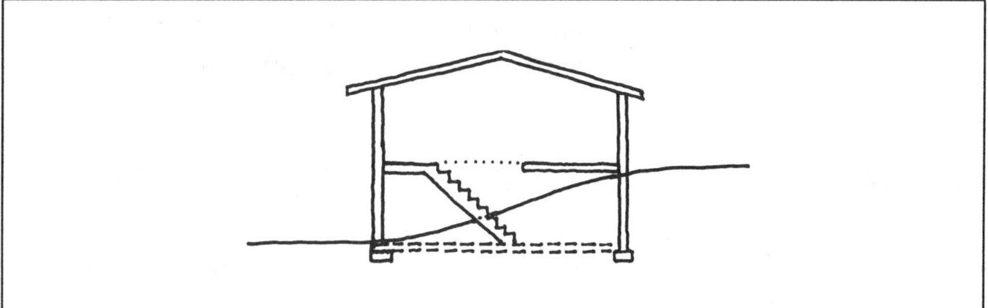

In matching your house to the lot, allow room *within the building setback lines* for outdoor decks, patios and porches. Properly placed in the plan, these amenities can enhance substantially the livability of a house.

Choosing the Best Garage

Do not forget the garage. If it is attached to the house, make sure it fits the lot without encroaching on the building setback line. Also ensure that the garage will conform to the slope of the lot.

On a side-sloping lot, if you lower the garage to meet the natural lot line, you may increase the requirement for steps from the house proper to the garage floor and lose a section of the garage because of the space required by the steps. On the other hand, if the garage is not dropped, the need for fill dirt to build up the garage floor, the driveway and portions of the lot may be substantial and may increase landscaping problems. The solution is usually a compromise.

FIGURE 2.3 Split Level and Split Foyer on Sloping Lot

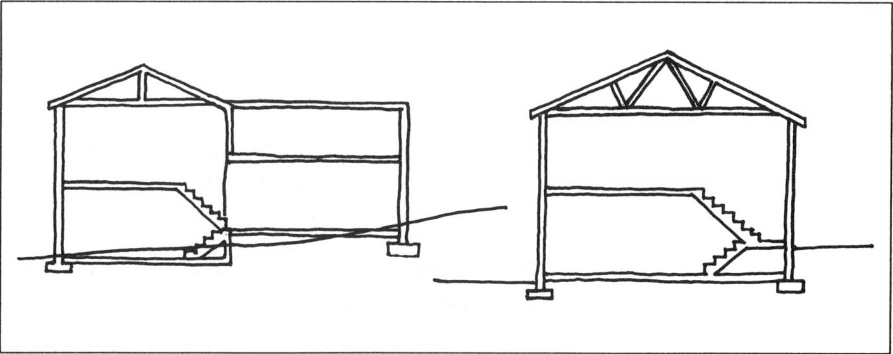

Matching the house to the lot is very important. If you feel the need for help, by all means consult a professional architect, engineer, landscaper, contractor or other knowledgeable person. If you have to pay a fee (the normal practice), it will be money well spent.

■ CHOOSING THE BUILDING SYSTEM

The three standard systems to consider in selecting the method to build your house are the modular, the paneled, and the stick built.

Building a Modular House Can Save Time

Great progress has been made in the design and construction of the modular house, and it has advantages that might be very important to you. Built in sections at the factory, it includes the complete structure with the plumbing, heating, and electrical work completed and the finished walls and floor already installed. Because the section size is limited to what can be shipped over the highway, the design of the house is somewhat restricted. By putting several sections together, however, some very attractive designs are achieved, including two-story houses and contemporaries with vaulted ceilings.

The package supplied by the manufacturer is quite complete. The owner furnishes only the site work, footings, foundation, final grading and water, sewer and electrical hookups. Many manufacturers provide their own erection crews or will recommend local crews to do the final assembly.

The two principal advantages of modular building are the speed by which it can be completed and the saving in cost, since the basic components are built on the assembly line at the factory. The principal disadvantage is the limit to the size, shape, exterior and architectural styles available from the manufacturer.

Paneled House Construction Is Flexible

The paneled house construction method is more flexible in its application since the materials are only partly put together at the factory. The framing is usually shipped with the walls assembled in panels of about 16 feet in width or less. Sometimes this includes the installation of windows, doors and insulation with the exterior siding partially installed.

Floor systems are partially assembled, and the roof framing may consist of prebuilt trusses. The remainder of the framing may be precut to some degree. The package supplied by the manufacturer may include the framing, doors, windows, shingles, electrical fixtures, plumbing fixtures, exterior siding and trim, finished hardware (medicine cabinets, doorknobs, towel and paper racks, and so forth) and interior trim material. The owner must provide the site work, all masonry and concrete work, all labor to assemble the materials in the package, electrical, heating, plumbing work (less any fixtures provided in the manufacturer's package), wall finish, flooring, tile, painting, final grade and water, sewer and electrical hookups.

In both the modular and paneled house, the material and labor provided by the manufacturer varies among the different companies and should be checked carefully in determining the final cost of the entire construction job.

The advantages of the paneled house are that it provides much more flexibility in size, shape, exterior finish and architectural style than the modular home. It should save one or more weeks in building time compared to the stick-built house, and the management of the materials is simplified because so much of it is provided in the package. The paneled house also offers cost savings in that materials are bought by the manufacturer in very large quantities.

Stick-Built Houses Are Traditional

Stick-built construction offers the greatest flexibility to the owner for house style, shape and size, and it gives him the best opportunity to control the quality of the labor and materials. With wood framing, the house is built mostly from uncut lumber. Thus it takes longer to complete and requires the owner/general contractor to spend more time and effort in working with a larger list of suppliers to ensure that the right materials are delivered to the site at the right time. If steel framing is used (see Chapter 7, Framing Your Project), some manufacturers will precut the steel members based on the house blueprint specifications, thus reducing the time and labor needed for its installation.

Because greater detail is required in supervising the construction of a stick-built house, the information contained in this book emphasizes that method.

The Log House Is Also an Option

The availability of log houses ranges from the modest backwoods cabin to complete year-round homes for the largest family.

Log homes differ from those built by conventional methods in that their exterior walls are built of logs with diameters from six to ten inches. The logs are the framing, the insulation, and the inner and outer finish.

Log homes are usually constructed in one of three ways:

1. ***Traditional:*** This system is the pioneer approach where the builder goes into the woods and cuts and trims his or her own logs or buys the unmilled logs from a supplier. This construction method requires a great deal of skill. A lot of work is involved in the on-site cutting and shaping of joints and corners. It can be very difficult, inaccurate and time consuming. In addition, because the logs are not symmetrical, large gaps between them must be filled to make the structure weathertight. This method is not recommended for amateurs.
2. ***Round Log Method:*** In this method, the builder buys logs that have already been milled to remove the bark and shaped to a uniform diameter. The problem of how to fill the varying width spaces between the logs has been substantially reduced, but the task of cutting and shaping the joints and corners still remains.
3. ***The Engineered System:*** With this method the builder is provided the log material already cured, cut, shaped, and ready for installation. The work is substantially reduced, and the sealing of the house is much more effective. Figure 2.4 illustrates three of the many variations in milling logs to provide the basis for a tightly sealed house. Note that the pattern on the right has been shaped to drain the water away from the joints between the logs. In addition to the shaping, an airtight seal is obtained by applying suitable caulking material between the logs.

The R-value of a log wall may be increased by installing rigid foam insulation sheets against the interior of the wall and finishing it with paneling or Sheetrock®. Or a 2×3 or 2×4 stud wall may be built on the inside of the wall, insulated with fiberglass and covered with a plastic vapor barrier, and finished with paneling or Sheetrock. If it is important to retain the appearance of logs in the interior of the house, the additional stud wall with insulation may be covered with half-round logs instead of the paneling or Sheetrock.

A log wall will store and retain heat much better than the standard conventionally built wall. Therefore it can be more effective when used with passive solar heating systems. (See Chapter 14, Heating with Sunshine (Solar Energy).

It is not practical to run plumbing, heating ducts and electrical wiring inside the exterior walls of a log house. Most log house plans can be accommodated by using interior walls for this purpose. Some log house kit manufacturers provide milled slots at the bottom of the inside of the exterior wall in which electrical cable can be run and covered.

FIGURE 2.4 Typical Log Patterns

Log house manufacturers will provide a great deal of information in their brochures.

FINDING A SOURCE FOR YOUR PLANS

To properly build a house you must, of course, have a good set of plans. There are several sources you may choose from, but before you arrange for your plans, visit as many houses as is practical to get the feel for room sizes, traffic flow among the various rooms, details of finishes and other information that goes into the design of a house.

Using Plans from a Professional Architect

A professional architect's plans will probably be the most expensive initially but may be the least expensive in the long run, particularly because they will ensure that your house design fits your lot and uses the maximum benefits of modern approaches to construction, particularly in the field of efficient energy. This subject is discussed in detail in Chapters 12, 13, 14 and 15.

A professional architect can provide a plan more closely matching your needs, especially if you have an unusual house design in mind or if you want accuracy in your selection of a particular architectural style. The architect's specifications will more accurately and thoroughly define the options of acceptable materials and construction methods and thus give you greater assurance of quality building.

Because architects often personally favor a particular style, try to find one whose style matches your tastes. Don't hesitate to ask to see some of his or her work.

Using a Mail-Order Plans Service

One of the more popular sources of plans is the use of various mail-order plan services. Many of them do excellent work. You may not find exactly what you want, but most plans can be modified to some extent by a competent draftsperson. Be cautious here because what may appear to be a simple change may actually cause major structural problems. Avoid changing load-bearing walls in the foundation and framing (extending or shortening non-load-bearing walls is a fairly simple change) and avoid major changes in the roof line.

You should be aware that mail-order plans do not relate to any particular lot. Be prepared, then, to have to decide on the foundation modifications to adapt the plan to your lot (especially for sloping lots). If this is necessary, get some professional advice.

If you select the modular or paneled house, most manufacturers provide house plans as part of the package.

Using Local Plans Sources

There are usually many local sources for plans through draftspersons and designers with various skills. Check with local general contractors and building inspectors for recommendations. Many of them do good work, but investigate before selecting one. If your local building code requires certified plans, you will have the additional task of getting this certification, and it can be provided only by a professional architect or engineer.

Learn How To Read Blueprints

Learning to read house design blueprints is not difficult, and the homeowner/general contractor should make an effort to do so. If you are using a local architect, engineer or designer, through your contacts with them (involving many visits), you should have a fair ability to read the prints when they have been finalized. But in any case, know your plans. You will be working with them for several months and living in the results for many years. A glossary of terms relating to the house-building business is in the back of this book.

CHAPTER 3

Arranging Contracts, Financing and Insurance

DEVELOP A GOOD BUILDING CONTRACT

Building a new house is the most expensive project that most people undertake. It is very important, therefore, that care be used in developing the building contract to ensure that the house is properly built and your investment protected.

The laws and customs governing construction vary from state to state. A well-drawn contract for building in one state will not necessarily serve the owner adequately in another state. For this reason, before signing any building contract have it reviewed by a local attorney experienced in this type of legal work. If you are working with a professional architect or engineer, most of them are experienced in preparing building contracts.

If you are working through a general contractor, as a minimum your contract should contain the following:

1. A complete set of plans (blueprints) drawn by an architect, engineer or designer experienced in house construction and design, including the following:
   - Foundation plan
   - Floor plan for each floor
   - Elevation for each side

     Note: A *plan* denotes the horizontal or bird's-eye view, and an *elevation* denotes a vertical view.
   - Construction details of typical walls
   - Construction details of special features

- Electrical plans showing, as a minimum, switches, outlet receptacles, TV outlets, central vacuum outlets, electrical fixtures, fans and heaters
- Plumbing plan mapping, as a minimum, the location of all fixtures requiring water supply and/or waste piping, to include, for example, the icemaker in many refrigerators
- HVAC plan describing, as a minimum, the location of the major elements such as furnace, heat pump inside and outside element, major duct lines, air supply outlets, return air grilles, exhaust duct lines, and exits through the exterior walls for exhaust fans

2. A complete set of specifications: The blueprints contain much of the construction information, but not all, by any means. For example, what kind of heating system should you have? What kind of plumbing fixtures? To spell out this information you must have a detailed list of specifications. Appendix A illustrates a typical list of "specs" with an explanation of why each item is necessary. The remaining chapters of the book discuss choices of the various items with the advantages and disadvantages of each.
3. A plot plan: A scaled drawing showing, as a minimum, the exact location of the house on the lot with distances to each lot boundary, driveway location, building setback lines and all easements. Local building officials may require the location of sewer and water lines. Check with these officials to find out what exactly is required.
4. General contractor's name: The person who is responsible for liability insurance to protect him from workers' compensation acts for his company and covering all subcontractors.
5. At-Fault agreement: Who (owner or general contractor) is responsible for vandalism, theft of building material, damage to the house structure during the construction period, and liability not covered by the general contractor's workers' compensation insurance.
6. Time limits: Indication as to when construction will begin and approximately when the house will be ready for occupancy by the owner. These dates are usually guides not specific goals. In the event, however, that the completion date is very important to the owner, a penalty clause can be included to require the general contractor to forfeit a daily monetary penalty for each day beyond the contractual completion date. A penalty of this nature usually increases the contractor's bid price.
7. Conformance agreement: A statement that the house will be built in conformance with the plans and specifications.

8. Change agreement: A statement that changes to the contract made after signing the contract must be in writing and include any additional cost.

If you are acting as your own general contractor and building through the use of subcontractors, the same content should be included with the following exceptions (numbers relate to those contained in the general contractor's contract above):

4. Each subcontractor must carry workers' compensation insurance and must furnish copies of their insurance certificate.
5. Owner should be responsible and carry appropriate insurance.
6. It is highly unusual to have a time of completion penalty clause in a contract with a subcontractor because he has no control of the construction phasing except for his own part.

Remember that the principal purpose of good plans and specifications is to provide a firm base for costing the house, standards to compare bids and a finite guide for the actual construction.

BIDDING CAN MAKE OR BREAK YOUR PROJECT

Selecting the Bidders

Before you make the selection of contractors and suppliers to bid on your job, do some investigating:

- Suppliers can usually recommend contractors to furnish the labor for the materials the supplier sells.
- Ask for references of people for whom the contractor worked.
- Check with the local Chamber of Commerce and Better Business Bureau.
- Ask contractors of one trade the names of reliable contractors in another trade.

Handling the Bidding with General Contractors

If you are going to have your house built by a general contractor, you should ask for bids from at least three whom you have researched.

If you get only one bid, you will have no basis for comparison and will be in a position of having to accept this one without knowing if the bid is competitive. If you get only two bids and one is high and the other much lower, you will have the dilemma of not knowing if the high bid is overpriced or the low bid is underpriced.

On the other hand, three bids should provide you with a better basis for making the decision. If two are low and one is high, then you are probably safe in accepting one of the low bids. If two are high and one is low, you had better be cautious in accepting the lower bid. The low bidding contractor may have underestimated the work and may cause problems by either cutting corners or failing to finish the contract when he discovers his mistake. Consider getting a bid from a fourth contractor to help solve the problem.

All these bids will naturally ask for large amounts of money and should be carefully examined. Each bidder will require a complete set of plans and specifications.

Figure 3.1 is a sample bid letter to selected general contractors.

FIGURE 3.1 Sample Bid Letter

1 September 1995

Built-Rite General Contracting Company
24 High Street
Center City, NC 28000

Dear Sir:

I would appreciate your bid to furnish all material and labor for the construction of my house in accordance with the plans, specifications and plot plan attached. The house is to be built on Lot 17, Scarlet Drive, Brentwood Subdivision in Center City.

I expect you to be provide insurance covering all workers' compensation acts for your company and all subcontractors employed by you.

I will carry general builder's risk insurance covering vandalism, theft, fire and wind damage and general liability insurance.

If your bid is accepted, I would like to know approximately when you can begin construction and your estimate of when the house will be ready for occupancy.

If you have any questions please give me a call.

J. J. Jones
184 Central Avenue
Center City, NC 28001
Tel. (811) 234-8603

Because insurance coverage policies vary from state to state, check with your local agent for advice about the types of policies you and the general contractor should carry.

When you receive all bids from the general contractors, compare them closely. If the contractor you accept has replied in the form of a contract to the owner, have it checked by a local lawyer familiar with this type of contract before signing. If the reply is not in contract form, have one prepared for you by a lawyer and send it to the contractor you have selected for his signature.

Handling the Bidding with Trade Contractors

If you are undertaking the construction of your house as the general contractor, you will have to ask for bids from the trade contractors yourself.

Each category of work in the construction of your house should be offered to contractors and/or suppliers for bids. Get at least three bids for each item. See Appendix D for a listing of the work the trade contractors normally perform.

Some contractors prefer to furnish the material as well as the labor, and it is usually to your advantage to agree. This is particularly true for plumbers, electricians and heating contractors. It is important that you make no attempt to find "bargain" material and ask the contractor to do only the installation. By splitting the responsibility for the work between labor and material, you are creating a situation where, if anything goes wrong with the completed system, the contractor can always take the position that the malfunction is caused by the material furnished by you, the owner, and is, therefore, not his responsibility. Unless you are an expert, it will be difficult to prove otherwise.

Insist that bids be made in writing in sufficient detail so that you know exactly what you are getting. Give each bidder a complete set of plans and specifications and insist that he refers his bid directly to those plans and specifications. Request information as to how much notice the contractor would like to have before beginning his work and his estimate of the time it will take to complete the job. As a rule, bidders will need several days to give you their bid.

In those instances where work is phased, you should ask for the time of completion for each phase. For instance, plumbing work is usually done in at least two phases, the rough-in and the final. These estimates will help you in carefully planning the schedule of the various parts of the whole construction project.

Requests for bids from the trade contractors are handled in a manner similar to that for the general contractors.

HOW TO OBTAIN THE CONSTRUCTION LOAN

Financing is a complex issue and varies throughout the country primarily because of differences in state banking laws and regulations. Policies of lenders within the same state may even vary between small towns and large cities. Visit several lenders in your area to determine the best financing for you.

You will need two different types of financing. The first is the construction or short-term loan that is used as a source of money to pay for the house during construction, and the second is the mortgage or long-term loan that is used to pay off the construction loan after the house has been completed.

Some lenders will issue only short-term loans, some prefer to issue only long-term loans, and others may issue one to cover both the construction and the mortgage with only one closing required, which can save on the total closing cost.

If you are building your house by contract with a professional general contractor, your application to the lender for a construction loan is generally approved if (1) the contractor's reputation is a good one and known by the lender, (2) your financial statement indicates that the project is within your financial means, and (3) if you have at least a commitment from a lender for your mortgage if one is necessary. Get this mortgage commitment before you go shopping for the construction loan.

If you are your own general contractor, getting a construction loan may be more difficult if the lender does not know anything about your ability to manage the job. To improve your chances of getting the construction loan, consider the following:

- Have a complete set of plans with detailed specifications (see Appendix A) to indicate that you are completely knowledgeable of the product you are getting.
- Determine the total cost of the house including breakdowns of the various parts and back up this costing with bids from local, well-recognized trade contractors.
- Develop a detailed construction schedule for your particular job. See Appendix C, Construction Schedule.
- Offer collateral for the loan other than the house you are going to build, such as other real property, stocks and bonds, savings certificates or other tangible assets.

Making Payments During Construction

If you are building through a professional general contractor, the contract you sign with him should indicate in detail the method of payment. There are two systems in common use.

The first is the payment of certain sums at the completion of different stages of the construction. For example, assuming you have a $60,000 contract, the general contractor might ask for payment of $15,000 when the subfloor has been laid (which means that much of the site work, all of the footings, all of the foundation and the floor framing have been completed); $15,000 when the framing, siding and exterior trim have been completed; $15,000 when the drywall or plaster has been completed, and the final $15,000 when the house has been finished and the occupancy permit has been issued by the building inspector.

This is a simple system but it is not necessarily an accurate one. For example, the payment of the first $15,000 may be more than the contractor has put into the house if it is a simple rancher. On the other hand if the plan has a full or walkout basement, the $15,000 may be much less than the materials and labor put into the construction.

With the second payment method, the general contractor asks for a sum at the end of each month based on the status of the construction at that time. This will require him to submit to you or the lender a detailed billing showing the percentage of construction completed, broken down into the various categories such as masonry, carpentry and so forth. With this system, it is common practice for the owner or lender to retain 10 percent of the amount due to ensure that the contract will be completed.

Regardless of which method is used, actual payments will be monitored by the institution that loaned you the construction money. The lender will expect the contractor to use his own money to pay for labor and materials pending a payment by the owner or lender. The lender will also have his experts inspect the job each time a payment is due to determine if the amount of payment asked for is correct.

If you are your own general contractor, you should expect to make payments somewhat differently. Methods of payment should be a part of the final contract between you and each trade contractor. Most large supply houses will bill you at the end of the month and expect payment a few days later. Some offer discounts for prompt payments, but always ask about discounts because many suppliers do not advertise them. *Taking advantage of discounts can save you several hundred dollars.*

Most contractors will expect payment at certain stages of completion of the construction. For example, the plumbing, electrical and heating contractors usually ask for payment of about half the total after the completion of the rough-in and the remainder after the completion of the work, including the inspection by the building official's office.

Some contractors, such as masons and carpenters, may ask for payment at the end of each week based on the amount of work completed at that time. This is particularly true of small companies who need weekly payments to make their own payroll.

All of these systems are acceptable and used in the house-building business. The important point is that *whatever system you agree to, have it in writing and then abide by it.*

OBTAINING THE MORTGAGE

Once the house is finished, it is common practice to pay off the construction loan with a mortgage on the house. *Before you make any contractual commitment to build the house, you should have completed the arrangements for both the construction loan and the mortgage.* A mortgage is a valid contract and is fully enforceable. Be sure you fully understand all of the provisions of your mortgage before signing it.

When you first finance a home, you are likely to make a down payment on the property. But, because you financed the purchase, you are now in debt and the lender "owns" most of the property's value. In traditional mortgages, the monthly payments on the loan are weighted. During the first years, payments are largely *interest;* in time, more of each payment is credited to the loan itself, or the *principal.* Gradually as you pay off the principal you build up *equity,* or ownership. Your equity also increases if the value of the home increases. This process of gradually obtaining equity and reducing debt through payments of principal and interest is called *amortization.*

Until recently most mortgages had fixed monthly payments, a fixed interest rate and full amortization (or transfer of equity) over a period of 15 or 30 years. These features worked in the borrower's favor. Inflation made your payments seem less and your property worth more. So, although the payments seemed hard to meet at first, over time they became easier.

A variety of mortgage packages beside the traditional fixed rate are available. They may help you finance a home you otherwise couldn't afford, but they also may involve greater risks. For example, the interest rate and monthly payments may change during the loan to reflect what the market will bear. Or the interest rate may fluctuate while the payments stay the same and the amount of principal paid off may vary. The latter approach allows the lender to credit a greater portion of the payment to interest when rates are high. Some plans also offer below-market interest rates, but they may not help you build up equity.

In shopping for financing sources today, keep in mind the terms that are keys to the affordability of the home:

- The *total cost minus your down payment,* or amount you finance
- The length, or *maturity* of the loan
- The size of the *monthly payments*
- The *interest rates* or rate
- Whether the payment or rates may *change* and, if so, within what limitations, if any
- Whether or not *extra payments on the principal* can be made at any time
- Whether there is an *opportunity for refinancing* the loan when it matures, if necessary

What Size Mortgage Can You Afford?

Most mortgage lenders process and underwrite loans according to generally accepted standards. The lender will want to look at your financial situation, as follows:

- Monthly income and expenses
- Credit history
- Property appraisal
- Source of cash for down payment and settlement costs
- Employment history

These lenders will also make two calculations:

- Housing Ratio: Your total monthly mortgage payment (PITI—principal, interest, taxes and insurance) divided by your total monthly income. As a guide this ratio should not exceed about 28 percent.
- Debt Ratio: The sum of your total monthly mortgage payment and other monthly debt payments divided by your monthly income. As a guide this ratio should not exceed about 36 percent.

To determine the PITI, contact your bank and ask them to give you your monthly payment on principal and interest based on your mortgage requirements. The local tax office (city or county) can give you the tax, and the insurance company can provide the insurance payment.

Do your homework before you apply for a mortgage so you will have a better idea of where you stand.

What Type of Mortgage Should You Choose?

Many types of mortgages are available to the borrower. Take the time to shop around to determine the best for you. All mortgages have advantages and disadvantages, so select the one that best meets your particular needs. The more commonly used mortgages are:

Fixed-Rate Mortgage It has a fixed rate of interest, is usually long term (15 or 30 years) and is paid off in equal monthly installments of principal and interest until paid in full. This mortgage offers stability and the advantages of long-term payments, but interest rates may be higher than with other types of financing. New fixed-rate mortgages may not be assumable should you decide to sell in the future.

Adjustable-Rate Mortgage Based on a financial index, the interest rate will change resulting in possible changes in the monthly payments, the term of the loan (time to pay off) and/or the principal. Financial indexes may be the Federal Home Loan Bank Board's national average mortgage rate, the U. S. Treasury bill rate or the prime rate. If the financial index increases, the interest on your mortgage increases, or if the financial index decreases, the interest rate on your mortgage will also decrease. Some plans will have caps (limits to any changes). This type mortgage is readily available. Its starting interest rate is slightly below the market, but payments can increase sharply and frequently if the financial index increases. Payment caps prevent wide fluctuations in payments but may cause negative amortization. This means that your monthly payments may not be sufficient to pay even the interest. To make up for this deficit, you may lose some of your equity in the house.

FHA-Insured Loans Under the FHA and the VA (below) programs, the federal government does not make mortgage loans, rather it insures that the borrower will repay the loan according to the loan contract. This insurance covers loans up to about $120,000, but this limit varies throughout the country. Check with your local bank for the limit in your area. The interest rate is generally lower than that for conventional fixed loans.

VA-Insured Loans The VA offers a loan program similar to the FHA-insured loan program for veterans of the armed forces only. The limit of this insurance is for a loan of about $184,000. Like the FHA loan, the interest rate is usually lower than the fixed-rate mortgage.

Farmers Home Administration (FmHA) Loans This federal agency usually works through local offices to lend money to families with relatively low incomes to buy or build homes. The maximum amount of the loan varies throughout the country. Interest rates may run 2 percent below the rate for conventional mortgages. Contact your local Farmers Home Administration Office for details.

Balloon Mortgage Monthly payments are usually based on a fixed interest, and the loan is short term, usually five or seven years. The loan is amortized as a 30-year mortgage, but at the end of the term (5–7 years) the entire principal is due. Therefore, the balloon mortgage offers low monthly payments but possibly no equity until the loan is fully paid. When due, the loan must be paid off or refinanced. Refinancing may include higher interest rates.

The mortgage market generally also offers different types of mortgages than those discussed above. If your situation is unusual, consult your local banker or mortgage company to find out if they offer additional selections that better fit your requirements.

Calculating the Total Cost of Mortgages

In shopping for mortgages, many people neglect to consider the total cost of the mortgage. Often this cost can be substantially reduced by a modest increase in the monthly payments:

Loan Amount	Cost 30-Year Term	Add for 15-Year Term	Interest Saved
$ 50,000	$ 439/month	$ 98/month	$ 61,290
75,000	658/month	148/month	91,935
100,000	878/month	197/month	122,580
150,000	1,317/month	295/month	174,870

These figures are based on an interest rate of 10 percent. The table indicates, for example, that by increasing the monthly payments on a $75,000 loan by $148 per month for a total monthly payment of $806, the mortgage term can be changed from 30 years to 15 years with an interest saving of $91,935, because additional payments go directly to the principal.

Calculating Settlement (Closing) Costs

Almost every mortgage transaction involves settlement costs to cover additional expenses. A sample for a $100,000 mortgage follows.

Lender Fees:			
Loan arrangement fees	$500	to	$1,000
Discount points	0	to	3,000
Inspection fee (new house)	50	to	100
Document preparation	50	to	200
Mortgage insurance	0	to	1,000
Title Charges:			
Attorney's fees	200	to	400
Title insurance	300	to	400
Transfer tax	100	to	2,000
Recording tax	200	to	400
Miscellaneous Charges:			
Survey	150	to	200
Termite inspection	250	to	400
Prepaid Expenses:			
Odd days interest	0	to	800
Homeowner's insurance	250	to	400
Real estate taxes	200	to	1,500
Total:	$2,250	to	$11,800

■ YOU WILL NEED INSURANCE

During Construction

The following types of insurance are necessary during the construction phase of your project:

- Title Insurance: Needed to protect your ownership of the land and the house you are building. *The amount of insurance should include the market value of both the lot and the house when completed.* Usually the lending institute will require the insurance in the amount of the mortgage only, which does not fully protect the owner.

- Basic Homeowner's Insurance: Covers loss from damage, fire, theft and personal coverage to those injured on your lot. In some states an endorsement "additional extended coverage" is available at costs as little as $20. This endorsement dramatically broadens fire and extended coverage. Also, there are special construction policies that provide coverage for the dwelling and material stored on the job site.
- Workers' Compensation: Protects the owner from claims by workers injured while building your house. This type of insurance is particularly important if you are acting as your own general contractor dealing directly with the subcontractors. For additional protection, hire only those subcontractors who carry their own workers' compensation insurance and ask them to provide you with a certificate verifying that they do have this insurance.
- Flood Insurance: This insurance will also be required by your mortgagor in areas where a history of flooding exists. Again, make sure it covers your property fully and not just for the amount of the mortgage.

Discuss all your insurance coverages with an experienced agent because the details tend to be somewhat complicated.

After Completing Construction

Continue all of the insurance discussed above with the exception of workers' compensation. In addition, you may want to consider getting warranties to provide coverage of house breakdowns as a whole for up to ten years. In many cases coverage is not complete. For example, if a leak develops in a water pipe in the wall, usually the material and labor cost to replace or repair the leaky pipe are covered by the warranty, but this may not be true for the material and labor cost to replace the plaster or paneling that had to be damaged in order to get to the pipe. *Learn the details of your warranty before you sign it.*

CHAPTER 4

Starting the Construction

PRECONSTRUCTION TASKS TO ATTEND TO

Before you begin the actual construction of your house, make sure that the following tasks are completed. The list is a guide and should be reviewed to ensure that it includes the needs for your particular project. Tasks are listed generally in the order in which they should be done.

If you are working through a professional general contractor:

- Check with the local building official to see that the house plans are approved.
- Get the approval of plans by the local subdivision building committee if required.
- Roughly stake out the house and driveway on the lot following the plot plan you have previously developed. Again make sure that
  1. you have sufficient room for a septic system if one is required, and
  2. there is enough space between the house and the boundaries of the lot to meet the local building codes.
- Complete your financing arrangements.
- Have a signed contract with the general contractor you have selected to do the job.
- Write letters or make telephone calls to thank the other bidders. This is a matter of courtesy. Many of these bidders spent a lot of time, which usually means money, to give you the information you asked for.

In addition, if you are going to be the general contractor:

- Complete the cost of construction based on the bids you have received from the trade contractors and suppliers.
- Have a completed contract with the trade contractors you have selected to do the job.
- Write letters or telephone to thank the other bidders.
- Get the building permit. At the same time arrange for payment of any water and sewer hookup fees necessary for issue of the permit.
- Notify the electrical contractor to start the work to install the temporary electrical power to the lot.
- Notify the plumbing contractor to install the temporary water hookup.

Get All Your Permits

Usually a fee is required for a building permit. The fee is based on the size of the house or the cost of the construction. As part of the application, you will probably be required to submit a plot plan, blueprints and specifications that the inspection office will retain for their files. Most local building officials will review your plan and approve it or let you know if there are any code violations that will require changes.

If your plans include a subsoil disposal drain system and/or a well, you will need permits for their installation, usually issued by the local health department.

Arrange for Timely Inspections

Most local governments require inspections by them at different phases during the construction. This is for your protection. Be certain you have a list of these inspections and notify the building official when you are ready for each one. It could be very costly if you missed one and continued with the work. The building inspector could require you to rip out some of the work to expose areas that had not been inspected. If the inspector does not pass your job, see that the necessary corrections are made and a reinspection completed before you continue.

The following ten inspections may be required:

1. Footing and slab excavation before the concrete is poured
2. Floor framing before the subfloor is installed
3. Framing
4. Plumbing rough-in

5. Electrical rough-in
6. Heating, ventilating and air-conditioning (HVAC) rough-in
7. Plumbing final
8. Electrical final
9. HVAC final
10. Final building inspection (occupancy permit issued)

Inspections 3, 4, 5 and 6 must be done with the interior of the framing exposed. Be sure that the drywall or plaster lathing and the insulation are not installed until completion of these inspections.

Check Zoning of Adjacent Areas

Before you buy your lot, check with the local authorities or your real estate broker to determine if the zoning of the land you are buying is suitable for the type of construction you are going to build. *In addition, check the zoning around your area to ensure that construction that would detract from your house cannot be built nearby within the provisions of the current laws.*

Be Aware of Subdivision Restrictions

In some instances the covenants of residential subdivisions require that builders submit plot plans, blueprints and specifications to the subdivision building committee for its approval. The purpose of these committees is to provide economic protection for the subdivision. They want to be sure that the house you are going to build will maintain or enhance the value of the houses already built there and to ensure that the architecture of your house is not so bizarre that it will detract from the value of neighboring houses.

■ START WITH SITE WORK

Site work includes all of those operations that must be done before actual construction can begin. It usually includes some or all of the following:

- On a wooded lot, clearing the trees from the construction area
- Changing grades to fit your plan
- Excavations for basements
- Grading for the driveway; filling and compacting as necessary
- Removing excess dirt, trees, rock and other debris

- Installing the septic system or laying the hookup line to the public sewer
- Drilling a well or installing the hookup line to the central water system
- Laying out the batter board system to locate the house

Clearing the Land

If you have a wooded lot, remove only those trees necessary to permit construction unless you have already definite landscaping plans for the entire lot. Remember that trees can be removed quickly, but it takes years of growth to replace one.

Before getting bids on the work, determine the area to be cleared for construction of the house, driveway and septic system (if one has to be installed). One of the simplest methods is to locate the corners of the house with small stakes (you don't have to be too accurate at this stage—within a foot is fine), select an area around the house, driveway and septic system *plus at least ten additional feet* to allow room for the construction. Mark this area by tying tape on selected trees. Brilliant orange or red plastic tapes are excellent. This method of marking makes it easy for the site work contractor to identify the scope of the task.

"Locate" the House on the Lot

House location consists of (1) the temporary location to provide the basis for lot clearing, and, after the completion of the clearing, (2) the installation of the batter board system.

Situate the house to take advantage of the sun for light and heat. Face the side of the house with the most glass toward the south if your overall plan permits. In the winter the low-hanging sun's rays will penetrate the glass and add warmth and light inside the house. In the summer, a properly designed roof overhang can block the high-hanging sun's rays and thus prevent the heat from these rays adding to the air-conditioning load. See Chapter 14, Heating with Sunshine (Solar Energy). If you are using solar heat extensively, consider the possible blockage of the sun by future construction on adjacent lots.

In high wind areas place your house to take advantage of the reduction of the wind by trees, particularly evergreens, which retain their "leaves" during the winter.

FIGURE 4.1 Types of Culverts

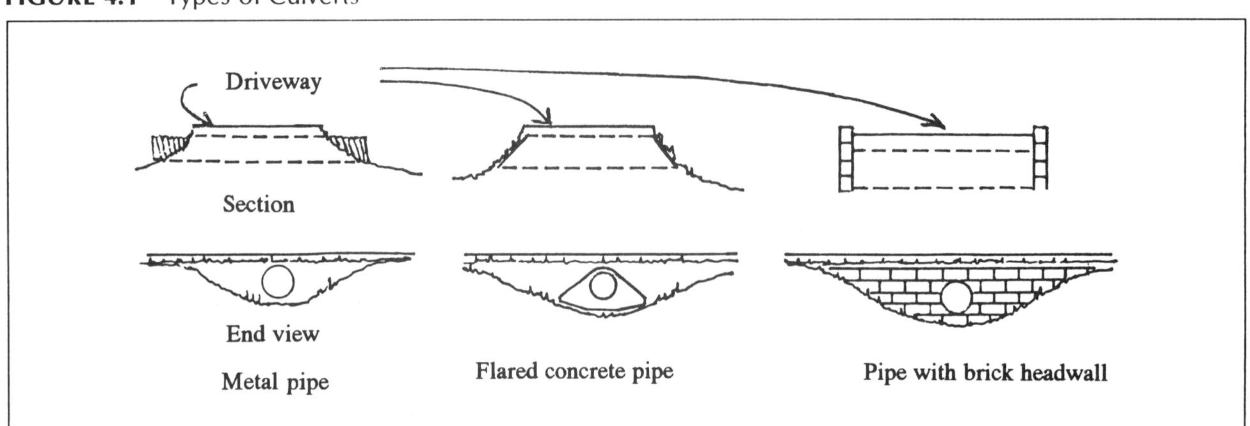

Prepare the Driveway

In clearing space for the driveway, allow a wide area at the street end. If your driveway is about 10 feet wide, its width at the curb should be not less than 16 feet to permit cars to turn into it easily.

Construct Culverts

Many lots require a culvert pipe to run under the driveway for proper drainage. If this culvert is located on city/county property or right-of-way, check with the appropriate government office for the proper size and method of installation of the pipe. In some communities, the highway department will install the culvert pipe at no cost to the homeowner. If not, ensure that the installation is included in the site work contract and that it also includes the establishment of the driveway base. During construction the heavy concrete and lumber trucks will pack down the base and make it stable by the time you are ready to put on the final surface.

Figure 4.1 shows the three types of culvert pipes in general use. For a finished look, the metal and nonflared concrete pipe need head walls made of brick, stone or concrete.

Move and Store Topsoil

As part of the clearing, have the site contractor scrape off the topsoil in the construction area and stockpile it on the lot out of the way of the construction. This topsoil will then be available for placement back onto the cleared area during the final grading.

FIGURE 4.2 Foundation Buildup

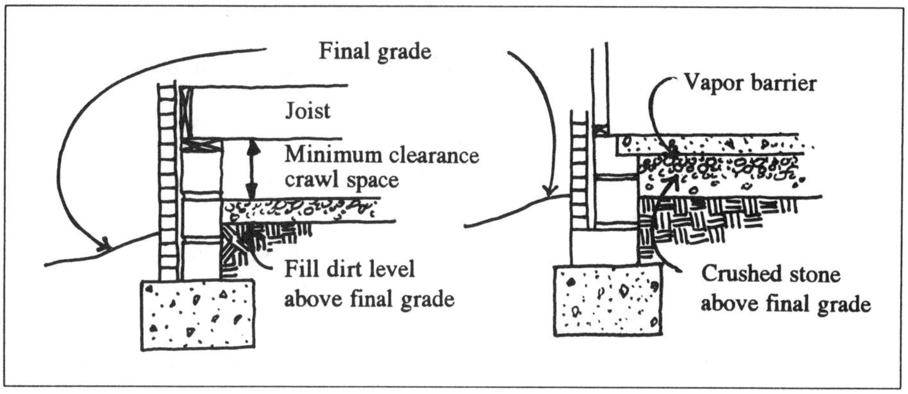

Protect Remaining Trees

All trees that are removed should be taken out completely, including the root system. You may be able to sell some of the cut trees to a local sawmill. Also consider having the site work contractor cut them to length for use in a fireplace or stove, but be sure he stacks the cut logs where they will not interfere with the construction to follow, including the final grading. For more permanent storage later, place the cut logs on a frame (pipe or salt-treated wood) several inches above the ground so the fireplace logs will not be eaten by wood-boring insects such as termites.

Remove from the lot all stumps, tree limbs, brush, rocks and excess soil.

Solving Flat-Lot Problems

If your lot is very flat with little or no natural drainage, you can avoid creating a moisture problem by bringing in fill dirt to *raise the lot elevation under the house above the final exterior grade.* This is a safeguard against standing water problems after the house is complete and is especially important if your house is to be built with a crawl space. (See Figure 4.2.) Check with the local building codes to determine the minimum clearance required in the crawl space.

STARTING THE HOUSE

Do the House Layout with Exacting Care

The purpose of the house layout is to provide a measurement base on which the house is to be built by establishing the following:

- The exact lateral dimensions of the exterior walls
- The height of the floors and their levelness
- The squareness of the house to ensure that all corners are 90° or whatever angular dimension your plans call for

The most widely used system involves the installation of a series of batter boards whose function is to hold in place a network of string lines that accomplish the above.

Because the house layout task is somewhat complicated, it should be carried out by skilled hands. Most surveyors and many lead carpenters have the skills to install a batter board system.

Excavating Basements or Lower Levels

If your plan requires a basement or a partly underground lower level, the site work contractor will need to know the elevation of the bottom of the excavation and the lateral dimensions of its sides. He will also want to know where the excess dirt is to be put. If you have him spread it around the lot, your site work cost will be less than if it has to be hauled away. Often this excess dirt can be used to build up undesirable low spots.

Sewage Disposal System

If your lot is served by a community sewage system, you only have to hook up to it. This work should be included in the plumbing bid. It can be done at any time during the construction process as agreed upon between you and the plumber, but *allow several weeks for settling of the ditch that carries the pipe from your house to the sewage system before final grading of the lot.*

If no public or community sewage system is available, you will have to install on your lot an individual sewage system designed for the local conditions including the porosity of the soil. Among the various systems are leaching cesspools, subsoil disposal drains and sand-filter systems. (Because leaching cesspools are not used much

FIGURE 4.3 Septic Tank System

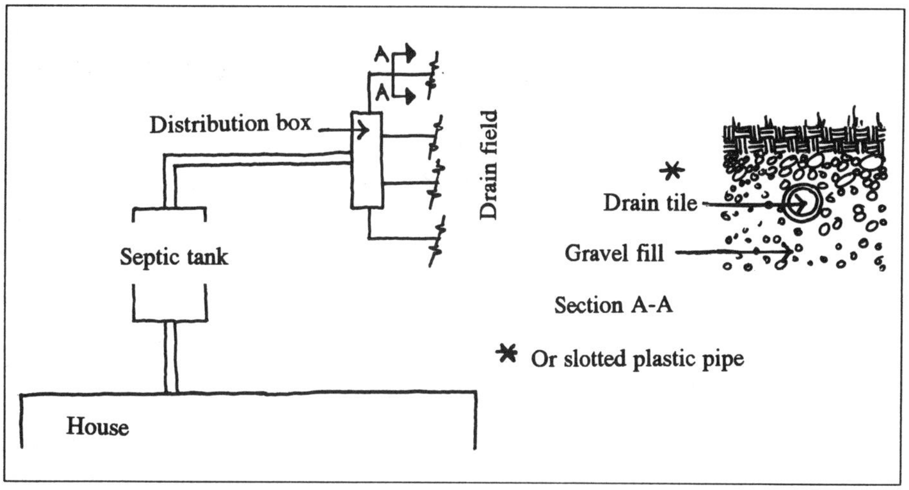

these days, they will not be described here.) Whatever system you choose will probably have to be approved by the local health authorities.

Septic Tank System

One of the more widely used systems is the subsoil disposal method or "septic tank," as illustrated in Figure 4.3.

The principal components are as follows:

- The concrete septic tank that collects the sewage, decomposes the solids and passes the liquids on to the distribution box
- The small distribution box that divides the liquid sewage and distributes it evenly among the drain lines
- The subsoil drain lines (drain field) that carry the liquid sewage to the various parts of the field where it is absorbed into the soil

The specifications for this system are usually determined by the local health department. After analyzing the soil and considering the size of the house (usually the number of bedrooms determines in large measure the number of people that could be expected to live in the house), the health department will issue a septic permit that will include the size of the tank, the number of subsoil drain lines, their length, and the width and depth of the trench holding each line.

The area to be used by the septic system should be cleared of all trees and other heavy growth to ensure that the system's capacity will not be reduced by future damage from roots. Weeping willow trees, in particular, have a way of working their roots into the pipelines and clogging them.

Check your lot size and house location to ensure that

- the lot will provide enough room to accommodate the house and the septic system;
- there is enough room, if your plans require a well, to provide a minimum lateral separation of 100 feet between the well and the nearest point of the septic system, as required by most building codes; and
- the size of the lot will permit the movement of machinery (primarily a backhoe and a small bulldozer) to the septic area after the foundation of the house has been built. If this is not the case, install the septic system before you begin the foundation.

Sand-Filter Disposal System

If the soil conditions of your lot do not permit the use of a subsoil drain system, you might consider installing a sand-filter system. These are miniature sewage systems that operate on principles similar to the large public utility systems and discharge water that is close to being drinkable. Their efficiency is not related to soil conditions, but they require a place to drain the discharge. They are more expensive than the subsoil drain system.

Install a Temporary Water Supply System

Before masonry work can begin, you must have a source of water for mixing the mortar, cleaning the brick and other related masonry tasks. Check with your masonry contractor and determine what the requirements will be.

The following are various ways of supplying temporary water:

- Have the plumber install a temporary hookup to the local water supply. This is a simple task if the supply line is already installed on or near your lot.
- Arrange to get water from a neighbor.
- Haul in water by truck using 55-gallon drums or other suitable containers.
- Install a well. Of course, this is to be done only if your plans call for a well as a permanent source of water. The masonry requirement for water, however, may dictate the timing of the well installation.

Install a Temporary Electrical Hook-Up

Before the framing of the house can begin, you are going to need a temporary source of electricity for saws and other equipment. This hookup is normally installed by the electrical contractor. He will rig up on a pole a temporary service box that must be inspected by the local building inspector. Then the power company brings their lines to the service box. This process may take two or three weeks, so planning for this service should begin early. In an emergency, a gasoline-powered generator will suffice, but in the long run it is better to have power on a more permanent basis.

Costing

Don't overlook the following costing details prior to starting construction:

- The cost of labor and materials for clearing, grading, excavating and laying the driveway base is included in the site contractor's bid.
- The cost of the culvert pipe is provided by the supplier and the labor for its installation is part of the site contractor's bid unless the highway department does the job. Labor for brick or stone head walls is contained in the mason's bid and the cost of the materials is provided by the masonry supplier.
- The cost of the materials for the house layout is provided by the lumber supplier, and the labor is included in the bid of the contractor given the job.
- The cost of the building permit and the water and sewer fees can be obtained from the building official.
- The cost of the materials and labor for the septic or other disposal system are included in the bids of the trade contractor.

Management

To make sure the construction gets off to a good start, don't overlook the following:

- Get the building permit and pay fees for the sewer and water hookup.
- See that the appropriate trade contractors get the permits for electrical, plumbing and HVAC work. Post these permits on the

site as required by local codes. Contact the site work contractor and have him begin his job.

- Line up other site work contractors (well digging and septic system) as needed.
- Minimize soil erosion by placing hay bales or other suitable material at probable water run-off areas. Disturb the original grade only as necessary for construction.
- Have the culvert pipe on site if the driveway needs one.
- Have house layout materials on site when needed.
- Start a daily log of construction events including work done and materials delivered. The daily log will be very useful in keeping a check on progress and in keeping a record of materials ordered, including those not in the original estimate. It will be important for you to know when and if you exceed your budget and by how much.

■ — CHAPTER 5 — ■

The Importance of Footings

The footing is the part of the structure that provides the base and the contact with the ground for the house. Most footings are made of concrete reinforced with steel bar. In all-wood foundations, however, the footings are usually composed of gravel.

The two most important aspects of footing construction are:

1. They must be emplaced on firm, undisturbed soil. If your lot has been filled, the fill should be compacted by mechanical means.
2. The top of the footing must be below the frost line. Check this requirement with the local building code.

Build on Solid Footings

If your house plans have been prepared for your lot by an architect or engineer, they will show in detail the size of the footings and the size and amount of reinforcing bar needed. If your plans came from a general source, such as a plans service or paneled home manufacturer, the footings will not necessarily be suited for your particular lot and its soil conditions. It is very important that the footings and foundation be specifically designed for your lot. Get some help from a professional architect or engineer, if necessary. In many cases the local building officials will advise you on code requirements for footings and foundations. As a general rule and as a *minimum* requirement

- the footings for a one-story house should be not less than 16 inches wide and 8 inches deep.

FIGURE 5.1 Footings

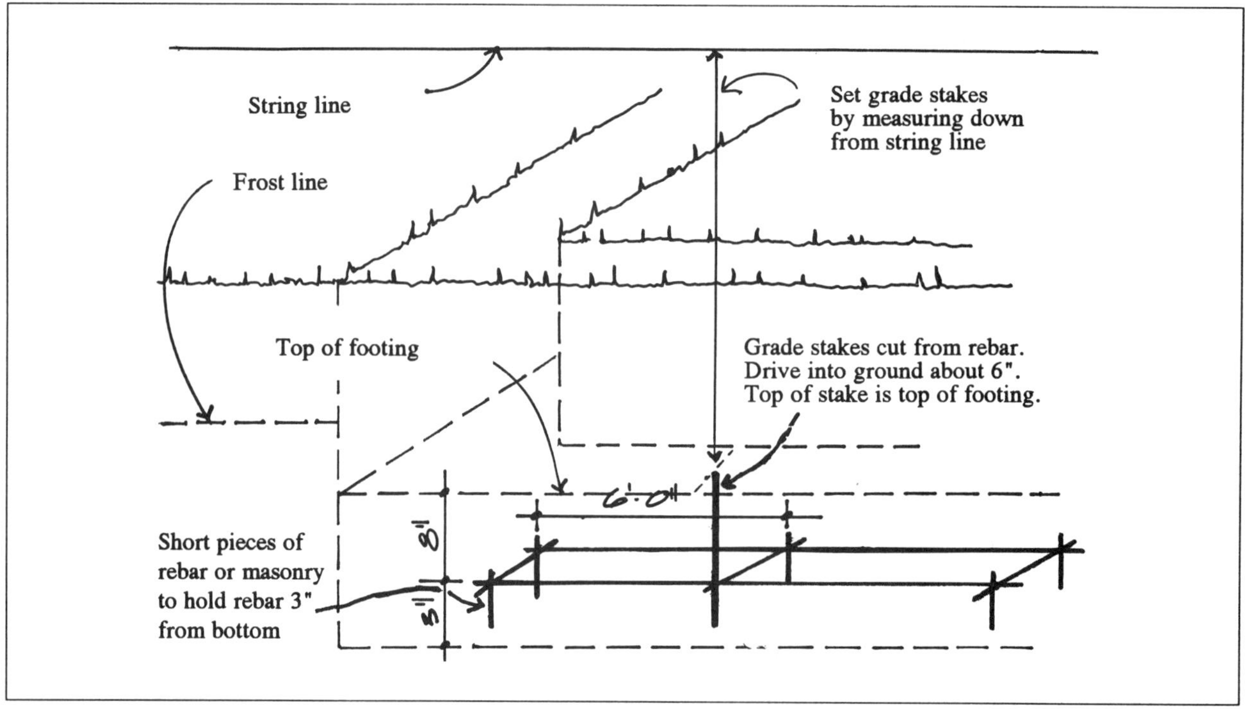

- for a two-story house or a one-story house with a basement, the footings should be at least 24 inches wide and 12 inches deep.

These are *minimums.* Check your plan with a local professional.

In all footings, whether or not the plans call for it, install reinforcing bar. This is a relatively inexpensive addition and provides insurance against possible problems that can be quite expensive to correct after construction.

Figure 5.1 illustrates a typical footing consisting of poured concrete reinforced with steel bar. The sides of the excavated trench provide the forms for the concrete.

You will need to know the quantities of materials used in the footings because they are usually provided by the owner/general contractor.

Determine the amount of concrete by multiplying the depth × width × length of the footings and convert this figure to cubic yards. (There are 27 cubic feet in a cubic yard.) Do not forget to include the concrete pads under piers, fireplaces, columns and other areas shown on the blueprint. Having calculated the total amount of concrete, increase it by 25 percent to 30 percent. You will probably have about this much waste created primarily by digging out unexpected soft spots and some collapse of the trench side walls. Use 3,000 pounds per square inch (PSI) concrete and order it by the cubic yard.

The reinforcing steel bar (rebar) requirement is based on the length of rebar needed. Allow at least a foot of overlap where the different bars meet. Rebar is usually supplied in 20-foot lengths.

You will need stakes to hold the horizontal reinforcing rebar *within the bottom third of the concrete during the pouring.* Install these vertical supports at about 6-foot intervals.

You will also need grade stakes to indicate the top of the concrete footing. Measure down from the batter-board string line the proper distance to establish the correct placement of the top of the stake.

Both grade stakes and the vertical supports for the horizontal rebar should be metal or masonry. For example, pieces of concrete block can be used to keep the rebar well up into the bottom third of the footing. This is not as good a system as the one using metal support stakes because the rebar can slip off the piece of block during the pouring. Do not use wood. It will weaken the concrete, particularly after it has rotted away. Rebar is an excellent material for support purposes. Most suppliers will cut the rebar for you, so compute the number of grade and vertical support stakes needed before ordering the material and add in a few extra. Vertical supports of about 8 inches are all right, but the grade stakes should be long enough to allow about 1 foot to be driven into the ground plus the thickness of the footing. You will also need some malleable wire to tie the rebar to the vertical stakes. Do not forget the rebar for the pads for the fireplace, piers, etc.

If your lot has any slope, you will need to install your footings with steps to compensate for the differences in grade, as seen in Figure 5.2. For a block foundation, the height of each step should be 8 inches, the height of the block. To form these steps, you will need material, such as plywood, to hold the fresh concrete as shown in the illustration. The plywood pieces should be 8 inches high and about 4 inches wider than the footing so that it can be forced into the dirt sidewalls of the footing trench for stability. You may need some small stakes (1 × 2 × 12 inches) to hold the plywood in place if the soil is soft. When poured, concrete for these steps should be fairly stiff.

Footing Costs

Most contractors who specialize in footing work prefer to furnish only the labor and tools with the owner/general contractor supplying the concrete and other materials. If this is the case, be certain in your bidding that each bidder knows exactly what he is bidding on. You may want to ask for two bids, one for the complete job including the materials and the other for the job with you furnishing the materials.

FIGURE 5.2 Stepped Footings

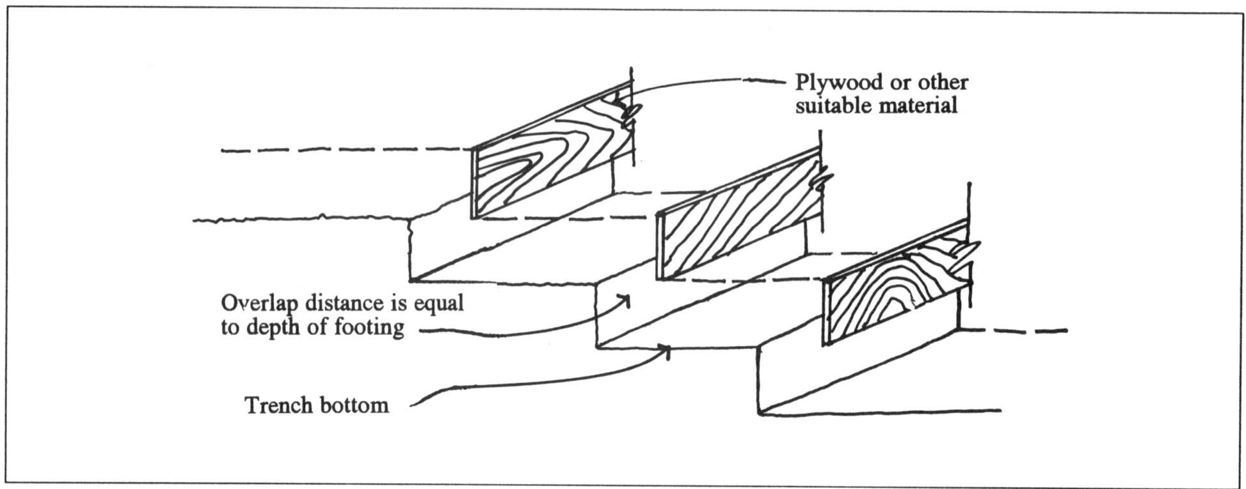

Enumerate your labor requirements in detail to the bidding contractors as follows:

1. Dig the footing trenches (and other areas such as fireplace base, column and pier pads). Digging may be done by hand, or done in part by machine (usually a backhoe) and finished by hand. Hand digging usually results in less waste of the concrete because there is less collapse of the walls. Machine digging may provide lower labor costs. The labor price should also include corrections to the excavations directed by the local building inspector in order to get approval.
2. Install the rebar, vertical supports and grade stakes, including tying this material.
3. Pour and distribute the concrete and finish it with a float (a wood trowel that levels the top with a rough finish).

Some footing contractors prefer to give a labor price based on a certain charge for each cubic yard of concrete poured. This method is acceptable, but it is preferable to get a fixed price for the job because a price for each yard encourages the contractor to exaggerate the size of the footing trenches and thus increase both the labor and the material costs.

In summary, to get the total cost of the footings, both labor and material costs can be provided by the contractor, or the labor cost can be provided by the contractor with the material furnished by you from the supplier. You will need to know the quantities of concrete by the cubic yard, rebar to include the grade stakes and vertical supports, tie wire for the rebar, and the material for the steps, if any.

Footing Installation Plan

Installing the footing can be simple or complex depending on your house design and the lot. Whatever the case, you must have a plan for the footing operation. Consider the following:

- How will you get the concrete truck to the footing trenches? These trucks carry from seven to nine yards of concrete. Their flotation is not the best, and they tend to be top-heavy. Get advice from your footing contractor. If your lot poses a very difficult problem in getting the concrete trucks to the footings, your concrete supplier may be able to offer additional advice.
- In some circumstances, the best way to get the concrete to certain areas of the footing trench may be to move the truck across another trench already dug. If so, pack the inside of the trench with concrete block to prevent the side walls from caving in. When it is no longer necessary to cross this trench, remove the block and dress up the trench.
- On occasion, the best solution to reach the footing trenches is to build a makeshift wood trough and use it as an extension of the truck trough, or to use several wheelbarrows.
- In very troublesome situations, you may have to rent a concrete pumper at extra cost and pump the concrete into the footing trenches.
- Make sure that the material is on the site before the arrival of the contractor and his crew (less the concrete, of course).
- Allow a full day to dig the footing trenches for the average-size house.
- Check the plans carefully with your actual layout to insure that footings for fireplaces, masonry steps, piers and column bases have been dug and are accurately located. It will be costly if these footings are inadvertently omitted and have to be poured later.
- Line up the building inspector. The local code will probably require *an inspection of the footing trenches before the concrete is poured.*
- Order the concrete when all inspections have been passed and the contractor is ready to pour.
- Once you have placed the order and the truck has left the mixing yard, the concrete is yours. You usually have one to two hours from the time the truck leaves the plant until it must be emptied.
- Plan on pouring all of the concrete the same day unless you have an unusually large house. If the job requires more than one day, plan to pour so that concrete poured the second day does not structurally link up with the concrete poured the first day that has already "set up." For example, on the first day pour the

house footings, and on the second day pour the pads for the fireplace, piers, columns and masonry steps.

- Check on the weather to ensure that both precipitation and temperature forecasts are favorable. After the concrete has set for four hours or more, rain should have little effect on the curing process. Concrete should not be poured when temperatures are expected to fall to near freezing. Don't forget that temperatures tend to drop after sundown.

Allow at least two days for the concrete to gain sufficient strength before beginning the construction of the foundation.

In all cases, have a workable plan before you order the concrete.

Management of the Footing Job

Management of the footing installation should include the following:

- Make sure that the footing trenches are dug along the correct lines. Sounds ridiculous, doesn't it, but mistakes do happen. To avoid this problem, mark the ground under the string lines where the footing trenches are to be dug. Use colored plastic tape or lime.
- Make sure that all loose spoil is removed from the trenches.
- Check to see that the bottom of the trenches are down to firm undisturbed soil. Be particularly wary of those areas that originally contained a large tree root system. If the soil is still soft, continue digging until firm soil is reached.
- See that the sides of the trenches are more or less vertical.
- Be sure that the foreman knows where you want the spoil thrown. Without being told otherwise, most crews will place the spoil where the least effort is required. Generally, spoil should be thrown outside the house area where it can be easily handled by machinery when the final grading is done. If spoil is placed inside the house area in which a concrete slab is to be the first floor, it may interfere with the preparations needed to give the concrete slab a good base. If the plans call for a crawl space, piles of dirt will interfere with the work of crews who will be moving around in the crawl space later.
- Before the concrete is poured, make one final check of the trench alignment by placing the batter-board string lines in place to mark the foundation location. Then check the alignment of the trenches.

There is a tendency for workmen to add too much water to the concrete so that it will flow easily through the trenches and thus require less labor to place. Most concrete trucks are equipped with water tanks to permit thinning. Although some modest thinning may be required, thinning to the extent that the concrete flows easily will drastically reduce its final strength. If required, water should be added only to the extent that the concrete mix is still able to stand without spreading out flat due to its own weight. There should be no visible pools of water in the concrete. With the proper consistency, most of the concrete will have to be more or less placed in the trenches by constantly moving the truck trough, or by shoveling, or by wheelbarrow, or by a combination of all three.

A more accurate method of properly controlling the concrete/water mixture is the slump test. This test is performed on the concrete just before it is poured at the site. It consists of the use of a metal cone open at both ends with a base diameter of 8 inches, a top diameter of 4 inches and a height of 12 inches. The cone, provided by the concrete supplier, is filled with concrete from the truck and packed tightly to remove all pockets. The cone is then removed and placed alongside the concrete. Without the cone, the concrete will slump or fall to some degree. The amount of the slump is measured. If it falls between 2 inches and 4 inches, go ahead and pour. If it falls more than this amount, the concrete has too much water in it. If the fall is less than 2 inches, the concrete is going to be difficult to work and needs a little more water.

If loose dirt should fall into the concrete, have it removed with a shovel. The dirt will weaken the concrete at that point.

Your computations for the amount of concrete needed may not be the same as the actual requirement. For example, running into large amounts of soft soil will call for more excavation and thus more concrete than planned. Keep the concrete moving to the job, but hold off ordering the last truckload until all other trucks have been emptied. Then estimate how much more you will need and order that amount. You should be able to keep the waste to half a yard or less.

Keep the concrete supplier's trip tickets. They will give you the exact number of cubic yards of concrete delivered and provide a firm record for labor payment if your contract is the per-cubic-yard basis.

CHAPTER 6

Foundations

If your plans were prepared by an engineer or an architect for your particular lot, they should show all the necessary details of construction, including required reinforcing.

On the other hand, if your plans were provided by a plans service, it is unlikely that the foundation design fits your lot. If the plans and shape of the lot permit foundation design not exceeding four or five courses of block, you should not need any extra strengthening. Should your situation require a full or partial basement (particularly if this is a modification of the original plan) or if the lot slopes steeply and your crawl space requires walls of six or more courses of block, it is probable that additional reinforcing is needed. You should consult with a professional architect or engineer to get safe design criteria for your foundation.

The following are samples of the more commonly used reinforcement systems for higher foundation walls:

- Horizontal Block Reinforcing (Figure 6.1) is applied as the mason lays the foundation. It can be used for each course (it is buried in the mortar), every other course or just every third course. Generally, the greater the backfill that will be placed against the wall, the more horizontal reinforcement is required. Horizontal reinforcing can be supplied in different widths to match the widths of the block or block/brick combination used in the foundation wall.

FIGURE 6.1 Horizontal Block Reinforcing

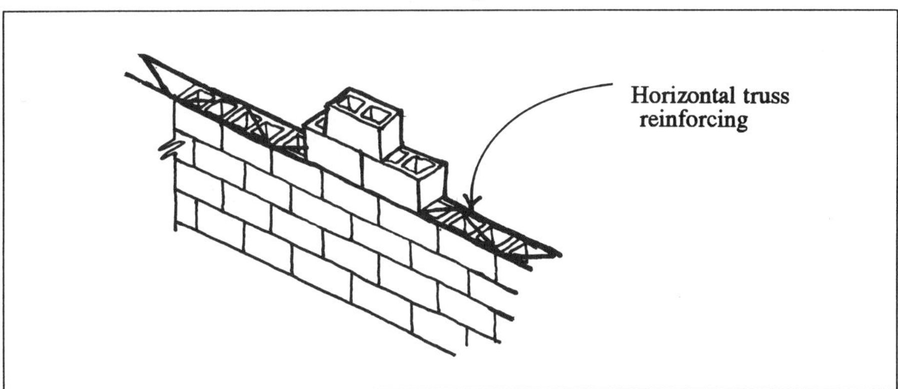

- Vertical Block Reinforcing (Figure 6.2) is applied in two commonly used methods. One is the use of reinforcing bar and concrete to build a solid steel and concrete column. The other is to build into the walls pilasters of extra block to give the wall greater thickness at selected points.

If your plans are based on a poured concrete foundation, the above remarks apply equally as well. With poured concrete, however, the horizontal reinforcing will most likely be made of rebar rather than the special truss designed for block.

Check with your local contractors to determine which type of foundation, concrete or block, is best for you. Block is usually better if your plans call for many corners in the foundation or many openings in the foundation for doors and windows. On the other hand, concrete is usually stronger and more waterproof (it will need extra waterproofing, as discussed later in this chapter). Concrete becomes more important if you have underground living space in your plan, but it may be more costly.

■ USING A BRICK/BLOCK CRAWL SPACE FOUNDATION

The crawl-space foundation made of block or a combination of brick and block (see Figure 6.3) has three forms:

1. The first method is the use of block by itself. The exterior of the block can be left as is or it can be painted or stuccoed.
2. The second form is the block/brick combination, where the brick forms part of the load-bearing foundation and thus supports the wood framing structure in conjunction with the block.

FIGURE 6.2 Vertical Block Reinforcing

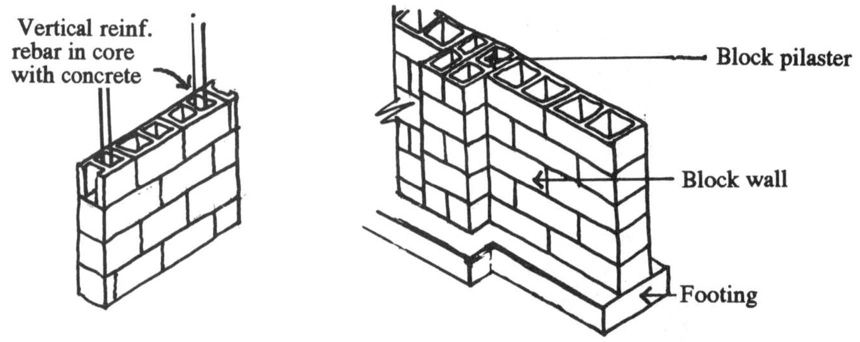

This form of foundation is best used where the exterior walls are to be finished with wood, aluminum or vinyl siding.

3. The third form is used when the exterior wall is to be completely covered with the brick veneer as a finished surface. The bricks of the exterior walls are actually an extension of the brick veneer of the foundation wall. The brick does not support the structure. Actually the structure (foundation wall and wood frame) supports the brick.

Crawl spaces must be vented to allow the circulation of air to the outside. Foundation vents, usually made of aluminum, are 8 inches × 16 inches, the size of the concrete block. During cold weather these vents may be closed to retain the heat in the crawl space.

The number of vents and their spacing is usually indicated in the blueprint. As a general rule, at least one vent should be close to each corner of the house, and there should be cross ventilation for at least two opposite sides. If you live in an area of high humidity, install at least one vent for each 15 linear feet of exterior foundation wall.

In addition, access to crawl spaces must be provided by doors not less than 18 inches × 24 inches. Ready-made steel doors of various sizes are usually available from masonry suppliers. These doors can also be made of wood by the carpentry crew during the framing job. Use salt-treated wood.

If your crawl space is large (over 2,000 square feet) or if the shape is unusual, you should consider installing more than one crawl space access door for the convenience of the crews who must work in this area during construction and later when repair or servicing of the house requires work in the crawl space.

If you are building your house in a very cold climate, you may want to install a trapdoor in the floor (perhaps in a closet area) to provide

FIGURE 6.3 Foundations with Crawl Spaces

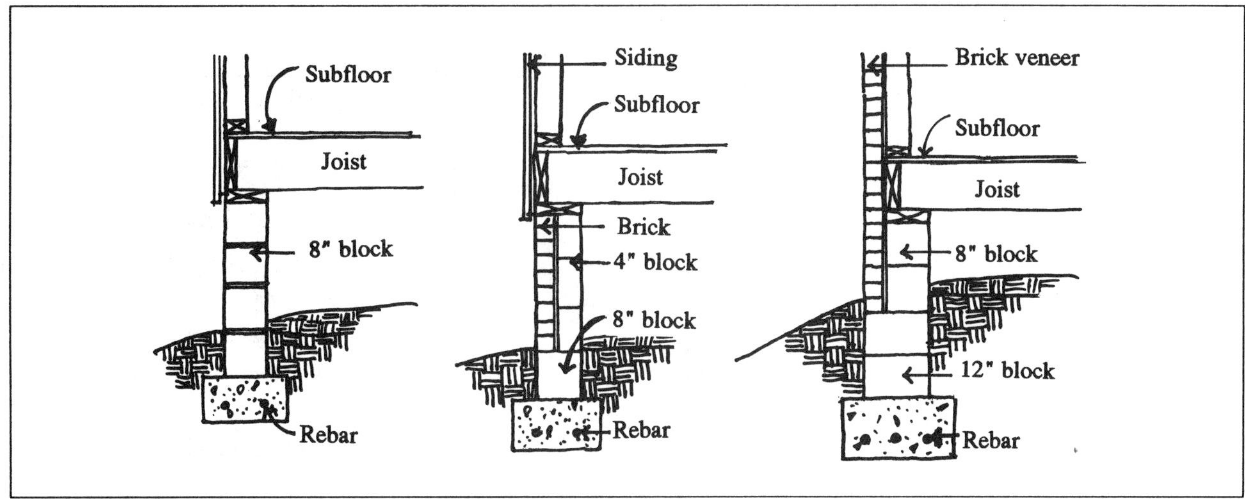

entry into the crawl space from inside the house. This additional access makes it easier to work on plumbing when pipes freeze.

■ USING A BASEMENT FOUNDATION

The basement foundation wall can be built using the same three forms shown in Figure 6.3. The details of the various elements of the basement foundation are illustrated in Figure 6.4.

Waterproofing material should be applied over the exterior of the basement wall below grade and a slotted drain pipe in a gravel bed added at the base of the footings to take away the water and prevent pressure buildup.

Waterproofing may consist of several layers of tar and building paper or several coats of waterproof masonry material or a combination of both.

A recently developed, more effective waterproofing material is a synthetic rubber waterproofing membrane. When used over concrete block, it is best to first apply parging (a layer of mortar cement about ½ inch thick) over the block, then follow with the synthetic rubber sheeting after the parging has dried.

The waterproofing must be protected during the backfilling process or rocks and other hard material in the backfill may penetrate it and allow water seepage into the living area. Large sheets (4 × 8 feet or 4 × 10 feet) of impregnated sheathing (an inexpensive compressed fiber material ½ inch thick) are excellent for this purpose and should be applied against the waterproofing before the backfilling is begun.

FIGURE 6.4 Basement Foundation

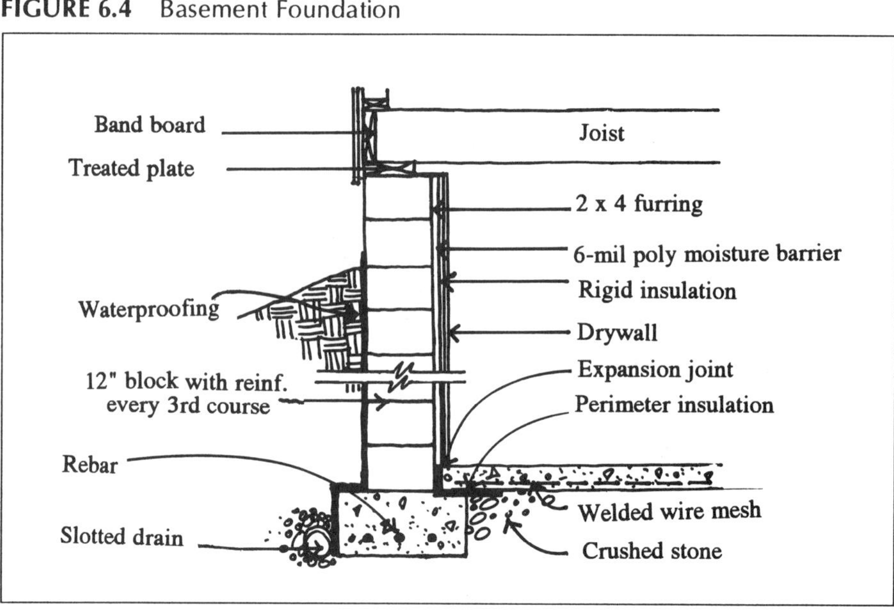

Backfilling must not be done until the floor framing of the first floor has been completed including the laying of the subfloor. Without this bracing, the foundation wall could collapse.

Costing

The cost of labor for the foundation walls is provided by the mason. He may also prefer to furnish the materials as well. If not, get the supplier to "take off" (determine the quantities needed) the foundation materials and price them.

If your choice of waterproofing is the building paper/tar system or the rubber membrane, most roofers will give you the cost of both labor and materials. If one or more coatings of cement-based waterproofing compound is required instead, the labor can be priced by the mason and the material by the masonry supplier.

The backfilling is usually performed by the site work contractor with the owner/general contractor furnishing the impregnated sheathing. Have the lumber supplier give you the cost of the sheathing.

In the above discussion of foundation walls, the poured-in-place concrete wall can be used instead of the precast concrete block. Under these circumstances, you should get the concrete contractors to bid on the basis of providing all of the materials for the forms, the reinforcing and the concrete. If this approach is not feasible, then ask one of the contractors to determine the materials needed and give you the list.

Then get the price for these materials from the masonry and lumber suppliers.

Management

Make sure that all the materials (less the concrete for poured foundation walls) are on the job before the masonry crew arrives. If your contract calls for the mason to furnish the materials, it is his responsibility to have them on the job.

Visit the job site at least once a day. Survey the material and talk to the head mason to be sure that the supplies are adequate. For some strange reason, many contractors realize they are running out of materials only when they actually do so. This usually means the loss of one or more days work.

Before the mason begins laying the block or brick, be sure that the batter-board string lines are installed in the proper slot. The footings contractor has probably cut additional slots to measure the outside limits of the footings. This can cause the mason to begin laying the block on the wrong line position.

The following is a list of materials needed:

Block	Horizontal reinforcing
Brick	Vertical reinforcing
Mortar cement	Anchor bolts
Masonry sand	Concrete and steel lintels
Brick ties	Crawl space door
Foundation vents	Window, door frames for basement

Anchor bolts are set into the masonry with enough of the threaded end projecting upward through the wood sill plate so that a washer and bolt may be installed to hold the sill plate to the masonry wall. Lintels are those devices used to span openings in masonry work for doors and windows.

If your foundation has these openings, you will need a concrete lintel to span each one. The simplest type of concrete lintel is the precast version that you can get from the masonry supplier. Its height and width are matched to the block, and its length should allow at least an 8-inch overlap on the bearing blocks on each side (see Figure 6.5).

Another method is illustrated in which the lintel is made on the job using a special bond block formed like a "U" (see Figure 6.5). It is much more complicated than the precast lintel and requires rebar and a wood form to hold the bond blocks in place until the concrete has set.

If your wall has a brick veneer over the block, you will need steel lintels to support the brick over the door or window opening (see

FIGURE 6.5 Masonry Lintels

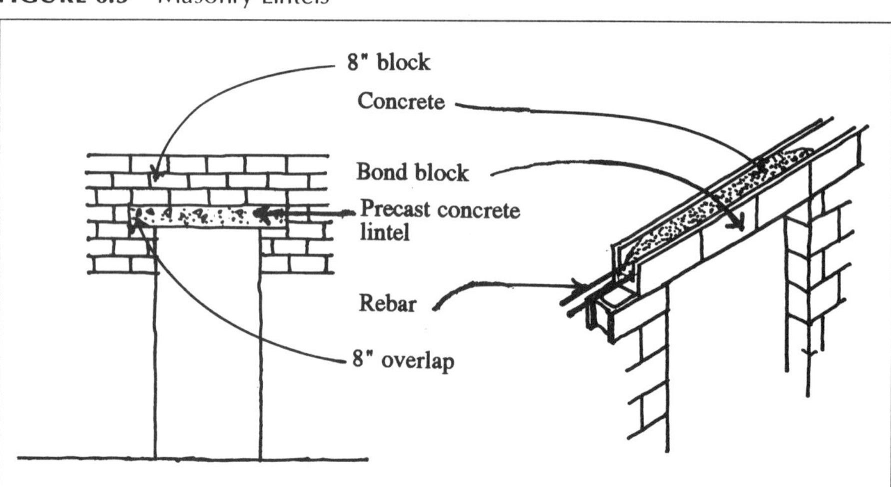

Figure 6.6). Steel angle iron whose sides are wide enough to support the brick are fine for this job. With standard brick an angle iron with 3½-inch legs works well. Again, allow at least an 8-inch overlap on the supporting brick below.

Discuss with the head mason the type of mortar joint you want in the brick and block. Some of the various types are flush, struck, concave, beaded, weathered and grapevine (for colonial work—requires a special tool). The mason can illustrate the various types for you on the job. This point should have been covered in the specifications and used for the bidding. It is wise to check again, however.

Mortar cement is manufactured in several shades and colors. Consult with and get your brick supplier's recommendation for the best mortar/brick combination.

Before the job begins, find out where the head mason wants the brick, block, mortar cement and sand placed on the site. This is important to minimize the mason's labor. Once this has been determined, place a sign at each location and, when ordering the material, ask the supplier to tell the driver to unload at the appropriate sign.

Brick and block should not be laid when they are wet or when temperatures are near freezing. Provide some sort of cover at the job site so this material can be protected when not being used. Polyethylene sheet material is excellent for this purpose.

Although mortar cement is packaged in what is supposed to be waterproof bags, the cement should have additional protection. Most suppliers deliver mortar on a standard wood pallet. Ask them to include a waterproof cover with each pallet. They are worth the extra cost.

FIGURE 6.6 Steel Lintels

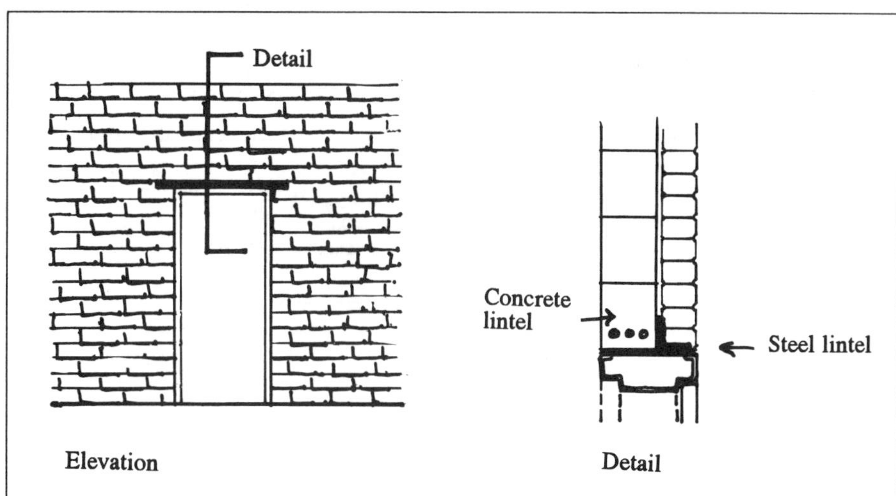

The trucks that deliver the brick and block are very heavy and are equipped with special unloading cranes. It is important that they be given sufficient space for operation. Discuss this problem with your mason, who is familiar with these trucks and their requirements. If your lot has little space for storing materials, you should consider having the material delivered in more than one trip with a day or two in between to allow the mason to use up the supplies on the job and release storage space for the additional material.

If your plans require windows and doors in the foundation walls of a basement, have them on hand so they may be installed by the mason. Having them on site during the masonry work also permits the mason to check the openings required in the masonry with the items to be installed.

■ USING A BLOCK/SLAB FLOOR FOUNDATION

Figure 6.7 illustrates the block foundation wall with a concrete slab floor poured over compacted fill.

In addition to the obvious differences when compared to the crawl space design, note the following:

- The top course of the block is a header or shoe block in which a portion of the block has been cut out by the manufacturer to provide a base for the concrete slab.
- The slab is laid on the top of the rigid perimeter insulation (see Chapter 13, Energy-Saving Insulation Options).

FIGURE 6.7 Block Foundation with Slab Floor on Grade

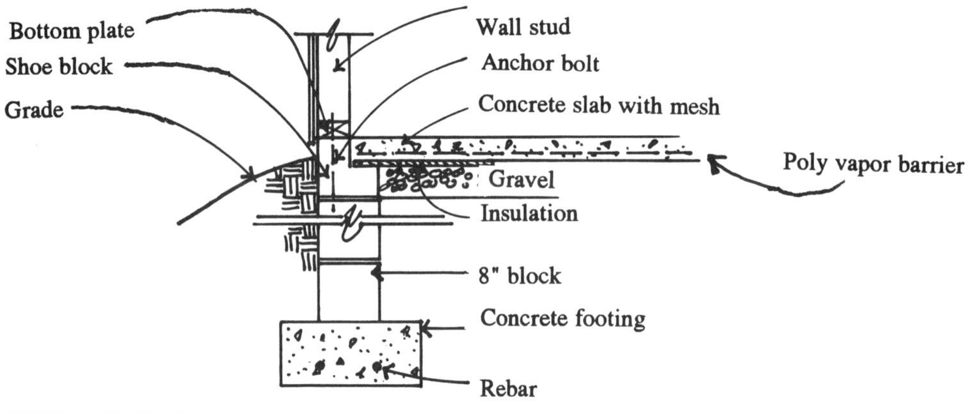

- There is a vapor barrier of 6-mil polyethylene below the concrete and on top of the fill.

Compared to the crawl space design, the slab requires less insulation and it is more solid and less prone to problems from ground moisture. On the other hand, the crawl space design will make later changes to the structure much easier; it is readily adaptable to a nonlevel lot and is less tiring on the feet.

Although the illustration shows the foundation wall as concrete block, this same design can be built with a combination brick/block foundation wall. Use the brick as the form for holding the slab floor rather than the header block. It can also be modified for a complete exterior brick wall as shown in Figure 6.3. The header block is used, but a base for the brick veneer is needed, either by laying the brick on the footing or by laying a larger block for the first course or two and then laying the brick on top of this wider block.

Costing

The cost of the labor and materials for the block and brick is provided as indicated in the discussion of the crawl-space foundation.

The cost for labor and materials for the concrete work is given in the bids of the concrete contractors. Again, you may find that the contractors prefer that the owner/general contractor furnish the materials. If so, have the masonry supplier give you a take off of the materials and provide a price for furnishing them.

Management

Make sure that all the materials are on hand before the crew arrives. Determine the proper placement of these materials as discussed in the crawl-space foundation section.

You will *not* need the following materials for a slab floor:

Vents	Vertical reinforcing
Crawl space access doors	Concrete lintels
Horizontal reinforcing	Steel lintels

Additional material needed for the slab:

Wire mesh (6 gauge, 6 × 6)	Concrete
Fill material	Rigid insulation
Polyethylene	

The eight-step order of the construction after the footings have been poured is as follows:

1. The foundation is laid.
2. The under-slab fill is brought in and compacted.
3. Any rough-in of plumbing, electrical and HVAC is installed *and inspected by the local building inspector.*
4. The polyethylene vapor barrier is put down.
5. The perimeter insulation is installed.
6. Wire mesh is laid.
7. *The work is inspected again.*
8. The concrete is poured and finished.

If the amount of fill is substantial (more than a 4-inch layer of sand or gravel), you should have the site contractor build up most of the grade before the footings and foundation walls have been built. The concrete crew will spread and compact the final top layer of the fill (including any spoil from the under-slab mechanical work), dress it up and lay the floor.

You will need a definite, workable plan for pouring the concrete, as previously discussed in Chapter 5, The Importance of Footings.

If the concrete contractor uses wood grade stakes (needed to give him level points throughout the slab area), make sure that these stakes are removed and the holes filled with concrete during the final finishing. Wood will eventually rot and weaken the slab.

The footings received only a float finish, but in most cases the slab must be given a trowel finish that is much smoother and requires the

FIGURE 6.8 Integrated Slab Foundation/Footing

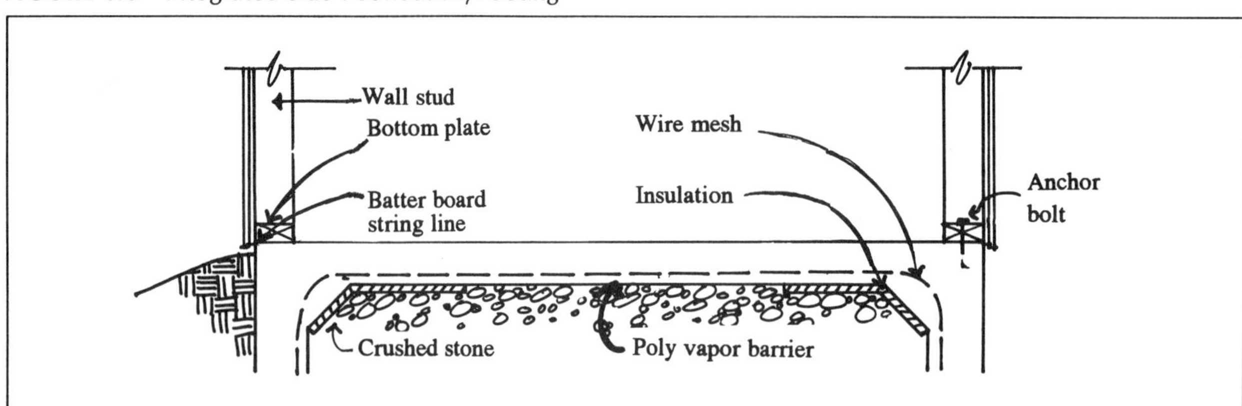

concrete to be more "set up." Consequently it will take more time. Consider this point in your scheduling. Start early in the morning.

The slab finish is much more sensitive to damage from rain or freezing precipitation than the footings. Watch the weather forecast. Have additional polyethylene sheeting on hand to cover the slab after it has been finished. This covering will not only protect the slab from the weather, but it will also provide better curing because it keeps the moisture in the concrete longer.

■ USING THE INTEGRATED CONCRETE FOOTING AND SLAB

Figure 6.8 illustrates a combination of the foundation and footings into a single piece of concrete. This method is simple and relatively inexpensive. The design should only be used on a flat lot. Even then it usually requires some site work to prepare the ground to properly receive the concrete.

Once the site work has been completed to provide the proper grade and compaction, the batter boards are installed. The next step is to dig the footing trenches. Because the footings and foundation walls are one piece of concrete, the string lines of the batter boards show the exterior line of both the footing and the foundation. The string lines indicate the level and dimensions of the finished floor.

The next step is to install the forms for the outside of the slab that will appear above grade. At this stage any under-slab plumbing, heating and electrical work is installed by the trade contractors. The grade for the slab is dressed up in preparation for the concrete pour. The rebar, mesh, insulation and vapor barrier are then put down, and *all work is checked by the building inspector.* Finally the concrete is poured.

Costing

Preparation of the grade, including both labor and materials, should be included in the site-work contractor's bid. It is much less costly to do this type of work by machine with the final dressing by hand.

Again, in determining the costs for the concrete work, you have two choices as to who provides the material. In this case, however, it is to your advantage to have the concrete contractor provide the form material. If you furnish this material, it will be used only once and discarded. The concrete contractor uses the forms over and over again, consequently his cost for them is low.

Management

To avoid wasting time and materials when laying the foundation, pay special attention to the following:

- Have on hand the following materials:

  Fill material
  Rebar and tie wire
  Wire mesh (6 gauge, 6 × 6 inch)
  Rigid insulation
  Form material
  Polyethylene
  Anchor bolts

- *When ordering concrete for slabs, specify that fiber mesh material be added. It will effectively reduce cracking in the finished product.*
- Have a plan for getting the concrete trucks to the job.
- Make certain that the under-slab plumbing, heating and electrical work has been completed and that the footings and slab work are checked by the inspector before the concrete is poured.
- Keep track of the weather and avoid pouring on days when freezing or near-freezing temperatures and precipitation are expected. A common rule of thumb is to pour if the temperature is 40°F and rising.
- Plan to start the pour early in the morning. The work should be continuous until the trowel finish is complete.
- After the troweling, cure the floor by covering it completely with polyethylene or by coating it with a spray-on curing compound. Leave the poly cover on at least three days. The spray-on coat will become part of the concrete. In very dry climates, keep the concrete moist by spraying with water as needed.

FIGURE 6.9 Block Bond Wall

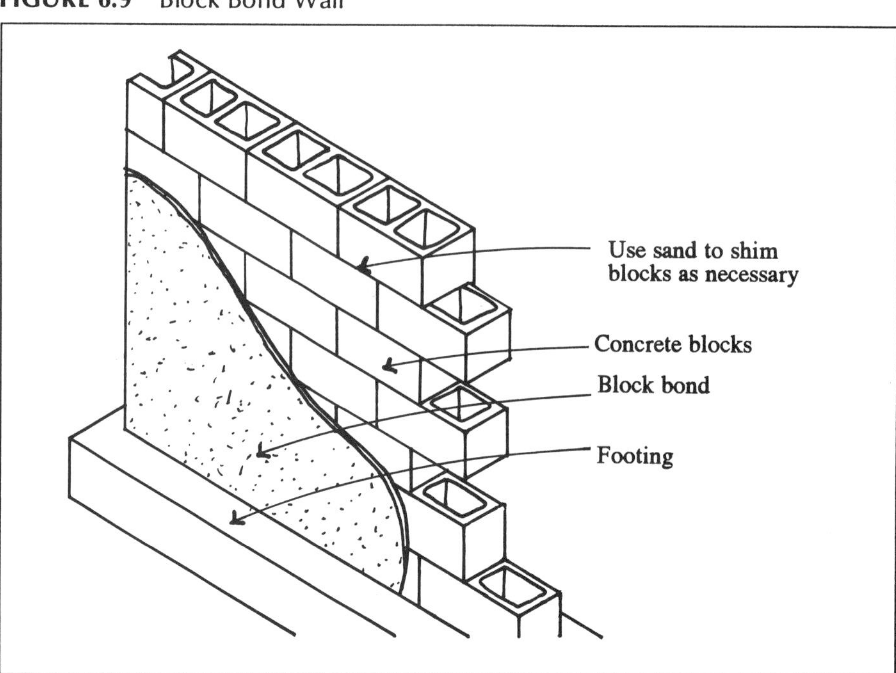

USING A BONDED-BLOCK-FOUNDATION WALL

Bonded block is a method of building a block wall without using conventional mortar (see Figure 6.9). If you use this system, construct the concrete footings in the usual way, then have your mason lay only the first course of block using mortar as he normally does. The rest of the foundation wall is then laid dry without the use of any mortar. To maintain a plumb, level wall, small amounts of sand may be inserted to raise blocks where required to keep the alignment.

When the dry laying of the block is complete, *both* vertical sides of the wall are covered with a thin layer (about ⅜ inch) of a special mortar consisting of hydrated lime, portland cement and a special fiberglass material. Most masonry suppliers carry this material. If you follow the instructions of the manufacturer, you should have no trouble.

The advantages of this system are that it requires less skill, and the wall is made waterproof by the application of the masonry/fiberglass coating. Its strength is at least equal to a wall laid fully with mortar. Horizontal reinforcing is not normally required, and the wall will present an attractive, easily painted stucco-like finish. This wall should not be covered with brick veneer. Since the mortar is missing from the joints of the block, the top of the brick veneer and the block will almost always be of different levels.

Costing

The cost of the block and the fiberglass binding material is provided by the masonry supplier with the labor cost furnished by the masonry contractor. Because little mortar is used, the block requirements will increase. The information sheet published by the bonding material manufacturer gives instructions as to how to compute the additional block and the amount of bonding material needed.

Management

All the management tips discussed in the previous sections will apply here as well.

■ USING A POLYSTYRENE-BLOCK FOUNDATION

A new substitute for concrete block is polystyrene block, a very lightweight block. The standard polystyrene block is 40 inches long (compared to 18 inches for the concrete block), 10 inches wide and 10 inches high.

Blocks are available that provide widths for the poured concrete of 4, 6, and 8 inches. Each side of the polystyrene block is 2⅛ inches in width, and the blocks are 10 or 12 inches in height.

The polystyrene block is laid by hand on the dry concrete footing and is held together by interlocking teeth (see Figure 6.10). Then concrete is poured into the cavities in the block. Both vertical and horizontal rebar may be installed as required. To reduce pressure on the polystyrene forms, the concrete should be poured to heights not exceeding 4 feet with intervals of approximately one hour between successive pours.

Polystyrene-block construction can be used for the foundation walls in a crawl space design or the full wall for basement living space.

Exterior walls can be finished with almost any exterior siding such as wood, shingles, stucco, brick and so forth. Interior walls (such as in a basement) should be covered with Sheetrock. Then paint, paneling or wallpaper can be applied.

Advantages of the polystyrene-block system compared to concrete block and concrete poured into wood forms are:

- Cost of labor and material is reduced up to 40 percent.
- The "wet curing" provided by the polystyrene seal improves the curing of the poured concrete so that the walls end up with a 50 percent greater compressive strength than standard concrete walls.

FIGURE 6.10 A Typical Polystyrene-Block Foundation Wall

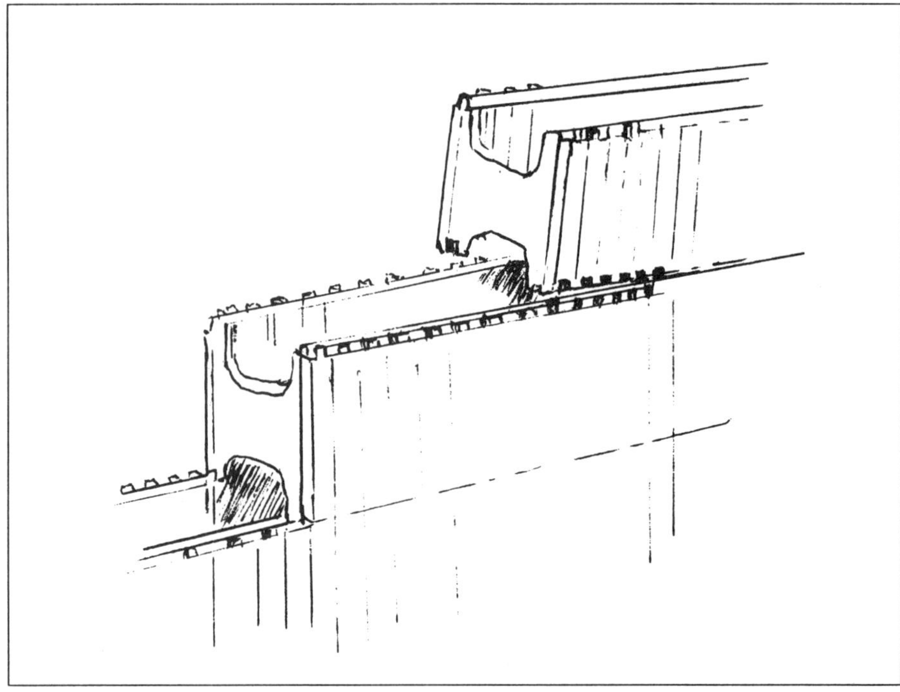

- The polystyrene provides a thermal insulation level of R-22 and sound insulation. Both of these qualities are important if the foundation walls are built to include basement living space.
- Labor skills to install polystyrene block are much less than those need to lay concrete block or to build the wood forms for conventionally poured concrete walls.
- In a fire, although the polystyrene will be consumed, the concrete wall will remain standing.

Costing

Material costs are obtained from the supplier. Labor costs are provided by the subcontractor.

Management

Polystyrene-block foundation construction may require some special management considerations, including the following:

- Use only subcontractors with experience in handling polystyrene block.

- Make sure the vertical rebar protrudes from the footings at least 1 foot to tie the concrete of the footings to the concrete of the foundation or basement wall.
- Have the polystyrene block and necessary rebar on the job before the crews arrive.

USING AN ALL-WOOD FOUNDATION

Figure 6.11 illustrates both the crawl-space and full-basement version of the all-wood foundation, a method of building footings and foundations that uses gravel and treated wood. It usually requires less time than the more conventional masonry method and should cost less. It can be installed in temperatures below freezing and thus permits construction in weather conditions that would halt concrete and masonry work.

The exact, proper construction of this type of foundation and footing is very important, particularly if the plan calls for a below-grade living area or basement.

The wood used in the construction must be salt-pressure treated, and the below-grade fasteners (nails and bolts) must be stainless steel. The pressure treatment for all lumber below grade should be .60 CCA (pressure treated with .60 pounds of chromate copper arsenate salt solution per cubic foot of lumber. See page 63), which is 50 percent higher than that recommended for normal ground contact.

The key element in this type of foundation is moisture control. Roof-water runoff must be directed away from the foundation by properly installed gutters, downspouts and splash blocks or, better, an underground pipe drain system. The joints between the plywood panels must be caulked. Final grading of the lot must be sloped away from the foundation, as it should be in any foundation construction.

In the basement version, plywood joints must be caulked full length and covered with a 6-mil polyethylene film to direct the water down into the footing drain system. As an added precaution, coat the foundation over the polyethylene with two coats of hot or cold tar with alternate layers of building paper or, preferably, coat the plywood with the rubber waterproofing membrane mentioned on page 47.

Footings may be gravel, crushed stone or sand at a minimum thickness of 4 inches for crawl space walls of a one-story house. For basement walls and two-story houses on crawl spaces, increase the thickness to 6 inches. Note in the basement version the need for the extra gravel around the base of the foundation and the drain pipe system.

FIGURE 6.11 All-Wood Foundation

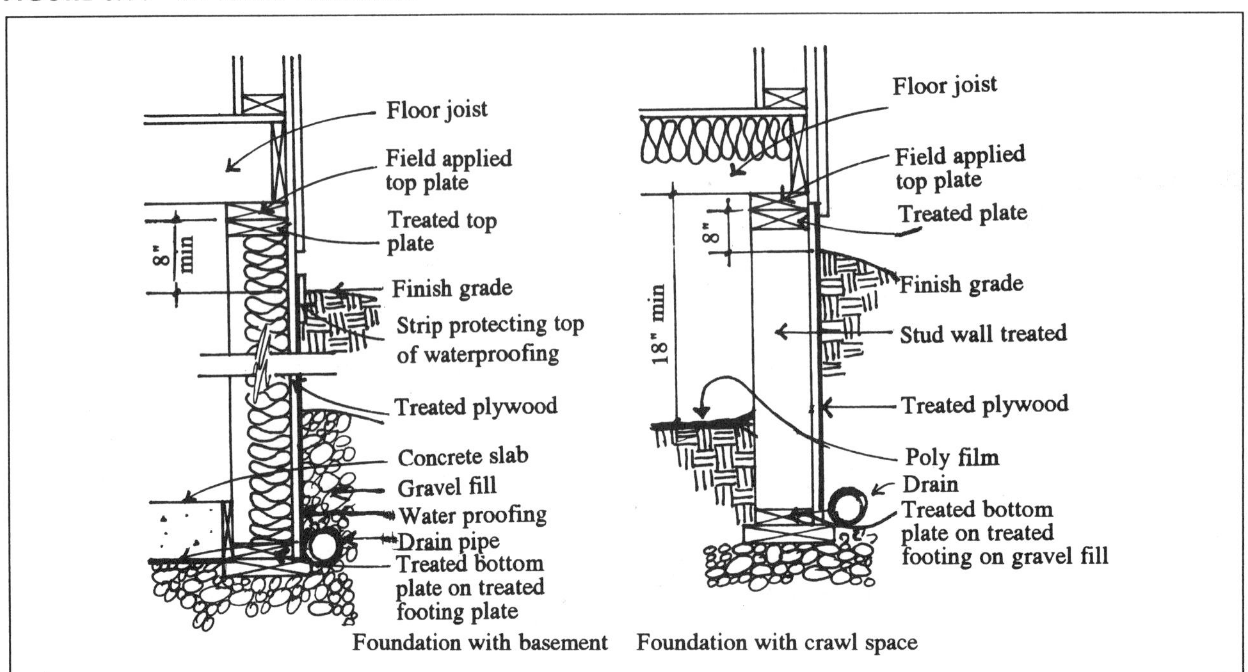

Costing

The labor cost for the footings is provided by the footing contractor with the owner/general contractor providing the gravel. In the basement version, the costs of labor and material should include the larger amounts of gravel and the drain-pipe system (corrugated plastic slotted pipe is fine) to be installed after the wood foundation walls are up and waterproofed.

The cost of the labor to install the wood foundation should be included in the framing contractor's bid with the lumber supplier doing the take off for quantities and price.

Management

Management of the all-wood foundation construction includes:

- Install the footings using the process similar to that for concrete, except that no rebar is required and the grade stakes can be treated wood.
- Determine how your footing contractor wants to handle the gravel. Should the entire load be dumped at one place, in several places or from the truck directly into the footing trenches?

- Check with the local building official in regard to inspections needed for the footings and any special requirements.
- Apply the management tips about carpentry work found in Chapter 7, Framing Your Project.

HOW TO CONTROL TERMITES

Termites can cause serious damage to houses if proper precautions are not taken. The most effective means of controlling termites is the poisoning of the soil around the foundation of the house by a professional contractor and the use of salt-treated wood in those areas where the wood could be exposed to moisture by contact with the ground, damp concrete, brick or block. See Chapter 7, Framing Your Project.

Have the contractor include a five-year guarantee that in essence says the contractor will pay for any damage to the house caused by termites and other wood-boring insects occurring in that time period. At the end of the five years, the guarantee can be extended for an additional fee.

Costing

The complete cost including labor, materials and the guarantee is included in the contractor's bid.

Management

If your house plan is based on crawl space construction, notify the contractor to apply the soil poisoning after the foundation is complete and the crawl-space grade is finished.

If your house plan is based on concrete-slab construction, notify the contractor to apply the soil poisoning after the foundation is complete, all the under-the-slab plumbing, electrical and heating work has been installed, the grade for the slab has been finished but before the concrete slab has been poured.

■ CHAPTER 7 ■

Framing Your Project

There are several methods of framing a house. Wood has been the most popular system for years, but steel framing is now making very rapid advances. In addition, concrete, concrete block and polystyrene block (discussed in Chapter 6, Foundations) can also be used to construct the outside walls.

■ WOOD FRAMING REMAINS THE MOST USED SYSTEM

The wood frame forms the shape and size and provides the strength of the structure. In a brick house (in modern construction this is actually brick veneer), the framing supports the brick, not the reverse, as many people think. It is very important that the framing be erected correctly. It is not an area in which to compromise to reduce costs. Errors discovered after the framing is complete may be expensive to correct.

As stated in the introduction, it is not the purpose of this book to teach you how to frame a house, but you should familiarize yourself with the framing system of your plans so that you know the major features and the names of the various parts. This knowledge will be very useful in talking to your suppliers and to your carpentry crew.

Selecting the Lumber

There are generally three choices in the selection of lumber for framing: fir, SPF (spruce, pine and fir mixture) and southern yellow pine (SYP).

Fir is an excellent lumber. It is strong and easy to work, but it may be expensive and not readily available in your area.

SPF is a mixture of several species of lumber and generally consists of various proportions of white spruce, Engleman spruce, lodge pole pine and Alpine fir. Expect the bulk of the wood to be spruce. SPF is a moderately strong lumber, but less strong than either fir or SYP and may require, in certain load-bearing roles, a larger structural dimension with increased costs. SPF lumber works very well, so you may save on labor costs. Like fir, it is very stable and will not usually twist or warp after installation. SPF should be available in most areas of the country.

SYP is a strong species and is less costly than fir or SPF. It is harder to work, however, and may cause labor costs to be higher. SYP also has a greater tendency to twist and warp after installation in the framing system. With proper blocking (a possible additional expense), it will usually perform within acceptable limits.

Considering the pros and cons of these types of lumber, a good compromise is a selection of fir or SPF for studs and top and bottom plates, and SYP for the joists, rafters, headers and all other elements of the system. All lumber should be kiln dried (KD).

For those parts of the framing where the lumber is to be exposed to moisture or to damage from termites and other wood-boring insects, you should use pressure-treated lumber to prolong its life. Pressure-treated wood should always be used for the sill plate (horizontal 2×8 on top of the foundation wall; see Figure 7.1). There are three different degrees of treatment as follows:

1. .25 pounds of salt solution per cubic foot of lumber for above grade, such as decks and railings
2. .40 pounds of salt solution per cubic foot for lumber in contact with the ground, such as columns supporting decks
3. .60 pounds of salt solution per cubic foot for lumber below grade, such as the all-wood foundation

Wet, salt-treated wood should be handled with gloves and a respirator, and a dust mask should be worn when using a power saw to cut it. *Scrap pieces should not be burned. Their fumes are toxic.*

FIGURE 7.1 Platform Framing

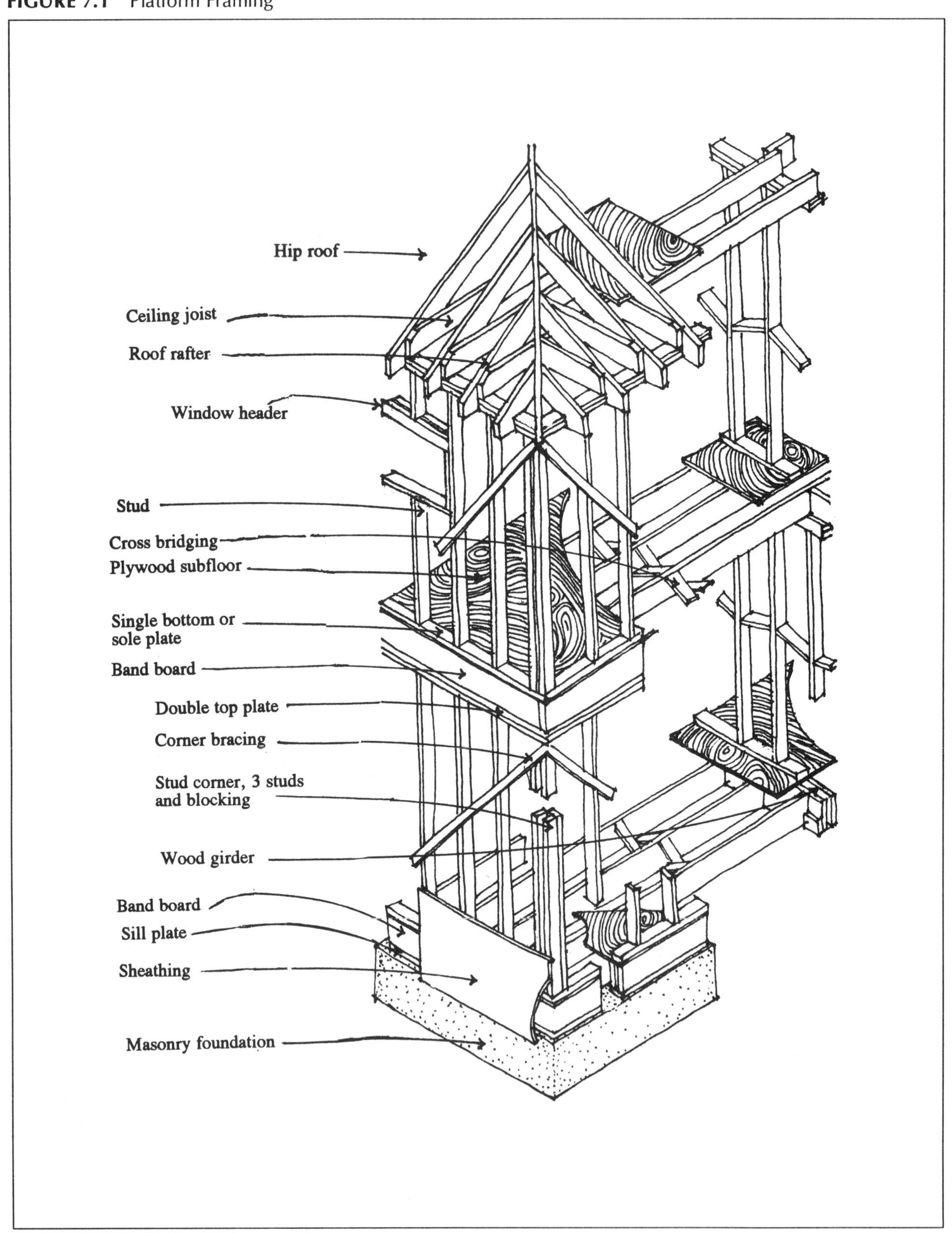

Selecting the Framing System

The three framing systems usually used are:

1. *Platform Framing:* In this system (see Figure 7.1), each floor is built separately with the first floor providing a work platform for the structure to be built above. Platform framing is the most widely used system.
2. *Balloon Framing:* This system is illustrated in Figure 7.2. Note that the studs of the exterior walls are continuous from the sill plate of the first floor to the top plates of the second floor. This type of framing is more costly in material because one 18-foot stud is more expensive than two standard studs of 93 inches. Labor costs are also higher because the structure requires much greater use of scaffolding.
3. *Plank-and-Beam Framing:* Shown in Figure 7.3, this type of framing uses greater spans for lumber and requires fewer pieces, but with greater dimensions. It is very popular in contemporary styling where exposed beam ceilings are desired.

Exterior Wall-Framing Systems Are Evolving

Until recently, before the cost of energy became so important, practically all wood-frame houses were built with 2×4 studs placed 16 inches on centers (OC), and were covered on the outside with an impregnated-fiberboard sheathing with little insulating value, and on the inside with drywall or plaster. In colder areas, a 3½-inch batt of insulation was placed in the wall. Today, in many areas of the country, the insulating value of this type of wall construction is inadequate.

Additional insulation can be obtained in two ways. First, use the 2×4 stud wall 16 inches OC but replace the impregnated sheathing with an insulating sheathing of polyurethane or similar product. Hang 3½-inch insulating batts between the studs. For even greater insulation, use 2×6 studs installed 24 inches OC, the polyurethane sheathing and 5½-inch insulating batts between the studs. Because fewer studs are used, the cost of the lumber remains about the same, but the 5½-inch batts will cost more than the 3½-inch batts.

If the geographical area in which you are building warrants the greater insulation, then by all means go ahead and use it. If it is not needed, there are advantages in staying with the 2×4 wall because it reduces window and door installation problems. All other dimensions remaining the same, the use of the 6-inch stud wall reduces the interior dimensions of the rooms of the house. This amounts to about 17 square feet of living space in a 2,000-square-foot house.

FIGURE 7.2 Balloon Framing

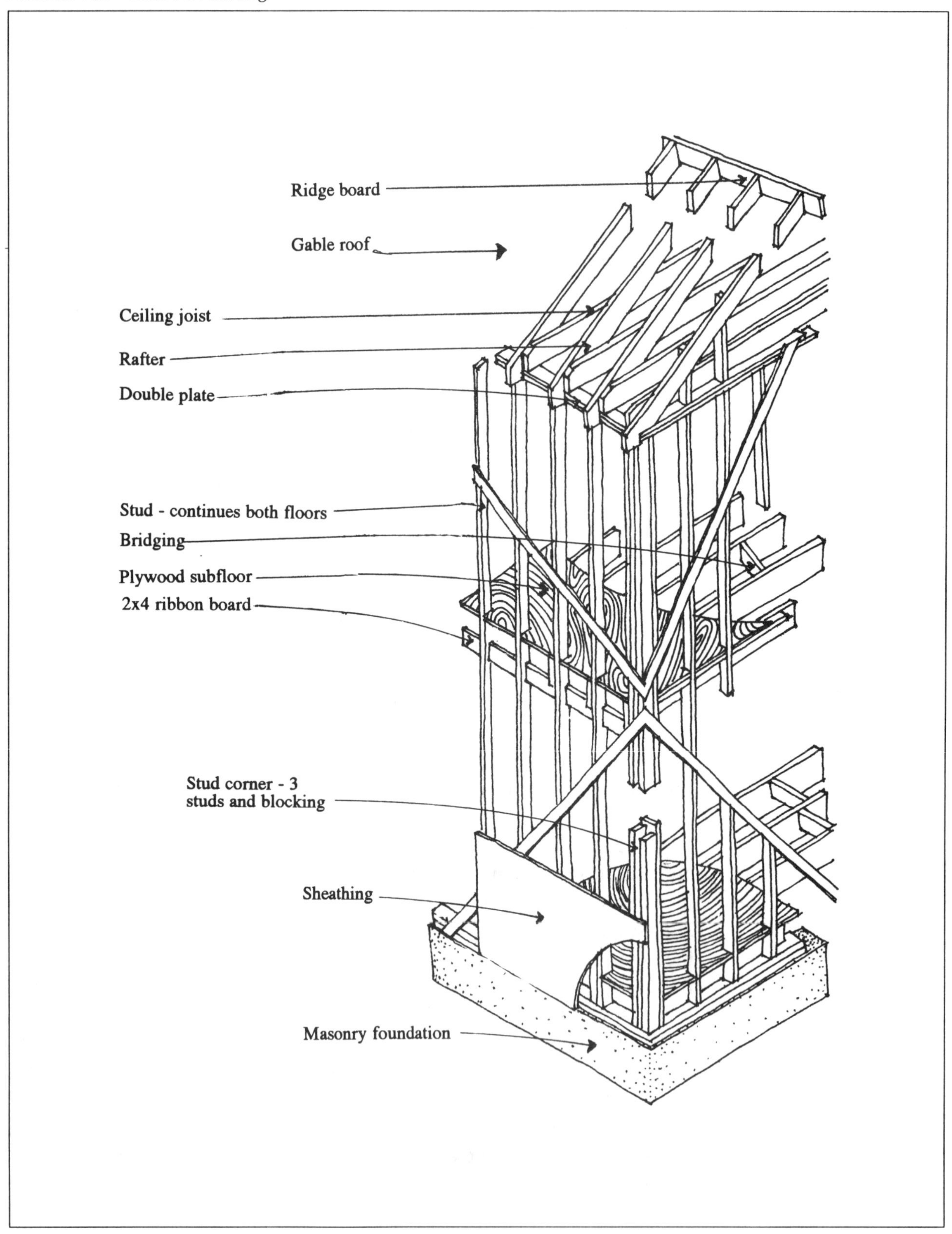

FIGURE 7.3 Plank-and-Beam Framing

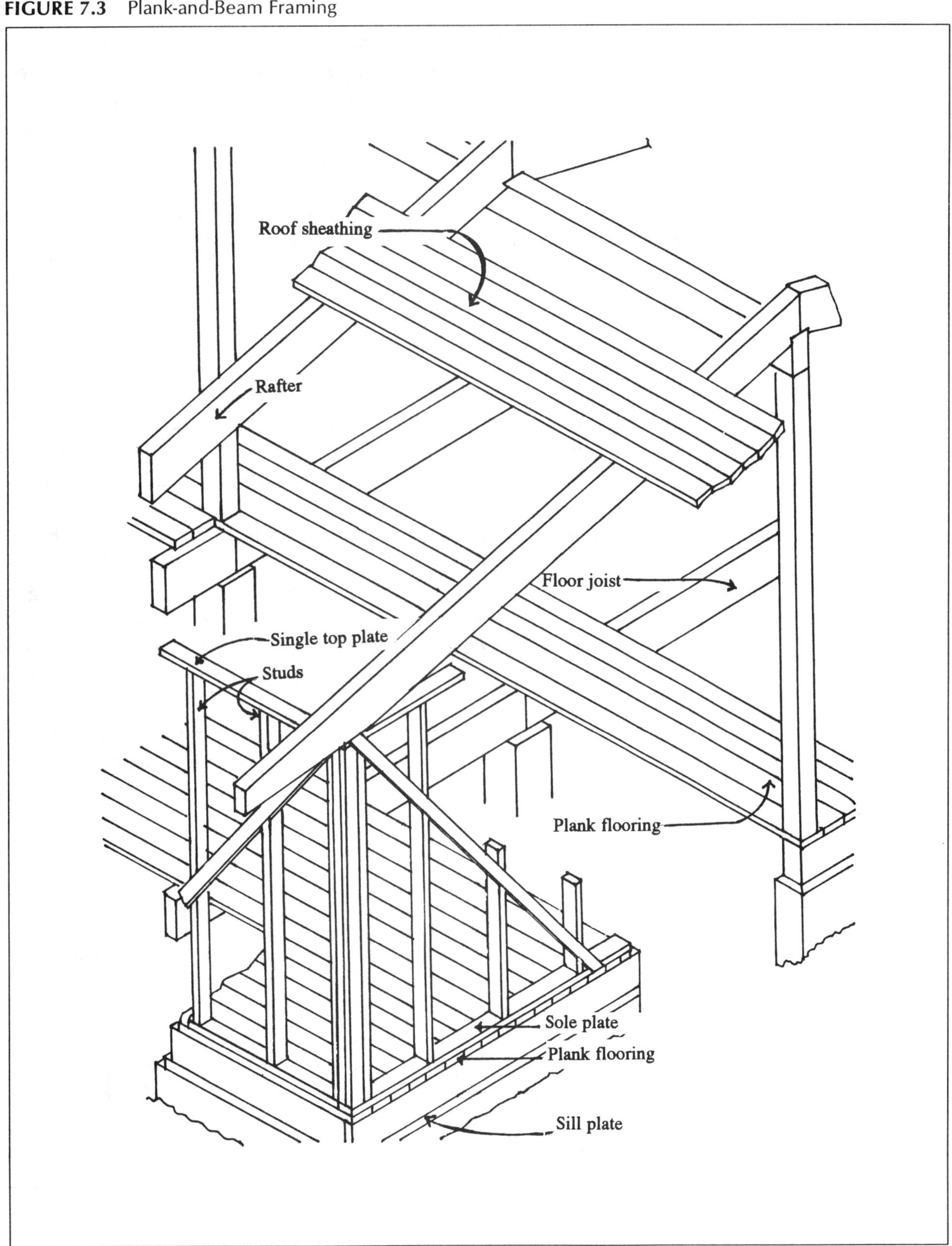

Long-Span Lumber Framing Innovations

Not shown in the previous drawings on framing are specially manufactured pieces of lumber for long spans (see Figure 7.4). All of these beams are well suited for long spans, such as in floor, ceiling and roof joists. They are becoming more popular in the building business and are easy to install, generally eliminate squeaking floors and are stronger than conventional lumber. When used as ceiling joists in a two-car garage, they can provide sufficient strength so that the usual girder with its pesky pipe column in the middle of the garage is not necessary.

Tips on Good Framing

Glue the subfloor to the floor joists in addition to nailing or stapling. This provides a much sturdier floor system for little additional cost. Check with the framing crew to determine what size glue cartridge they use before buying the adhesive. Two sizes of caulk/glue gun are in general use.

If you are installing a plywood subfloor, leave a ⅛-inch gap between the sheets. Plywood absorbs moisture and will buckle if it does not have room to expand. It also tends to delaminate when it gets wet. These delaminated areas must be replaced when the house is made weathertight. To eliminate this problem, use waferboard instead of the plywood. It is waterproof and thus not affected by the rain or other moisture.

Waferboard can also be used for roof sheathing, but it is slippery and may cause problems for the workers if the roof is steep.

FIGURE 7.4 Long-Span Lumber Beams

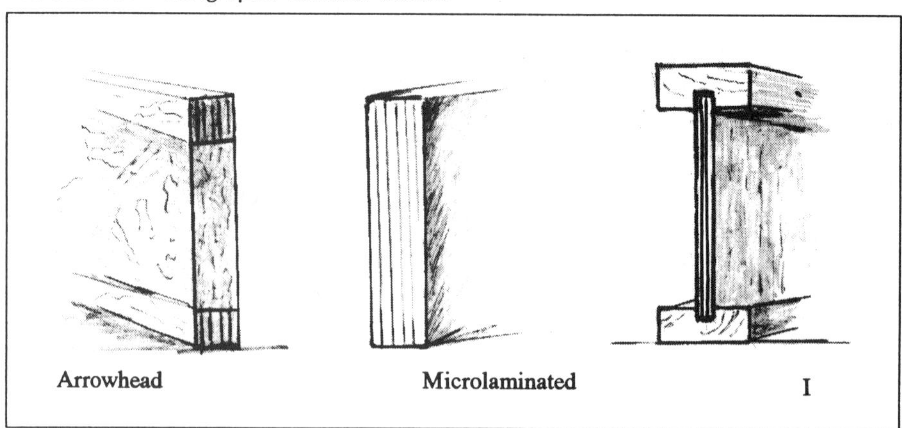

FIGURE 7.5 Crowning Joists

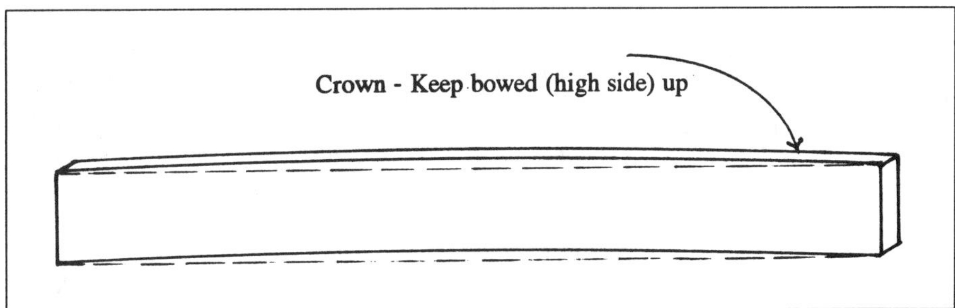

Run two parallel strips of caulk between the top of the subfloor and the bottom plate on all exterior walls. This will reduce the loss of heat by air infiltration. (See Chapter 12, Air Infiltration.)

Check with the framing crew on the best size of floor joist before ordering the lumber. The size of the joists required by the code is perfectly safe, but at the outer limits, the floor may be springy and have more bounce than you would like. Assume that the local code permits a 2×10 floor joist installed 16 inches OC to cover a span of 15 feet with the type of lumber you are using. This will be a safe floor, but it will be bouncy. To stiffen the floor, you have the following options:

- Use the manufactured long-span lumber discussed above.
- Install the 2×10-inch joists 12 inches OC.
- Go to 2×12-inch joists.
- Install additional piers and girders in the foundation system to reduce the span to about 8 feet. Change the size of the joists to 2×8.

Consider the cost of these choices (or combination of choices) and select the one most advantageous for you.

Make sure that the framing crew "crowns" the floor and ceiling joists and the roof rafters, as illustrated in Figure 7.5. Almost all lumber of any length has a crown in it. The lumber should be installed with the high side up. Most framing crews will do this without being told, but it is worth checking.

Wood or metal bridging or blocking should be used to stabilize joists and rafters and to properly align them so that the subfloor or roof sheathing has a level base to lie on (see Figure 7.6).

Metal bridging is easier to install than wood bridging. Blocking is the most solid and can be used to align a stubborn floor joist and hold it firmly in place before the subfloor is applied. Because the nailing of the bottom end of the bridging is not done until the house is more or less complete, this method will not hold an out-of-line joist or rafter in

FIGURE 7.6 Bridging and Blocking

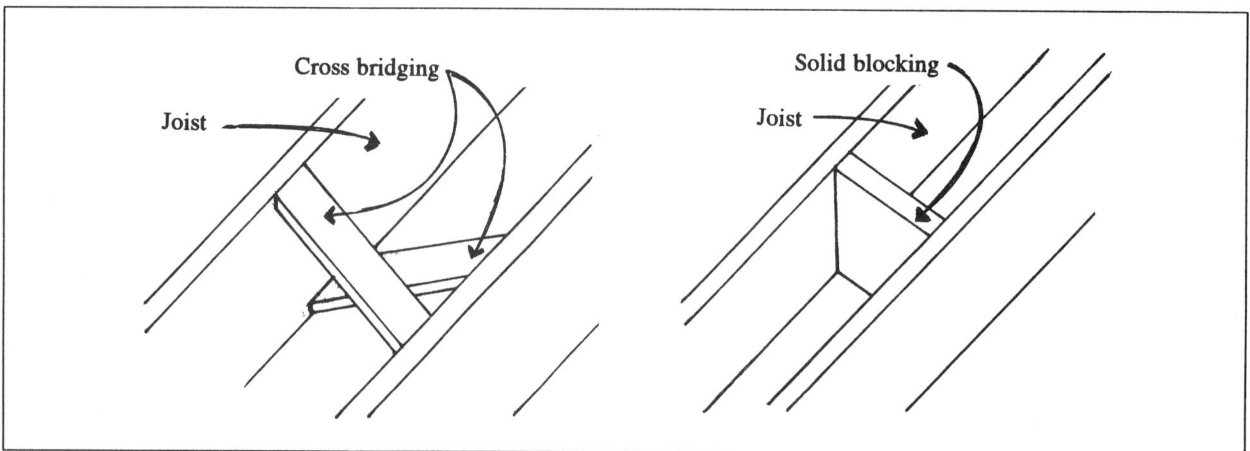

place as well as blocking. Either system should be applied between each joist and rafter at intervals of not more than 8 feet.

The most effective corner bracing, either 1×4-inch boards or special steel tees, is the diagonal brace "let into" the studs as shown Figure 7.7. The braces can be placed inside or outside the studs. This type of bracing should be used if the sheathing is polyurethane or polystyrene, because these materials have very little strength. Corner bracing of this type should be applied to all exterior corners and at intersections of exterior walls with interior walls. Sheets of plywood used as sheathing provide corner bracing also, but plywood is more expensive and has much less insulating value than polyurethane.

FIGURE 7.7 Let-in Corner Bracing

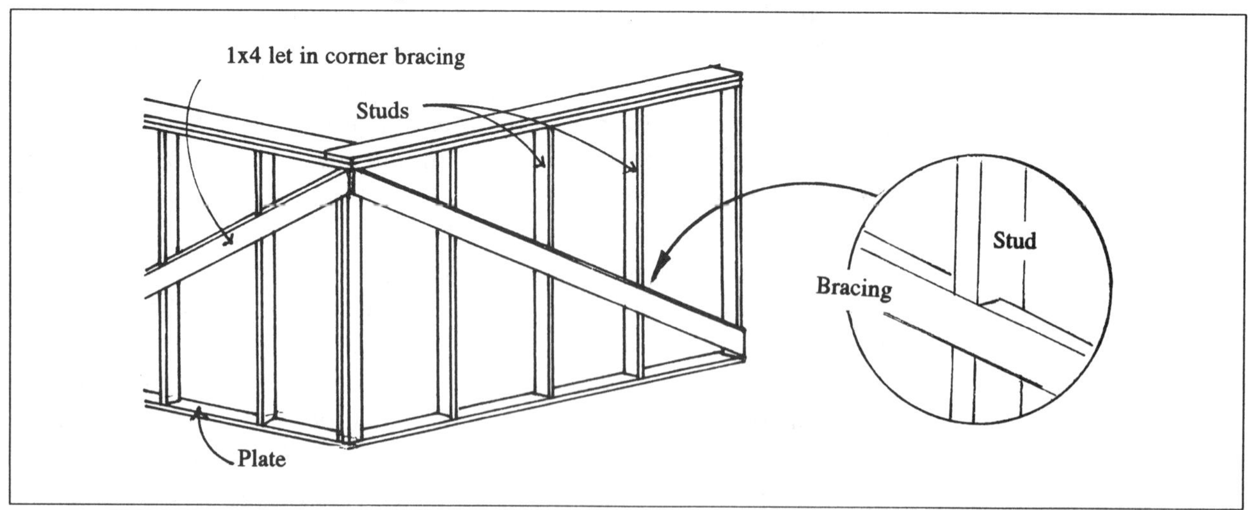

FIGURE 7.8 Dropped Floor Framing

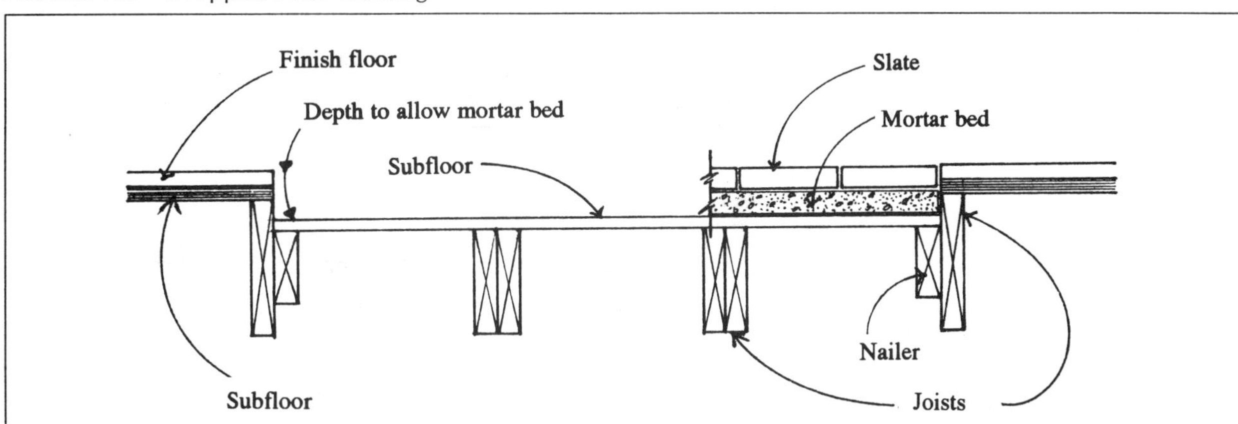

If your plans call for the use of slate, stone, earthstone or ceramic flooring in areas other than bathrooms, the subfloor must be dropped to allow additional space for setting of the flooring in a bed of cement.

As shown in Figure 7.8, this can be achieved by cutting out the top portion of the joist and by installing the subfloor on the top of the modified joists. Check with the tile setter to determine how much room he will need to have the finished floor even with the adjacent flooring.

In bathrooms, the ceramic tile is usually laid on top of the subfloor without lowering it. A marble threshold is set between the tile and the adjacent floor. The tile floor will be about an inch above the wood floor or carpet next to it.

Double the floor joists under the load-bearing interior walls. This measure will prevent sagging of the floor system.

Check to see that the framing crew has remembered to install nailers to which the drywall or plaster lathing will be attached (see Figure 7.9). At those junctures of ceiling and wall where the wall is at right angles to the joists, the joists provide the nailers on which to nail the drywall. On the other junctures, however, where the ceiling joists are parallel to the walls, there is nothing to attach the drywall to unless it just so happens that a ceiling joist lies at that point. If not, this is where you must provide the nailers.

Specify that exterior wall sheathing will be applied by hand nailing only. This material (polyurethane) is very easily damaged and torn by powered nailing systems.

A good framing crew will make accurate saw cuts. In particular, the cuts at the juncture of the roof rafters and the ridge board, cuts for the headers of the doors and windows and all intersections should be tight. If these cuts show large obvious gaps, the workmanship is sloppy and could weaken the framing.

FIGURE 7.9 Drywall Nailers

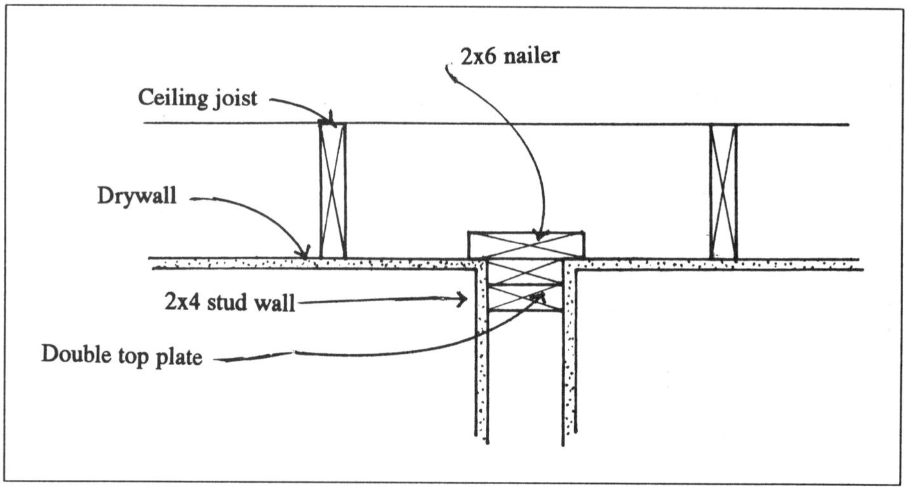

Apply a layer of housewrap (Tyvek is DuPont's brand) outside the sheathing to prevent air infiltration into and out of the house through the walls.

Use a long straight edge of 6 feet or more to check the alignment of the studs and ceiling joists to find those that bulge in or out excessively. Mark them and show them to the crew chief so he can have them corrected. An out-of-line wall may cause problems in the work to follow such as in hanging the drywall and, particularly, installing kitchen cabinets. It is relatively easy to make corrections before the framing is covered.

Install blocking to the right and left of each window between the studs to provide backing on which curtain rods can be mounted. Provide other backing in the baths for mounting towel racks and soap dishes. If you have any heavy objects such as large pictures or hanging bookcases, put up blocking in the walls to take the weight of these items.

If your plan calls for flush-mounted medicine cabinets in which the storage portion of the cabinet is recessed into the wall, additional framing must be installed to accept these cabinets. Select your cabinets well in advance so you will have the dimensions of the "rough opening" to give the framing crew.

The top portion of the top plate should not be built out of all the scrap lumber left over from other parts of the framing. The lengths of the pieces of the top portion of the top plate should be the same lengths as the bottom portions of the top plate, but stagger the joints. Both the bottom and top runs perform an important structural function.

FIGURE 7.10 Roof Framing–Stick-Built Construction

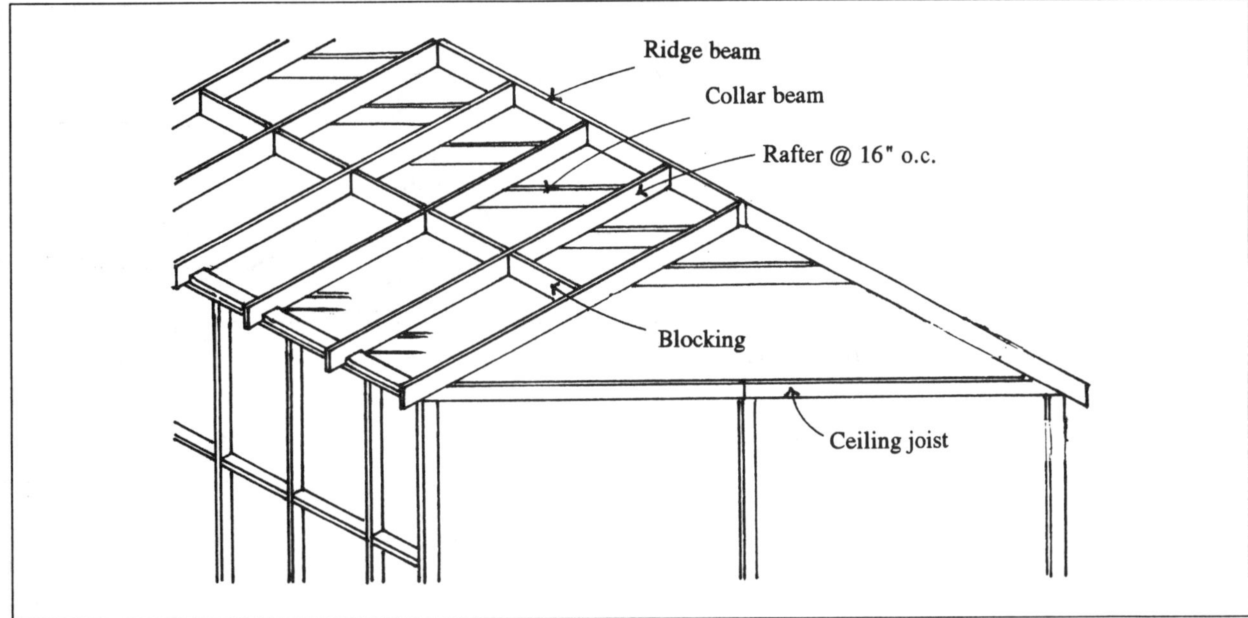

The size of the fiberglass tub/shower combination requires that it be installed during the framing. Arrange with the plumber to have them set it when the framing crew is ready.

Roof Framing Comes Three Ways

There are three generally used methods for providing support for the roof.

The first is the stick-built system using rafters, ridge board, ceiling joists and collar beams assembled on the job (see Figure 7.10).

The second is the prefabricated truss system in which the trusses are made off-site to your specifications by a fabricator specializing in this work (see Figure 7.11). The trusses are built using smaller dimensional lumber than the stick-built system, but despite this reduction and the fact that trusses are usually installed 24 inches OC, the truss design provides adequate strength to the roof. Savings in framing costs can usually be made using trusses because of the reduced costs for labor and materials. Trusses are normally designed to span the entire distance between opposite exterior walls. This arrangement provides more flexibility in interior wall location because only the exterior walls are load bearing.

The truss does have one disadvantage in that the diagonals used in its design drastically reduce the usable attic space.

FIGURE 7.11 Roof Framing—Wood-Truss Construction

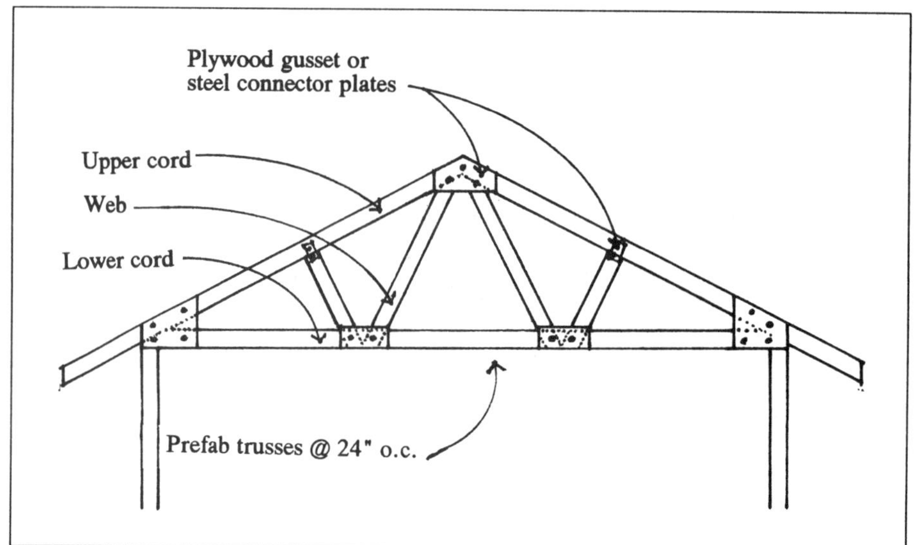

If your plans call for several dormer windows, the stick design will be the better choice because it is much easier to tailor the roof system to accept the dormer framing.

If the plywood roof sheathing is ⅜ inches thick on a truss system placed 24 inches OC, use metal clips (made for this purpose) between the sheets of plywood to reduce the potential sag of the sheathing between the trusses. Greater thicknesses of sheathing do not require the clips.

FIGURE 7.12 Roof Framing—Cathedral-Ceiling Construction

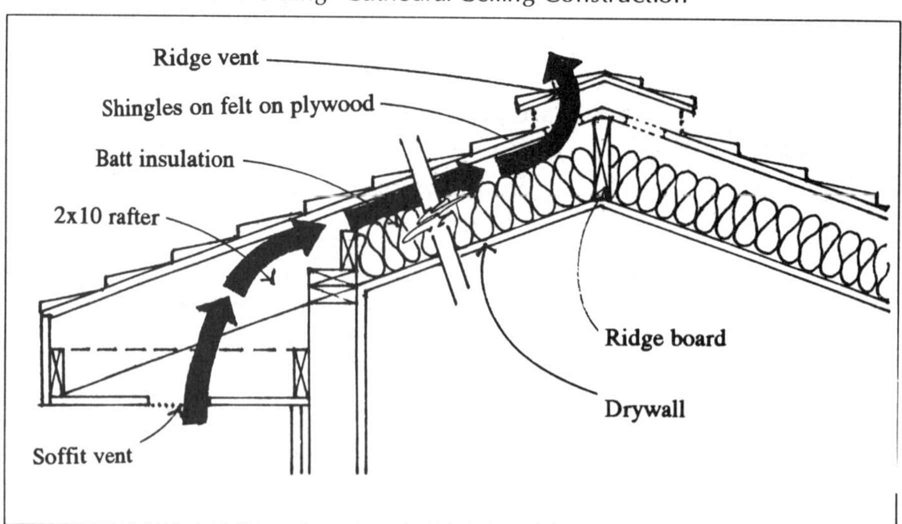

FIGURE 7.13 Cathedral Ceiling Alternate

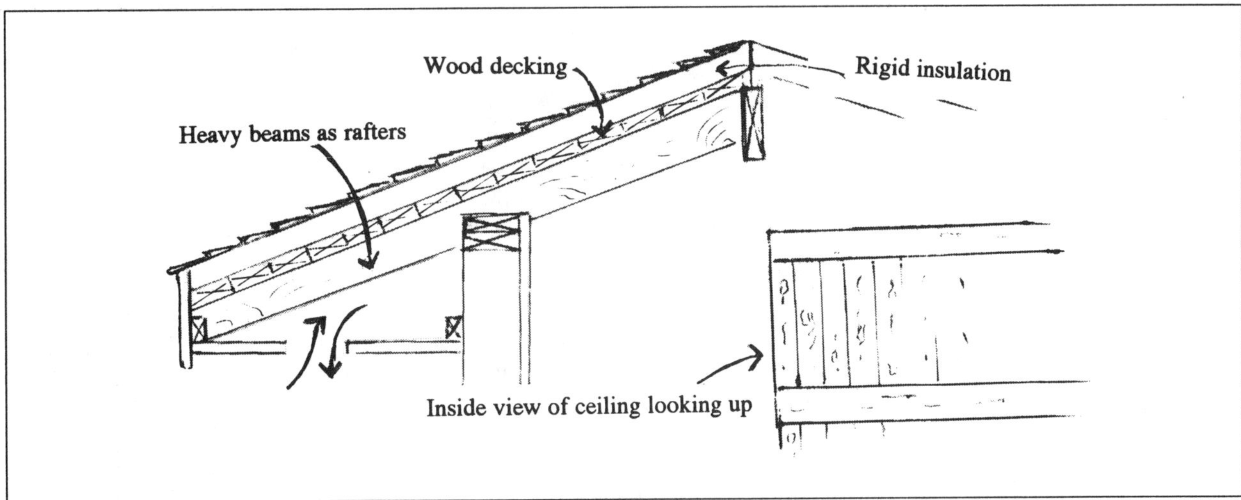

The third type of roof construction is the cathedral ceiling. It may be built of conventional lumber without exposed beams as illustrated in Figure 7.12, or it may be built using lumber decking with large timber beams as seen in Figure 7.13, or built using a combination of the two methods.

It is very important that the space between the ceiling and the roof be properly ventilated. With standard roof construction, either stick built or trussed, the attic is usually ventilated by the flow of air through openings in the soffit into the attic and then out through the vents in the gable.

FIGURE 7.14 Attic Ventilation—Gable Roof

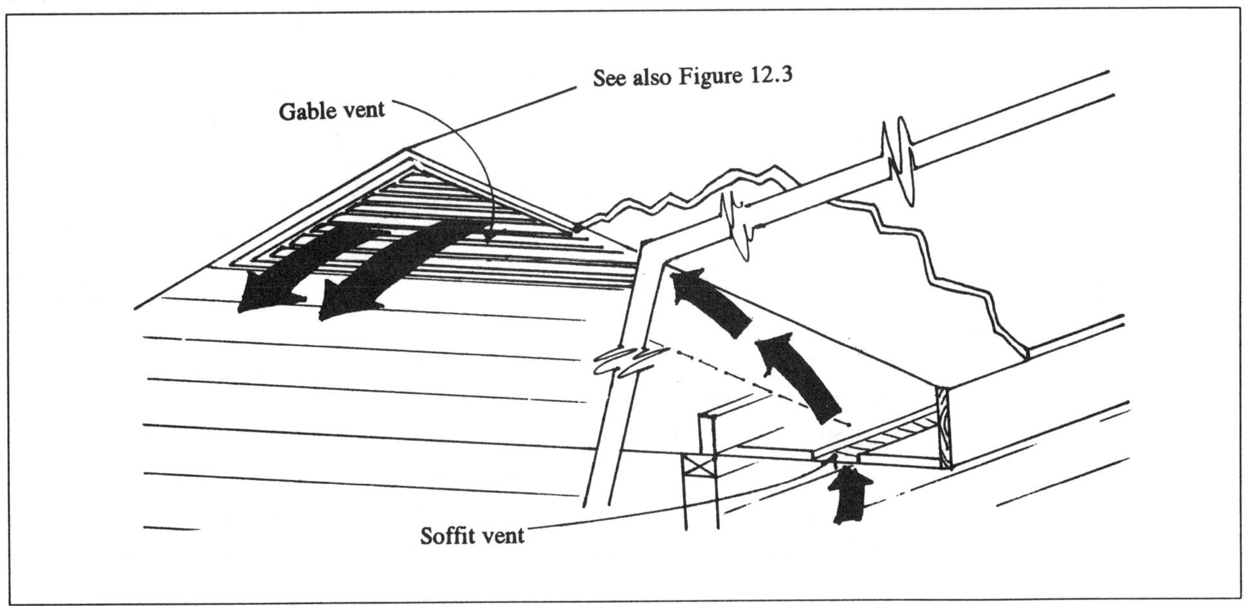

FIGURE 7.15 Typical Solid-Foam Panels

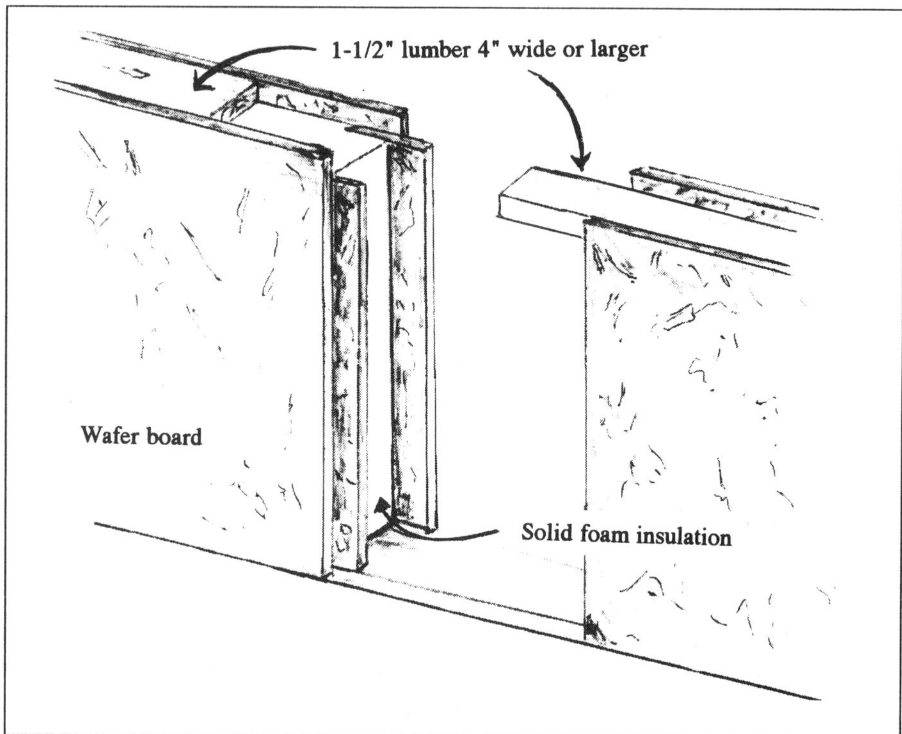

With a cathedral ceiling, the ventilation is provided by a flow of air through the soffit over the ceiling insulation out through a ridge vent (See Figure 7.12).

In a cathedral ceiling where the bottom side of the wood roof decking (used in lieu of sheathing) is the exposed ceiling, as in Figure 7.13, there is no air space requiring ventilation. The insulation, a rigid type, is applied above the decking with shingles on top.

If you plan to install an attic ventilating fan, make sure the size of the gable end vents or ridge ventilation is sufficient to permit the passage of the amount of air required for the fan to operate efficiently (see Figure 7.14).

Foam-Panel Framing Is New

A new method of framing a house has recently appeared and continues to grow. This new system uses factory-built solid foam care panels in lieu of stud construction for exterior walls and for application on top of the roof joists or as ceilings.

These panels range in depth from 3½-inch (R-14) wall panels to 11½-inch (R-44) roof panels. The usual size is 4×8 feet, but larger and smaller panels can be built. In Figure 7.15, note that the panels consist of waferboards glued to a solid foam core with 1½-inch lumber as top and bottom plates (4 inches wide or larger to accommodate various foam thickness). These panels are glued and/or nailed together and nailed to the subfloor to form the exterior walls. Roof panels with similar construction constitute the roof structure for cathedral ceiling design or the ceiling structure of the top floor in houses where attic space exists under the roof. Interior walls are conventional stick-built construction.

These panels are factory built at plants mostly located in the northern and eastern areas of the United States and in Canada, but they are sold by dealers throughout the entire country.

To enable the factory to properly construct the foam panels, you must submit complete house plans that include the desired thickness of the panels, the window and door cut-out locations and sufficient details of electrical, plumbing and HVAC plans so that cuts for cable, pipes and heat ducts can be made. As an alternative, these panel cuts can also be made on the job.

Advantages of the Foam-Panel System Compared to the stick-built house, the foam-built house can be built with lower labor costs. Built more quickly and easily, the house is weathertight sooner, suffering less damage to the structure by rain and snow.

The greatest gain, however, is the increase in thermal efficiency due to higher R-factors for the exterior walls and the roof and the decrease in air infiltration. Tests run in selected areas indicate heating cost reductions of up to 75 percent compared to heating costs for similar stick-built houses in the same area.

Disadvantages of the Foam-Panel System Material costs are higher than for the standard stick-built house. Some or all of these costs can be recovered, however, by the reduction of construction time and the substantial savings in heating costs.

Panel cutting at the job site to accommodate pipe, cable and duct runs is difficult and increases labor costs, but in complex house design it may be the best solution to reduce inaccuracies. Another solution, particularly for pipes and heating ducts, is to install additional wall framing inside the exterior panel walls and to run these pipes and ducts through the space provided. In any case, it is good building practice to run pipes and heating ducts through interior walls as much as possible to avoid the heat loss caused by installation in exterior walls.

Once the structure has been completed, changes to the electrical, plumbing and heating systems will be more difficult compared to the stick-built house.

FIGURE 7.16 Exterior Trim

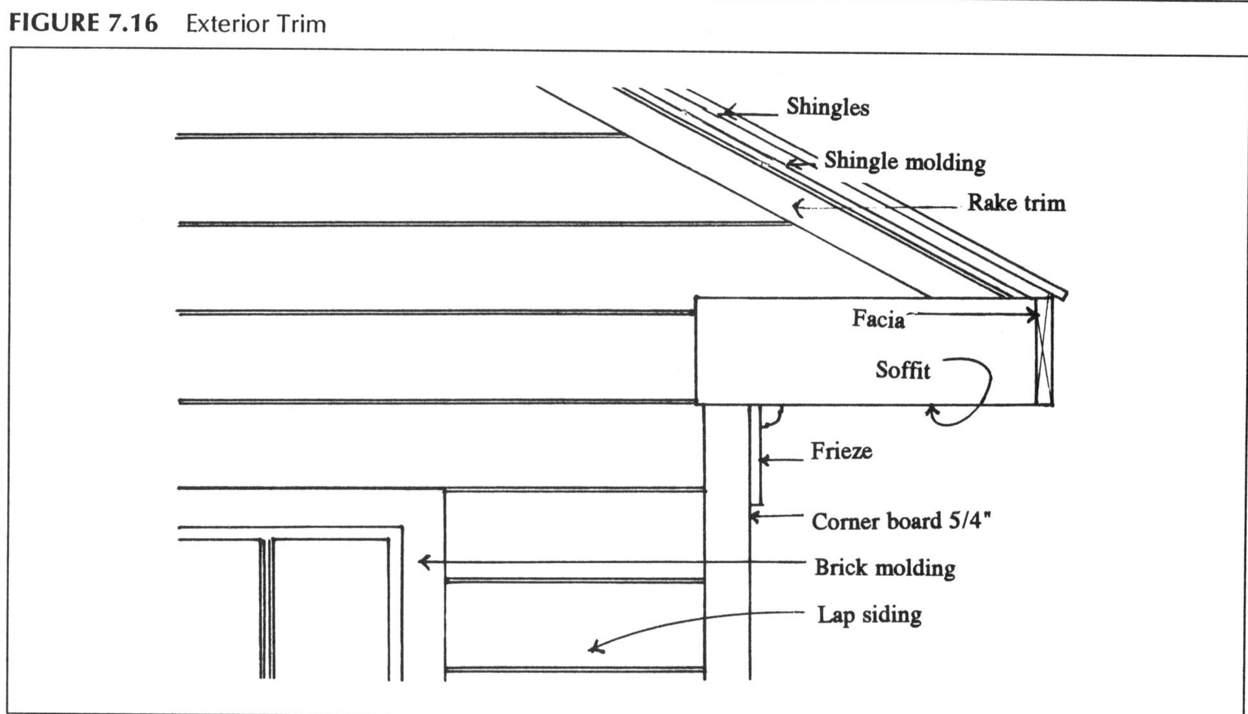

The foam-panel framing system continues to become more popular, although not all of the problems have been completely solved. Certainly this system should be investigated by the builder/homeowner. Discuss the system with those who have built a house of this type before you select the framing method for the house you want to build.

Exterior Wood-Trim Framing

Figure 7.16 illustrates the various parts of the exterior trim or cornice work. Familiarize yourself with the names of these parts and where each is applied.

Trim material is usually 1 inch nominal stock (¾ inch actual), and the finish and quality of the wood are better than that used in framing because it is exposed to view. Among the better choices for trim material are spruce, SYP grade "C" or better, redwood and fir. Select the wood that fits your budget and satisfies your taste. The cost per board foot will be more than the framing lumber. See Chapter 9, Considering Exterior Finishes, for a discussion of all types of siding.

All exterior wood exposed to the weather, such as exterior trim and siding, should be back primed, that is, sealed on the nonexposed side before installation to reduce cupping, other distorting and exterior paint peeling. One coat of the prime paint you will use on the exposed side will do the job.

Costing

In most cases, the framing crew will furnish the labor and tools. If they use a powered nail-gun system, they will also furnish the nails. The cost of the labor for framing and exterior trim, therefore, will be provided by the bids of the carpentry contractors.

Most suppliers will make the lumber take-off from your plans and will include the framing material, exterior trim, siding, doors, windows, interior trim and the rough hardware (nails, joist hangers and other metal pieces used to put the wood together). Have them break down the cost into each category so that you can take advantage of the best price in each case. In other words, you might want to order the framing lumber from one supplier, the doors and windows from another, and the trim material and roof trusses from still others.

Lumber is usually priced as so much per 1,000 board feet. A board foot is theoretically a board 12 inches wide, 12 inches long and 1 inch thick with all dimensions being nominal. To determine the amount of board feet in lumber, you must translate its dimensions (using nominal, not actual) into board feet. For example, a 2×4 that is 1 foot long is equivalent to a board 1 inch by 8 inches wide and 12 inches long; thus each linear foot of 2×4 equals .67 board feet. Following the same procedure, one linear foot of 2×6 equals 1 board foot, 1 linear foot of 2×8 equals 1.33 board feet, one linear foot of 2×10 equals 1.67 board feet and one linear foot of 2×12 equals two board feet.

Applying these factors to the requirements of a particular plan will give you the total board feet. For example, if the floor joist requirement is 24 pieces of 14-foot-long 2×10s, the total board footage for floor joists would be 1.67×14×24 = 562 board feet. If the price of SYP is $624 per 1,000 board feet, the cost of the floor joists would be $624×562 divided by 1,000, or $351.

Suppliers will do the pricing for you from your plans, but it is a good idea to know how to do it yourself so you can compute the cost of additional lumber needed during the building process.

Management

Electric power will be needed for saws and other tools used by the framing crew. Your electrician should install a temporary electrical hookup that is then connected to the local power source by the power company. In an emergency, portable generators can be used, but power from the temporary hookup is much preferred.

Get together with the framing crew chief to plan where the lumber and other materials are to be placed on site by the supplier. If you have a flat, open lot this will not be a problem, but if your lot is wooded with little open space or if the suppliers' trucks cannot move to the interior of the lot because of soft ground, you may have a storage problem. If so, the solution is to have the supplies delivered in phases—first, the floor system, then the wall material and finally the roof material. If more than normal hand carrying of the lumber is required of the framing crew, expect to pay more for the framing labor, unless this problem was included in the information you provided to all bidders.

Most lumber suppliers use flatbed dump trucks for delivery purposes. Expect to have your lumber dumped into one or two large piles. These piles will need to be sorted and restacked before framing begins. Have an understanding with your framing crew that this restacking will be their job.

Give the crew chief the rough openings of the windows and the size of the exterior doors you have ordered. He will need these dimensions before he begins the wall framing. If they are not in your plans, get the information from the door and window supplier.

If your framing crew uses conventional nails, include their cost. It is much cheaper to buy nails in 50-pound boxes (less than half price), so buy in these quantities if they are close to your needs.

Visit the job site daily to keep up with the work and to see that the crew does not run out of materials. Often the crew chief will forget to tell you of pending shortages, so ask each day how supplies are doing in each category. Be prepared to go after items that are needed immediately and can be carried in whatever car or truck you are using.

Before accepting the materials bid, find out from the supplier what delivery service you can expect. You will be wise to use a supplier who offers daily deliveries rather than one who delivers only twice a week, even if the former is somewhat higher in price. The ideal would be: Check on the job in the afternoon and then phone in any order to the supplier that day or before 7:30 AM the next morning for delivery by the first truck leaving the supplier's yard.

Windows and doors should be delivered to the site just before they are to be installed. If you have them sent out too early, there is more danger of breakage and absorption of excessive moisture by the wood frame. Order interior doors for delivery along with the rest of the interior trim material, after the house is weathertight and the drywall or plaster has been finished.

If your house has full-height exterior brick-veneer walls in whole or in part, it is easier for the exterior trim work to be done after the brick has been laid. Line up the brick mason at the proper time, but do not have the brick work start until the framing has reached the point where the brick work can be completed without interruption.

Use aluminum or hot-dipped galvanized nails for all woodwork exposed to the weather even if it is to be painted. The electroplated

FIGURE 7.17 Steel Structure Pieces

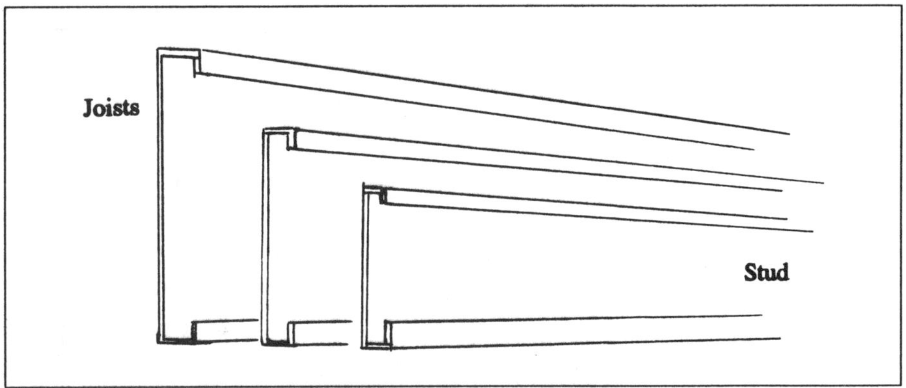

galvanized nails do not hold up as long, and they tend to rust through the paint or stain.

The method of placing the drywall or plaster lathing inside the house should be considered during the framing. Those heavy, awkward drywall boards will probably be delivered by a special truck with a boom designed to handle this material. In most cases, the best solution is to pass the drywall through a window opening where the window has not yet been installed. You can also create an opening by taking out an easily removed window. Another method is to leave off one or two sheets of sheathing and pass the drywall through the opening. Discuss this problem with your crew chief and drywall supplier.

STEEL FRAMING IS GROWING IN POPULARITY

Steel framing has been in use for several years, and in 1994 about 40,000 houses were built with steel framing. Steel framing used in houses does not consist of large heavy "I" beams like those associated with commercial buildings and large multistoried apartments. Steel framing for houses is manufactured by a cold-forming process in which strips of steel sheet are put through a series of roll-forming dies that form the sheet into desired widths and lengths. The strength of this form of steel comes from the material itself and how it is shaped.

Note that the cross-section of the stud, rafter and joist are in the shape of a "C," which gives these pieces unusual strength and retains lightness (see Figure 7.17). For example, the steel stud weighs only 60 percent of the wood stud, yet the steel stud is stronger. The stud is available in widths of 2½ inches to 8 inches with material thicknesses of 0.034 to 0.071 inches. Joists and rafters range in widths of 6 to 12 inches with thickness of material of 0.034 to 0.101 inches.

Steel Framing Methods

There are three methods of steel framing:

1. *Stick-Built Construction:* Steel stick-built methods are virtually the same as those used in wood construction except that the studs are usually placed 24 inches OC, to take advantage of their superior strength (see Figure 7.18). Note also that the studs must be installed directly over a floor joist because the track, which takes the place of the bottom plate in wood framing, is not a load-bearing part of the structure.
2. *The Panelized System:* Panelization consists of a system for prefabricating walls, floors and/or roof components into sections. Panelization is most efficient where there is a repetition of panel types and dimensions and it may include not only the steel framing but the exterior sheathing as well. Panels can be made in the shop or in the field. A custom jig is developed for each type of panel.
3. *The Pre-engineered System:* Because of steel's high strength and design flexibility, innovative systems are possible that are not possible using other materials. Engineered systems typically space the vertical primary load-carrying members more than 24 inches OC, sometimes up to 8 feet OC. These systems use either secondary horizontal members to distribute wind loads to the columns or lighter-weight steel fill-in studs between the columns.

   Most of the pre-engineered systems are fabricated by the supplier at his plant. When these systems are delivered to the building site, the framing of a typical house can be completed in as little as one day.

Rather than using nails, the steel framing system is typically put together using a powered screwdriver that drills the hole and installs the screw at the same time. Screws used in interior applications should be zinc plated, cadmium plated or phosphate coated. For exterior work, screws should be cadmium plated or copolymer coated. In addition, tin, or aviation snips, and a circular saw with a steel-cutting blade are also needed. Recently, nail manufacturers have developed nails that can be used to attach plywood and foam sheathing to the steel, or to connect steel-to-steel.

Corrosion protection can be provided by galvanizing the steel.

FIGURE 7.18 Lower Portion of a Typical Exterior Steel-Wall Frame

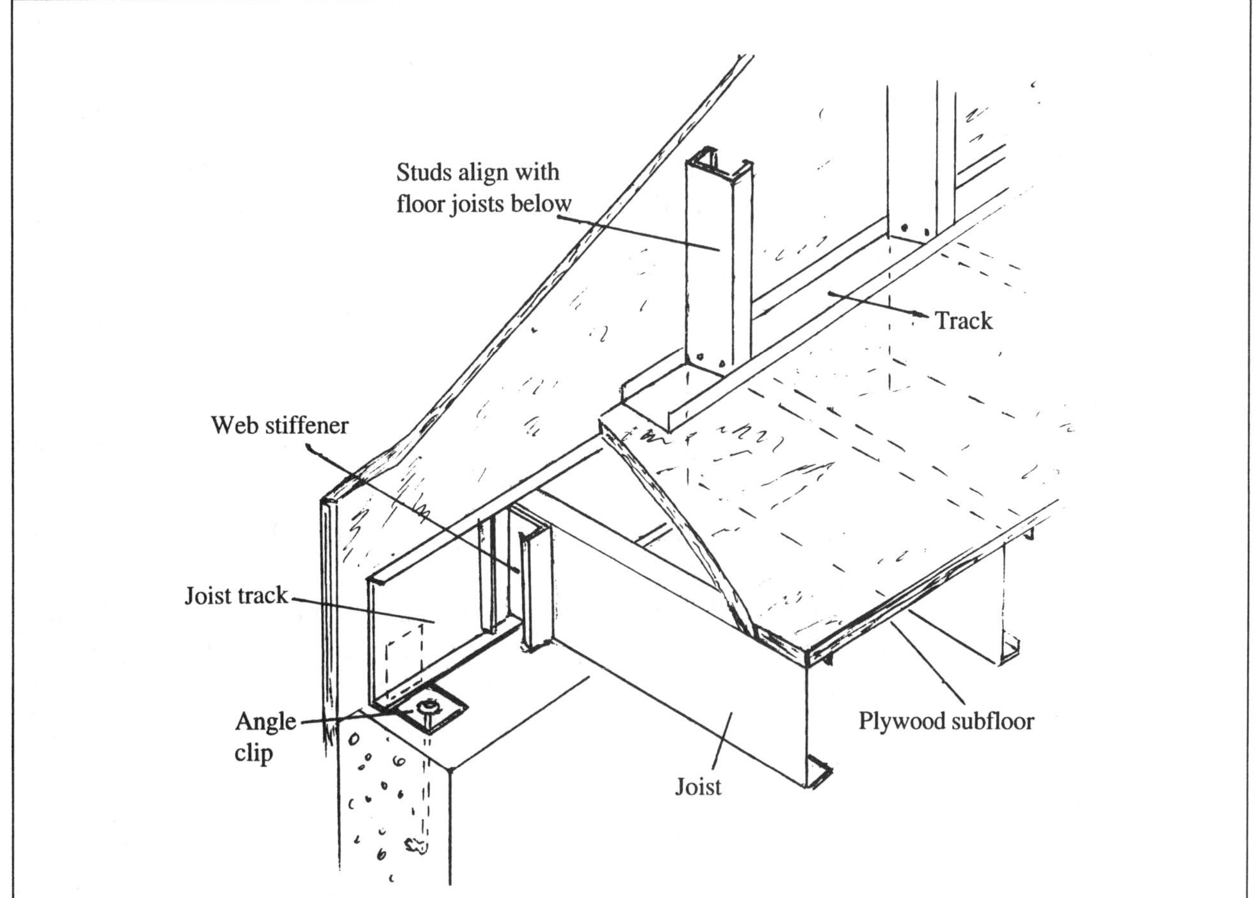

Advantages of Steel Framing

Steel will not shrink, swell, warp, and it is noncombustible. Steel is competitively priced and consistent in quality. The strength of steel results in fewer construction members that are available in a variety of precut, standard shapes and sizes as well as custom shapes and sizes, minimizing construction waste. Steel members weigh as much as 60 percent less than wood members. Framing members are manufactured with prepunched holes for running piping and electrical wiring. Steel's inherent strength and noncombustible qualities enable a steel-framed house to resist such devastating events as fires, earthquakes and hurricanes. Remodeling can be easily accomplished because nonload-bearing walls can be easily removed, altered and relocated. Termites and other insects cannot harm steel framing. Because of its strength, steel framing can span greater distances, offering larger open spaces and increased design flexibility without requiring intermediate columns or load-bearing walls. Steel products are recyclable.

Costing and Management

Costing and management as discussed for wood framing generally apply to steel framing. Of particular importance in steel framing, because it is relatively new, is to make sure that your framing crew is experienced in this field.

Call the American Iron and Steel Association at 1-800-79STEEL, and they will send you a copy of their directory that lists the location of manufacturers of steel framing and engineers and contractors who are experienced with steel framing for houses.

■ WALLS OF CONCRETE, CONCRETE BLOCK AND POLYSTYRENE BLOCK

Exterior walls can also be built using concrete, concrete block and polystyrene block. The walls will be very strong with a high capability to resist storms and will have a high resistance to sound transmission but, with the exception of the polystyrene block, will have very little insulation capability. In addition, concrete and concrete block present problems for installing pipe and electrical wiring unless special steps are taken to open channels for these systems when the walls are built.

CHAPTER 8

Selecting Your Windows and Doors

In these days of high energy costs, the selection of windows and doors assumes much more importance than a few years ago. In making your selection, consider: insulating and air-infiltration properties, ease of operation, maintenance and cleaning, a style to suit your architecture and a price to fit your pocketbook—in just about that order of priority. Do not buy cheap windows that will cause a loss of any savings through increases in heating and cooling costs and maintenance.

WINDOWS

Window types (see Figure 8.1) readily available on the market include the following:

- *Casement*: Operates like a door in that it is hinged on one side and rotates on a vertical axis by turning a crank. Along with the awning and hopper windows, it offers the best seal against air infiltration. Depending upon the particular design, interior and exterior surfaces can be cleaned from inside the house.
- *Double Hung:* This popular window is found in most houses. Its two sections move vertically in channels and are held in place by springs or friction. In the single-hung variation of this style only the bottom of the two sections moves.
- *Awning*: Operates very much like the casement window except that the hinged rotation (to the outside) is horizontal. The awning window is often used in combination with a fixed window above or below.

FIGURE 8.1 Types of Windows

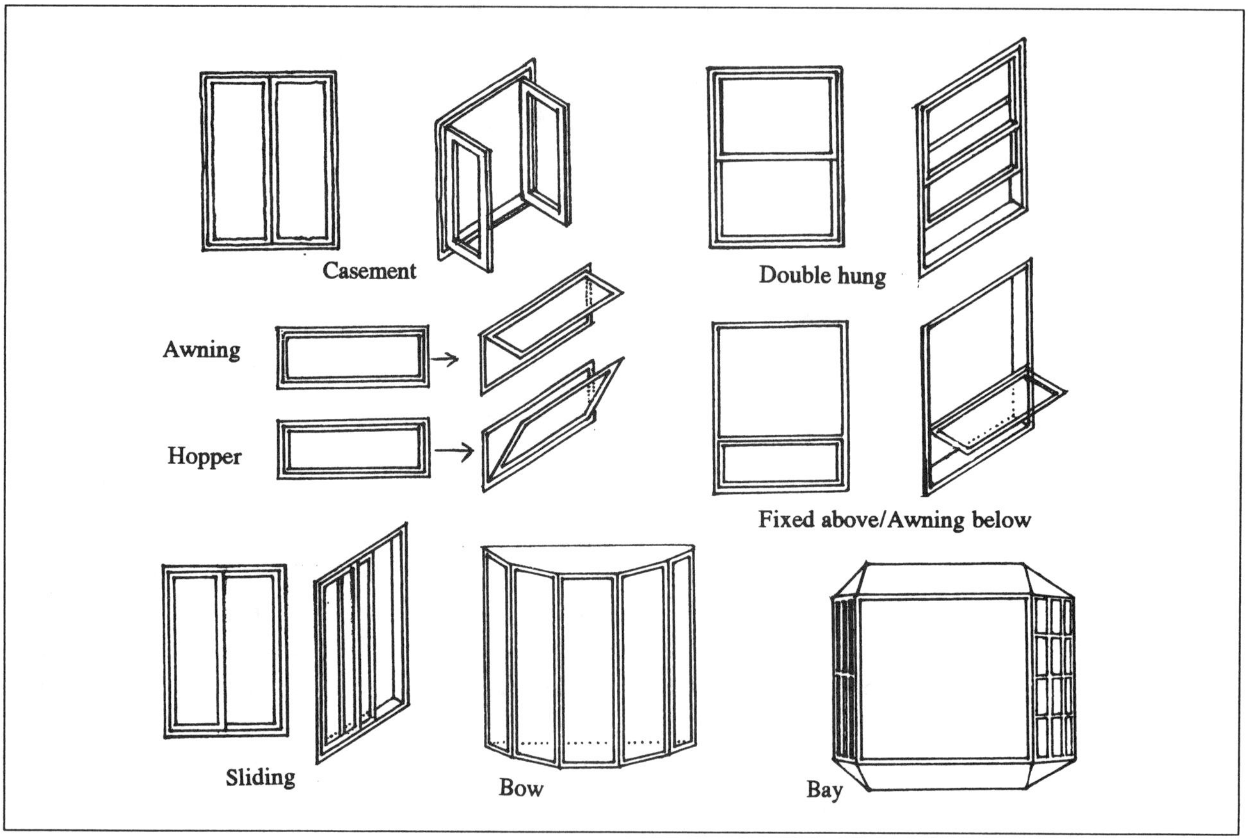

- *Hopper:* Operates like the awning window except the hinge is at the bottom with rotation to the inside.
- *Sliding Window:* Slides horizontally in a channel in the frame. One side is often fixed.
- *Fixed:* Glass mounted in a frame with no movement. May be ordered in a variety of sizes and shapes.
- *Bow:* A window made up of several elements in the shape of an arc extending out from the exterior walls of the house. All sections are usually fixed.
- *Bay:* Similar to the bow window except that it has two side sections that are angular instead of curved and a straight center section. May be composed of combinations such as casement or double-hung windows on the sides and a fixed center section.

Is Insulating Glass Worth the Cost?

This glass exists in two forms. One is a special double sheet of glass separated by an air space with the glass edges welded together to form an airtight center space much like the liner for a thermos bottle. The other consists of two sheets of glass held in the frame with an insulating air space in between. For most areas of the country, the windows you select to install in your house should be one of these two systems. The additional expense is well worth it, and you should save enough in fuel costs to more than make up for this expense in a few years and have a more comfortable house in the meantime.

Those who live in very cold climates should consider using windows with triple glazing, that is, three layers of glass with two separate air pockets in between.

Glass itself is a very poor insulator and will act as a high heat loss area unless air- or gas-filled spaces are interposed to block the ready escape of heat. Even then the insulating qualities of the double- and triple-insulated glass windows and doors will provide only ⅛ to ⅕ the insulating value of a 2×4 wall with 3½ inches of insulating batt and a 1-inch-thick polyurethane or polystyrene sheathing. On the other hand, windows installed to take maximum advantage of the sun to provide heat can be a definite asset. See Chapter 14, Heating with Sunshine (Solar Energy).

More Than One Type of Glass

A wide variety of glass types are available, including the following:

- *Tempered Glass:* This glass should be used in doors, glass panels adjacent to doors and other areas where it is likely that people, especially children, might fall against the glass and break it. Most codes require the use of tempered glass in wall areas that are within 4 feet of a door. When broken, tempered glass crumbles into more or less harmless granules.

  Tempered glass cannot be cut, so be sure that your measurements are correct before ordering. Allow about ⅛ inch on each side of the frame for expansion. Standard sizes cost less and are usually readily available from stock.
- *Annealed Float Glass:* Formerly called plate glass, it is used in house windows and it breaks easily into pieces that are usually very sharp. This glass is largely being replaced by Low E Glass, discussed below.
- *Tinted Glass:* This glass, usually annealed float, is designed to reduce the passage of solar heat. It is particularly useful in areas such as the seashore to reduce glare and in the southeast and southwest USA with similar environments.
- *Reflective Glass:* Serves a similar function to tinted glass but is more effective. It reduces solar heat passage to about 50 percent

of that of annealed float glass, whereas tinted glass only offers a 25 percent reduction. Reflective glass has been designed primarily for commercial buildings with large window areas to reduce heat loss to the outdoors in the winter and to reduce heat gain in the summer. From the outside, the windows look like mirrors, an effect that most homeowners will not want.

- *Low E Glass* (low emissivity): This glass is used in dual-glazed windows with a low E coating on the inside to reduce heat loss in the winter and heat gain in the summer. It is an excellent glass for houses.

Window Frames

Windows may be selected with the following choices of frames:

- *Wood:* Usually excellent quality woods are used. Because frames must be stained or painted, the maintenance cost is higher than other frames. Color of the finish depends upon the selection of the paint or stain.
- *Wood Clad with Vinyl:* A very fine long-lived window. The wood frame is completely encased in a thick layer of tough vinyl. Because no painting or staining is required, the maintenance on this window is very low. The choice of color is usually limited to white, brown or bronze.
- *Wood Clad with Aluminum:* Another fine choice with almost no maintenance. In this case, the wood frame is encased in a layer of aluminum that is coated with baked-on, factory-applied paint. Color choice is usually limited to white, brown or bronze.

  Cladding—vinyl or aluminum—is usually on the exterior surfaces only with the unclad wood frame on the inside of the house.
- *Aluminum:* Windows framed in aluminum are available in natural finish or several selections of anodized coloring. This is a long-life frame and inexpensive compared to other materials. Aluminum is an excellent conductor of heat, though, and will permit high heat losses from within the house through the window frame. It will cause excessive moisture condensation on the interior portion of the frame under conditions of large temperature differences between the outside and the inside. For these reasons, if you buy aluminum-framed windows, be sure to select a brand that has a thermal break using an insulating material to separate the exterior and interior sections of the metal frame.

- *Steel:* Windows framed with steel are sometimes used in basements. They have the same disadvantages as the aluminum-framed window without the thermal break and, in addition, they must be kept painted to prevent rusting.

Screens

Screens should be included in the window specifications for those parts of the window that will be opened. Nylon screen material is the most popular. It will not corrode like copper and aluminum. When the windows are delivered to the construction site, remove the screens and store them in a safe place for the duration of the construction period. They will probably be damaged if allowed to remain on the job. Screen doors should be provided for those entry ways that will be habitually open during the warmer months.

Storm Windows

Storm windows, when properly installed, provide additional insulation and present another barrier to air infiltration. They are difficult to operate, however, and it is preferable to obtain the additional insulation through double or triple glazing and the reduction of air infiltration by efficient design and construction than through the use of storm windows.

Skylights

Skylights are a form of fixed window mounted in the roof. They are particularly popular in contemporary styles and are useful in taking advantage of passive solar heating. Figure 8.2 illustrates the most commonly used skylight in house construction.

The preferred skylight is one made of plastic and double domed to provide insulation against heat loss through the roof. The type mounted on a job-built curb is preferred because it is less troublesome and is less likely to leak. Have the skylight on the job before its framing is begun to ensure that the skylight curb and the roof framing fit. To prevent water leaks, follow the mounting instructions of the skylight manufacturer explicitly.

FIGURE 8.2 Skylight Installation

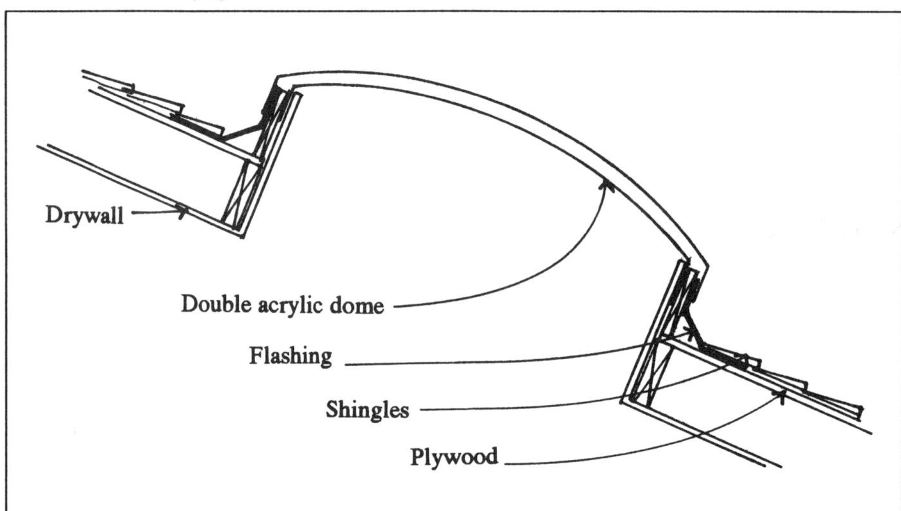

■ EXTERIOR DOORS

Like windows, exterior doors must perform a more important function in this era of high energy costs. They must effectively seal the opening against air infiltration, insulate against the loss of heat through the material and still provide easy movement through the wall. There is much more to door selection today than just appearance and style.

Wood Exterior Doors

Wood doors are made in a variety of styles to satisfy almost any taste. Figure 8.3 illustrates only a few of these styles.

Exterior doors are thick and heavy, as they should be, and they can be selected from a variety of widths and with heights of 70 inches (standard) and 84 inches. The two most popular styles are the flush door and the paneled door.

There are two types of flush doors: the solid-core door made with particleboard between the two outer surfaces, and the solid-lumber-core door with solid lumber between the two outer faces. The latter is the much better, much stronger door and is the most expensive.

Most wood exterior doors are made of high-grade fir. The advantages of wood doors are their beauty, particularly if stained to show off the grain, and the vast array of choices. To their disadvantage they may warp, crack, shrink or cause sealing problems. And other doors provide better insulation. Both paneled and flush doors are available with various amounts and shapes of glass panels.

FIGURE 8.3 Typical Exterior Doors

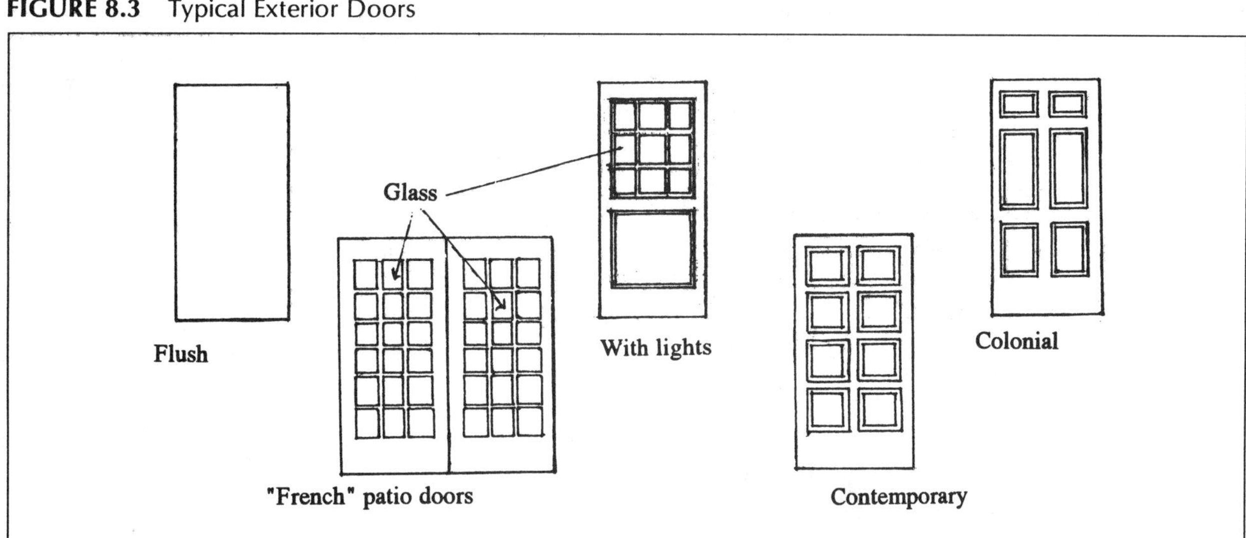

Molded Exterior Doors

Molded doors have an advantage over the wood door in that they are less likely to warp, crack or shrink. They usually cannot be stained, however, and show little, if any, grain.

Steel Doors

These doors are made with a steel outer shell filled with insulating material. They are usually prehung, that is, they are supplied with their own frame, jamb and hinges with all parts already assembled or set up for easy assembly on the job. The steel door provides an excellent seal against air infiltration, is well insulated, is more difficult to force open and is not affected by moisture. Its disadvantages are that it must be painted and that its panel embossing is often shallower and less handsome than that of a wood door. Plastic decorator panels can be applied to the face of the steel door to provide considerable variation in design.

Some steel door systems are made with magnetized weather-stripping (similar to that used on modern refrigerators) that clamps to the door when closed and forms an excellent seal. *This magnetized seal must not be painted.*

Make sure that the steel door is predrilled by the supplier to accept the hardware (knobs and locks) you have selected. Most carpenters do not have the tools needed to drill steel doors.

FIGURE 8.4 Sliding Patio Doors

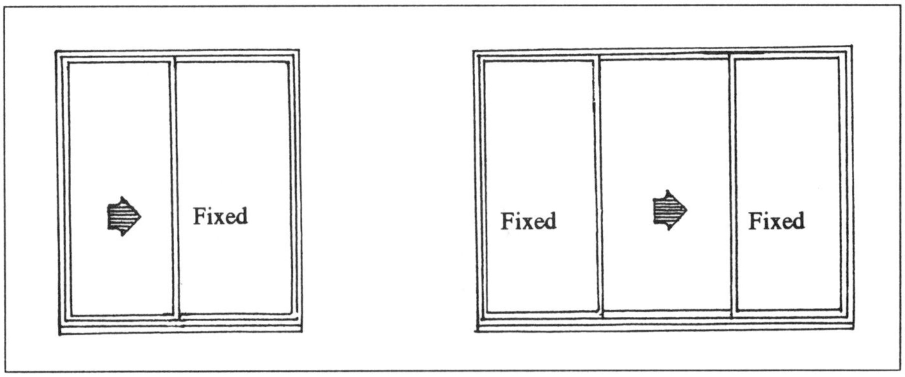

Fiberglass Doors

Fiberglass doors are made from a molded fiber skin with an etched wood grain wrapped around an insulating urethane core. When stained or painted the fiberglass looks very much like wood, but it has none of wood's warping and splitting problems. The fiberglass can be trimmed like ordinary wood doors.

Patio Doors

Most patio doors consist of sliding and stationary glass panels with widths of 3 feet or more per panel (see Figure 8.4). Their frames are available in the same choices as the windows discussed earlier and with single, double or triple glazing.

Sealing to stop air infiltration through doors is just as important as it is with windows. The sliding patio door has the same disadvantages as the slider and double-hung window. By nature of their design, it is difficult to properly seal sliding doors against air infiltration. Even with the higher-quality doors, the wear and tear caused by the door movement across the sealing material eventually causes leaks. Sliders are more likely to leak than conventional nonsliding doors.

If you desire a large amount of light and sunshine (see Chapter 14, Heating with Sunshine (Solar Energy), you can get it by using single- or double-swinging doors along the lines of the French door or, even better, by a combination of one fixed panel with a swinging door. If passage through the door is not needed, then you can use a whole completely fixed system and eliminate the air infiltration problem entirely.

INTERIOR DOORS

With interior doors, there is usually no problem involving insulation and air infiltration. These doors are not normally weatherstripped. In fact, if the house heating system depends upon the free flow of air, interior doors should be undercut at least ½ inch above the finished floor, threshold or carpet to permit this air flow. This does not apply in those rooms with both air supply and return outlets.

Wood Interior Doors

These doors can be purchased in various forms such as paneled, flush or louvered. The flush doors may be solid or hollow and be made with finished surfaces of birch, mahogany, pine or a composite hardboard. The hardboard cannot be stained, but it will take paint well. The paneled and louvered doors are usually made of a species of quality kiln-dried western pine.

Louvered doors are available as full louvered, top and bottom louvered or partially louvered with either the top or bottom paneled. They are particularly useful in those locations where the free flow of air is desired, such as in closets. They may be required for rooms that need ventilation because they contain mechanical equipment, hot water heaters and heating equipment.

Molded Doors

Interior doors molded of wood fibers are available primarily in the paneled form. They are much less expensive than the wood-paneled doors but will not take staining. They are hollow except at the points where the door hardware is to be applied, and they will not readily accept coat hooks or towel racks. They will not warp or split as wood doors occasionally do.

Prehung Doors

Because a prehung door is supplied already hinged to its frame, it saves some of the trim labor. Although it is more expensive than the nonprehung door, the savings in labor usually results in an overall cost reduction. Because prehung doors are supplied with part of the casing installed and part precut but not installed, you must select the type of door casing for the entire house before you order the doors.

FIGURE 8.5 Bifold Doors

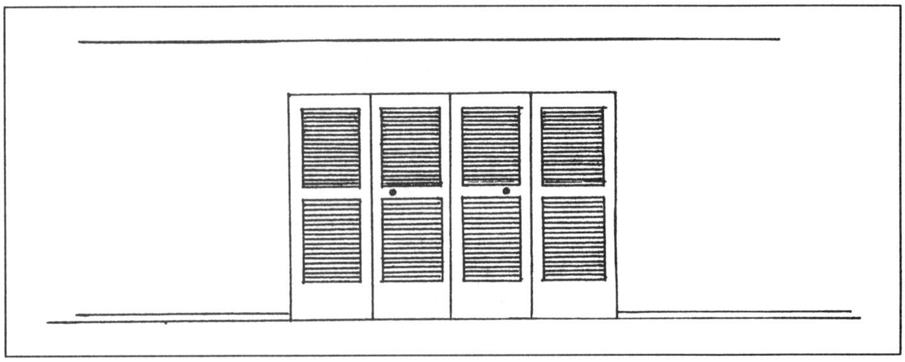

Pocket Doors

A pocket door slides in and out of a slot built into the wall framing. Like the folding door, it is very useful where little room exists to swing a standard door out of the way. On occasion, the pocket door can cause problems if not carefully installed with quality materials. In order to provide the pocket, the size of the stud is substantially reduced, producing a frame where warpage is much more likely. This warpage can interfere with the operation of the pocket door. To minimize the probability of warpage, use 2×6 studs in those walls in which a pocket door is to be installed.

Bifold Doors

The bifold door is made of two or more hinged sections (see Figure 8.5). For small openings it usually consists of two narrow panels hinged together forming one door. For large openings, bifold doors are made with wider panels, or four narrow panels (forming two doors) or a combination of both. These doors are designed to be operated from one side only and, consequently, are best suited for closets. They are most useful in providing wide doors to shallow closets, making the most use of the square footage available.

In the walk-in closet illustrated in Figure 8.6, note that the space used for the "walking in" cannot be used for storage. In the shallow closet with the bifold door, however, the user does not enter the closet, so that almost all of the space is available for storage. A disadvantage of the bifold door closet, however, is that much of the wall space is lost to the door and the flexibility of the room furniture placement is reduced.

FIGURE 8.6 Closet Designs

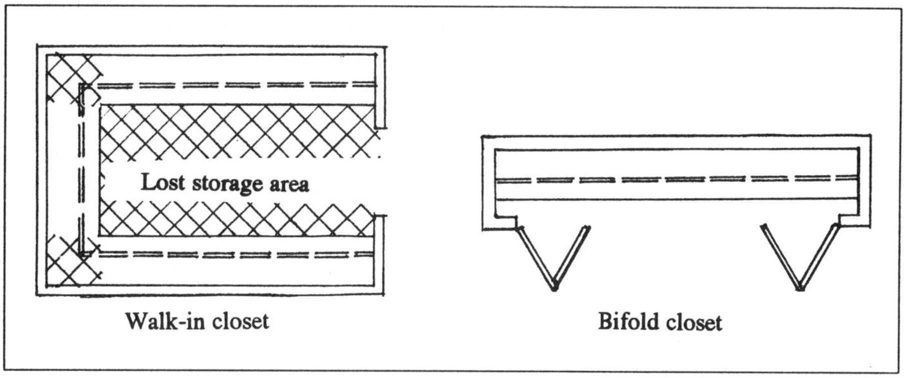

Lost storage area

Walk-in closet

Bifold closet

Folding Doors

The folding door (see Figure 8.7) can be made of wood, vinyl and many other materials. It is most useful where little room exists to swing a regular door.

Costing

The cost of the windows and doors will be provided by the supplier. The cost of the labor to install them should be included in the framing and interior trim bids. The cost of priming the exposed exterior wood should be included in the painter's bid. Make sure that this is understood before the bids for painting are made because the work involves a separate trip and a few hours of labor for one or more painters. If you have selected windows and doors that do not have exposed wood, make this fact known to the painting contractors also.

FIGURE 8.7 Folding Door

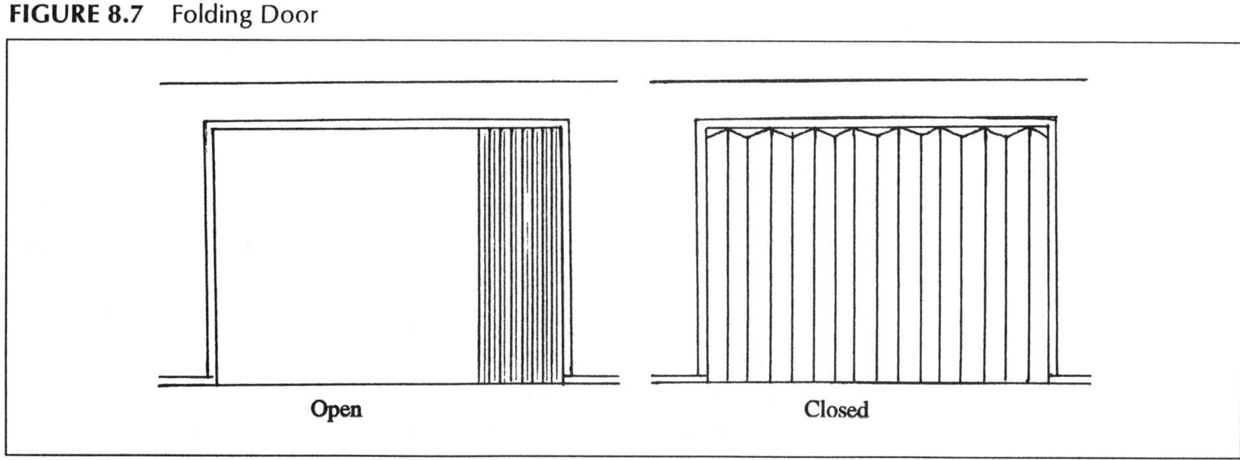

Management

Window and door construction management includes the following:

- Order your doors and windows well ahead of time. Many types are held in stock by the suppliers, but if your choices include some that are not stocked, delivery times may take several weeks. If 2×6-inch studs are used in the exterior walls, be sure that the windows ordered match that opening depth.
- Get the rough openings of both windows and doors from your supplier and pass them to the framing crew. They will need these dimensions during the framing to cut the correct size headers for the openings.
- If you have brick-veneered exterior walls, you will need to know the window and door widths to order the proper size steel lintels for the brick.
- Among those items most changed from original plans are the types, sizes and location of windows and doors. Be sure that the copies of plans available on the site have the correct placement of doors and windows and show the rough opening measurements for the actual doors and windows you have ordered.
- Do not request delivery of the windows and exterior doors to the site until just before they are to be installed. This reduces the exposure to theft, breakage and excess moisture absorption.
- As soon as the windows and doors arrive on site, large glass areas should be clearly marked with an "X" of masking tape or other suitable material to reduce the chances that someone will walk through the glass or push a piece of lumber through it. Unfortunately, this type of accident happens too frequently.
- Collect the screens, muntins and uninstalled hardware (such as cranks for casement windows, but leave one on the job so the carpenters can operate windows) and store them in a safe place away from the construction area to reduce the probability of loss or damage.
- Prime door and window exposed exterior wood shortly after (or even before) installation to protect it from the weather.
- After installation, check the operation of all of the windows and doors to ensure that they are not binding. If the operation is not smooth, correct the installation now. It may become a major problem to correct after the house has been finished.
- Check to make sure that the painters have painted both the tops and bottoms of wood exterior doors to prevent moisture getting into the wood and damaging it. Many wood and wood-material door manufacturers will void their guarantee if these two areas have not been properly painted.

CHAPTER 9

Considering Exterior Finishes

Almost any house structure can be altered to fit any of the available exterior finishes: brick, stone, wood, stucco, aluminum, vinyl or any other. In most cases, no change in the plan is required. The principal exception is the plan based on wood or similar siding that must be changed to accept brick or stone veneer.

To make the change to brick veneer from wood siding, you have two choices: (1) You can move the exterior wall inward about 5 inches to allow space for the full brick veneer and thus retain the same outside dimensions for the exterior walls, or (2) you can keep the exterior load-bearing foundation walls the same but install the brick veneer outside these walls. The first choice should require no changes in the roof structure, particularly the overhang and the exterior trim, whereas the second choice may require changes in these areas to accommodate the wider dimension of the outer limits of the exterior walls. In the first choice you will lose some living space in the house—roughly equal to about 5 inches multiplied by the length of the exterior walls of the living area.

If you choose to retain the exterior wall in its original position and move the brick veneer out, be sure to check the ceiling joists and roof rafters to see that their length will accommodate the change. The same applies to the dimensions of the roof trusses if your plans use them.

FIGURE 9.1 Lintels and Arches

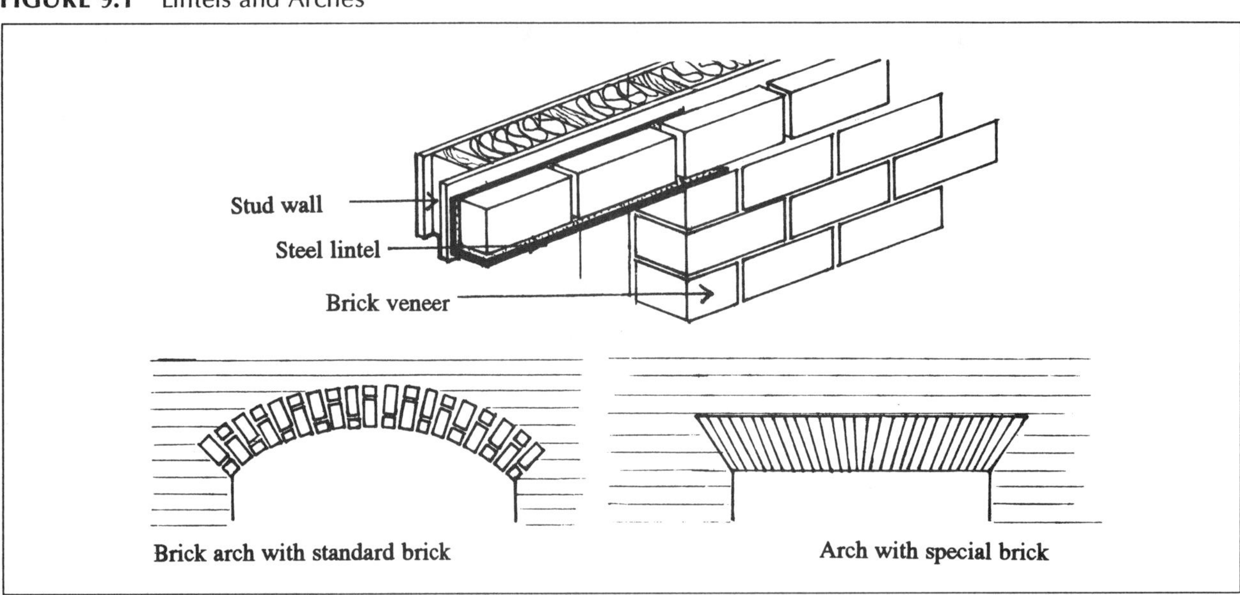

■ BRICK OR STONE SAYS SOLIDITY

Brick's Characteristics

Brick makes a very attractive exterior. It has a very long life and rarely requires any maintenance. It is, however, more expensive than wood, stucco, vinyl or aluminum. Although brick does not require painting, any wood trim of the house will require it. And the trim is relatively more expensive to paint than the siding because it takes more labor to cover smaller square footages.

A silicone sealer should be applied to the outside of the chimney (if it is made of brick) to prevent water leakage into the house. If the brick selected is very porous, a double coat of sealer may be required on the exterior surface of all the brick.

Openings over doors and windows require some special support to hold the weight of the brick above the opening. There are three methods (see Figure 9.1) in general use:

1. *Steel Lintels* are the simplest and easiest to install. The lintel consists of a steel angle iron about ¼ inch thick of the appropriate length with flanges about 3½ inches wide. It should be long enough to span the opening with not less than 8 inches bearing on each of the adjacent supporting walls. For larger openings, such as a double garage door, use a larger steel angle iron of

about 5 inches x 2½ inches and 5/16-inch thickness. The wider flange of 5 inches should be installed in the vertical position.

2. *Curved Brick Arches* can also be used to span the opening. Use bricks of standard size and shape. The arch must be supported by a wood form until the mortar has set so that the design of the arch can carry the load. Note, the curve of this arch requires that the frame and trim of the door or window installed under it be curved to match.
3. *Flat Brick Arches* if desired, require specially cut bricks. These bricks are expensive, and the cutting should be done by an experienced mason, one who has done this type of work before.

Brick Selection

To provide better adhesion with the mortar, much available brick is made with holes through it (see Figure 9.2).

These holes are concealed in a normal brick wall, but if your brick work requires that the bed of the brick be exposed (such as the end brick of a step), you will need to have some "solids," that is, bricks without the holes. Check with the supplier to find out how the manufacturer supplies these solids. Some include the solids as part of each packaged cube (approximately 450 bricks). Others require that they be ordered separately. Your mason should be able to give you an idea as to the quantities of solids needed.

Some bricks are made with a textured facing that appears only on the surfaces exposed in a running or common bond. If part of your masonry work requires exposure of the large flat surface or bed (again, the end brick in a step is an example), you will have a different texture and color that is quite noticeable. You have the choice of accepting this difference or selecting a brick that has the same texture and color on all sdes.

FIGURE 9.2 Brick Selection Problems

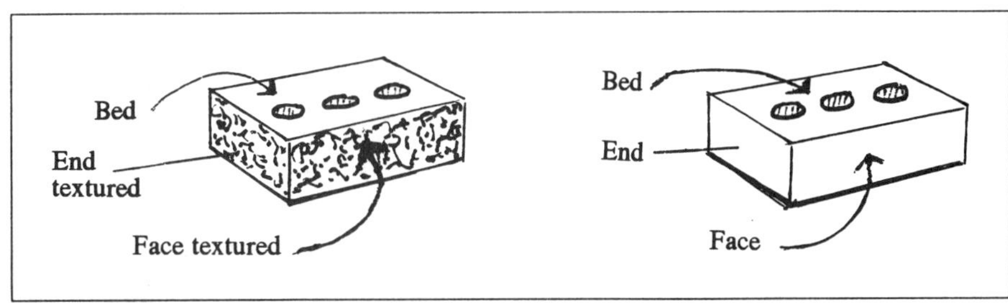

Stone Selection

Stone has most of the advantages of brick as well as the disadvantages, but it has no holes and has a uniform texture. Usually stone work costs more than brick work, but may be less costly if a lot of work with native stone is done in your area. Check with your local masons.

Costing Brick and Stone

The cost of labor is provided by the mason in his bid. The cost of the material is provided by the supplier. Don't forget to include the masonry sand, mortar and brick ties.

Management of Brick and Stone

Plan for placement of the material on your lot. If you have very little storage space, you might have to order the delivery of the material in several loads.

Check to be sure your supplier's stocks can provide the brick or stone at your site when you want it and in the quantities you need. If the brick you select is not normally stocked there, be sure that your supplier orders enough to complete the *entire* job and that it is either delivered to your site or held until you need it. Having to reorder from the manufacturer creates delay in the construction and may result in a mismatch of brick color or texture if the second order does not come from the same batch.

If your selection is an oversize brick, the quantities required compared to the standard brick are less, on a ratio of about 5 oversize to 7 standard.

Brick ties are galvanized corrugated-steel straps about 1 inch wide and 4 inches long used by the mason to tie the brick veneer to the house framing. One end of the tie is nailed to the stud and the other end is buried in the mortar between the brick and stone courses. Most codes require that one of these ties be used for every 4½ square feet of wall area. You will therefore need about 150 ties for every 1,000 standard bricks and about 110 ties for every 1,000 oversize bricks.

Two or three days after completion, the brick work should be cleaned with a muriatic acid solution by the masonry crew. (Use a ratio of 1 part muriatic acid to 10 parts of water). This work should be a normal part of any masonry work, but verify that your mason has included it in his bid. Muriatic acid is usually supplied in large quantities only. So it is best for your mason, who uses large amounts, to provide the acid.

FIGURE 9.3 Wood Siding

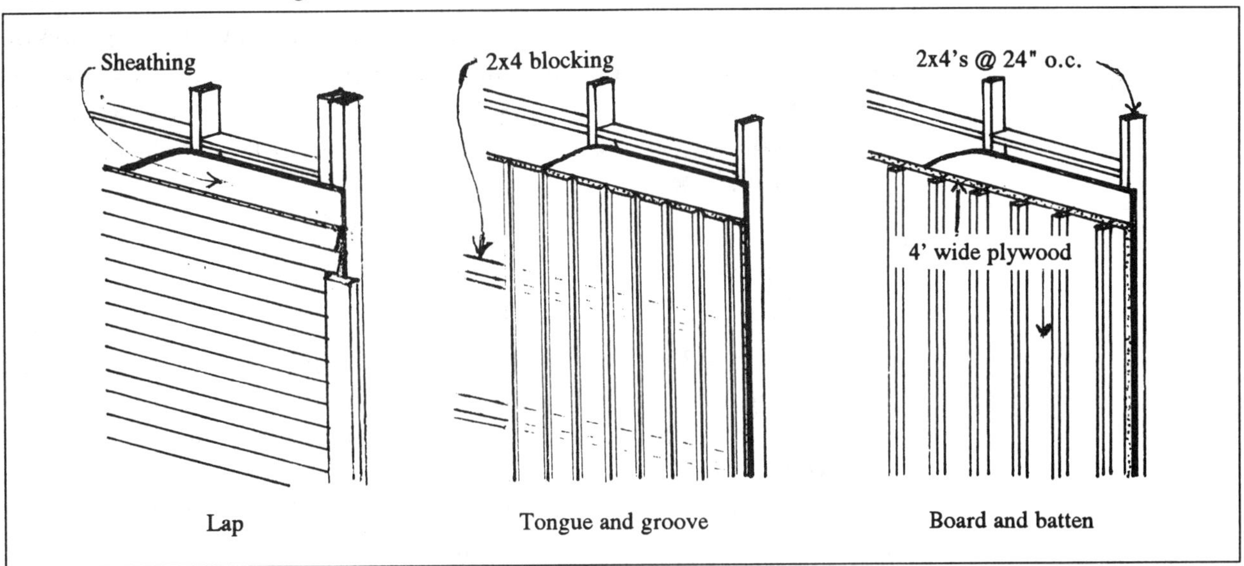

For other management suggestions, review Chapter 6, Foundations.

■ WOOD SIDING SAYS WARMTH

Solid Wood Siding

Figure 9.3 illustrates the most popular forms of solid wood siding. Almost any wood can be used for this purpose including such species as redwood, fir, cypress, pine, cedar, spruce and hemlock.

Lap Siding

Lap siding is normally installed over the sheathing (and the polyethylene wrapping, if it has been used) and nailed to the studs. For corner treatment, use either the metal corner pieces or wood corner boards. The thickness of the corner boards should be 5/4 inch or 1 inch actual. If the corner board is less than 1 inch thick, the lap siding may project beyond it. The results will not look good and will be impossible to caulk efficiently.

Vertical Siding

To properly install vertical siding, you will have to put blocking between the studs at a vertical interval not greater than 24 inches. Because most of the pieces of solid wood siding have widths less than the 16-inch interval of the studs, this blocking is necessary to provide a good nailing base.

Plywood Siding

Plywood siding can be supplied in many varieties of wood and pattern and at varying costs. Check with your local supplier to see samples. Plywood panels are made in various lengths—8, 10 and 12 feet. Match the length to the requirements of your house to have as few horizontal joints as feasible. They detract from the overall appearance and can be a source of air infiltration and water leaks if not properly installed.

There should be a ⅛-inch gap in the vertical and horizontal joints between the plywood panels to allow for expansion. Figure 9.4 illustrates methods for forming waterproof joints.

FIGURE 9.4 Horizontal and Vertical Joints in Plywood Siding

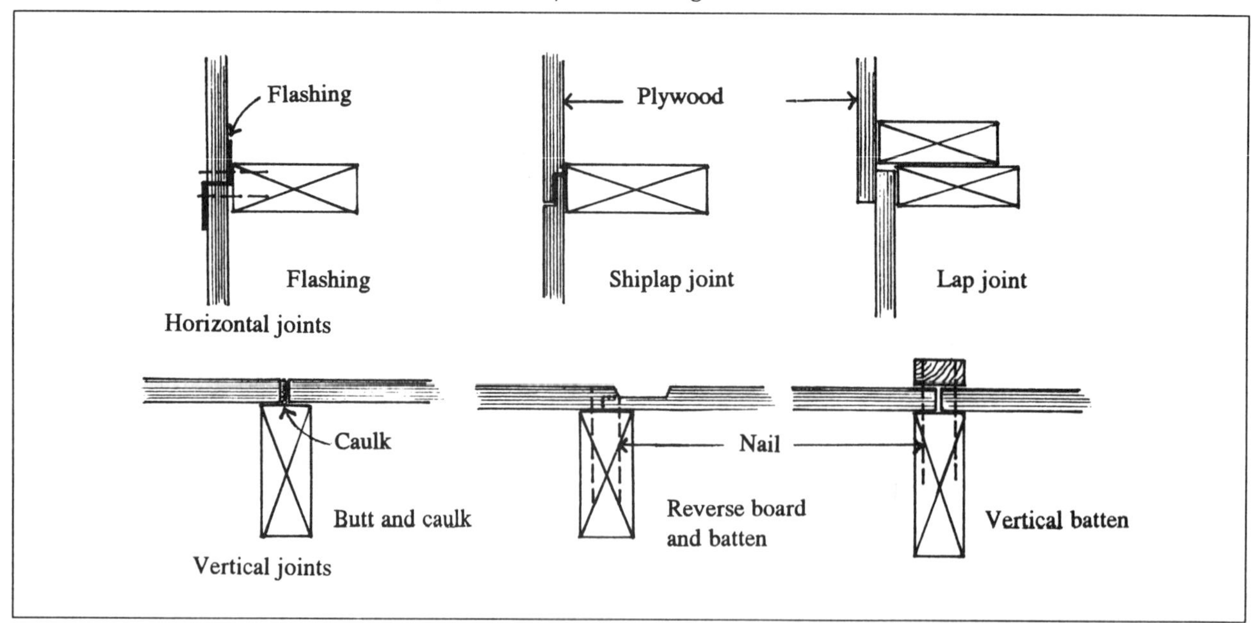

Costing Wood Siding

The price of the materials is provided by the supplier, and the labor costs are included in the bid of the carpentry contractor. Expect about 10 percent waste of material in excess of the actual square footage of the wall area.

Management of Wood Siding

Keep the following in mind when installing wood siding:

- Long lengths of wood siding (10 feet and 12 feet) may not be stocked by your supplier. If not stocked, order several weeks in advance.
- Handle the material carefully on site. It is expensive and may split if treated too roughly. This is particularly true of the relatively thin edges of lap siding.
- Store the material so that it will not warp. Put it on a flat surface and cover it to protect it from the elements. If your house has one, put the siding inside the garage to protect it until installed.
- Do not apply the siding over wet sheathing or studs, and do not apply it next to uncured concrete or stucco.
- All wood siding should be applied with aluminum or hot-dipped galvanized nails.
- As in all phases of the construction, be certain that the siding, nails, flashing and related material are on hand before you bring in the carpenters. If the framing crew is to install the siding, find out when the crew chief wants it on the job. The crew chief may want to do some siding work before the framing and exterior trim are complete.
- Prime paint the back of the siding before installation.

ALUMINUM AND VINYL SIDING SAYS PRACTICAL

Aluminum and vinyl sidings are available in different forms and textures for both vertical and horizontal installation. They can be used alone or in combination to cover all exterior wood surfaces to eliminate painting and to reduce maintenance.

Aluminum is an excellent siding that comes in a variety of colors from light tints to deep rich tones. Most manufacturers offer a guarantee of 20 or more years. Aluminum can provide additional insulation in the horizontal mode by the application of polystyrene backboards under each piece (this is in addition to the sheathing).

The disadvantages of aluminum siding are that it will dent if struck by a hard object, and the surface color can be scratched, exposing the bare aluminum.

With vinyl siding, the color selection is limited to the lighter tints. On the other hand, the color saturates the entire thickness of the material so that a scratch will do little harm. Vinyl will not dent.

Vinyl is not readily adaptable for covering exposed-wood trim, whereas aluminum is well suited for this purpose. Therefore, if you want vinyl siding and coverage of all wood trim, use a combination of vinyl for the siding and aluminum for the trim.

Costing

The cost of the material and the labor is normally furnished by the contractor. Many carpentry crews have experience in this line of work. If you choose this option, get the labor cost from the carpentry crew and the material cost from the supplier. Most suppliers are willing to do the material take-off at no cost to you.

Management of the Installation

Watch the following when installing aluminum or vinyl siding:

- The installation of these materials requires special skills and tools, and you should be sure that the installers have experience in this type work. This is particularly true if the job involves on-the-job forming of aluminum to cover exposed wood materials.
- If you are to furnish the material, order so that it is on the job before the installers arrive.
- Be sure that your bid for installation of this type of siding includes the cost of caulking. This task is normally performed by the painting contractor, but with aluminum and vinyl there is no painting involved. Include the caulking task in the specifications when you ask for bids.

■ STUCCO SAYS STYLISH

Stucco is an excellent exterior finish with long life and very little maintenance. It is a form of concrete and has most of its characteristics. It is made only in white, but can be coated with any paint recommended for application over masonry. You have a wide choice of colors.

FIGURE 9.5 Stucco Wall Construction

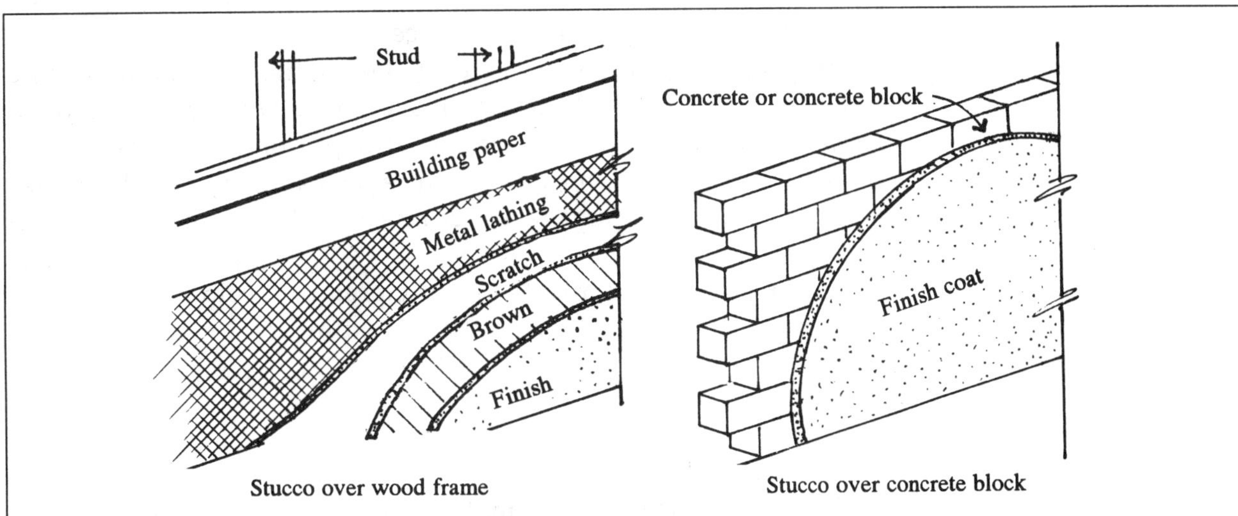

When applied over the sheathing of a wood-framed house, a layer of building paper is placed over the sheathing to protect it from the moisture in the stucco (see Figure 9.5). Next, metal lathing is nailed to the studs. The important point in the application of the stucco is that the scratch, or first, coat of material must be pushed through the metal lathing and behind it to form a solid layer between the lathing and the stud. The metal lathing provides a space between the lathing and the stud to permit the *scratch coat* to slip behind and thus anchor itself firmly.

A *brown coat* is applied over the scratch coat after allowing sufficient time for the first coat to dry. And finally, after the brown coat has dried, the *white finish coat* is applied with whatever pattern you have selected—smooth, stippled, swirled, etc.

In applying stucco over masonry, the finish coat is applied directly to the block or concrete. The mortar joints of the block should be flush to eliminate valleys that may show through the finish coat.

Outside temperature is critical: During the curing process, the stucco coats should not freeze. A safe guide is not to do the job when the temperature is expected to drop below 50°F.

Proper stucco application requires a special skill. Each step must be done correctly or the process may fail. For this reason, it is best to contract the entire process: the application of the building paper, the lathing and the three coats. It is also preferable that the contractor furnish all of the materials. Where stucco is applied over large uninterrupted areas, control joints should be installed to permit expansion and contraction of the stucco material. Without these control joints, the stucco will crack. As a general guide, control joints should be installed at least every 30 feet.

Recently, a fiberglass-reinforced, cement-board stucco system has become available. It is simpler to install in that a cement board is applied to the outside of the framing over the sheathing. A base coat of stucco is spread on, and the final coat is put on the next day. This system reduces labor costs. It also reduces cracking because this type of material can expand and contract more readily than the standard product.

The finish coat is available in many premixed colors (with custom color mixing as well) and four different textures.

Costing

The cost of both labor and material should be provided by the contractor.

Management

Don't overlook any of the following when stuccoing a house:

- If the contractor supplies the materials and the labor, it is only necessary to specify when the job is ready for the crew to go to work.
- If you provide the materials, the contractor should give you a list of the quantities needed. You must make sure that these materials are on the job at the proper time and protected from the weather.
- During the stucco process, it is important that no other work is under way, such as hammering inside the house, because it could cause the stucco to fall away from the lathing before the curing process has been completed.

CHAPTER 10

Building a Snug Roof

Shingles: Practical and Most Popular

Shingles are the most popular roofing material for a home. They should not normally be used on roofs, however, with a pitch of less than 3/12 (3 inches vertical rise for each horizontal 12 inches). At this flat angle, water may seep under the shingles, especially in high winds. If installed over a properly applied, two-ply underlayment (building paper), shingles may be used on roofs with a pitch of only 2/12.

Color Selection

If your roof is complex with many dormers and valleys and varying planes, a dark shingle will tend to pull it together.

Check the other houses on the street. If they all use more or less the same color, you may want to select a different one to break the monotony, but do coordinate the color with your house trim, etc.

A light color will reflect heat and thus is more desirable in those areas where air-conditioning is the greatest user of energy. In colder climates, because black absorbs heat from the sun, a darker color may be the better choice.

If you live in a mildew-prone area, avoid light-colored shingles because mildew will be most noticeable on them.

Choose from Many Types of Shingle Material

Some of the more popular types of shingles are the following:

- *Asphalt* shingles are made in many different colors by many different manufacturers. They vary in weight from 220 pounds per square (100 square feet of roof area) to 340 pounds. The heavier shingle is more expensive, has greater texture and longer life. Most roofers also charge a higher rate for applying the heavier shingle.
- *Fiberglass* shingles (single layered) are similar in appearance to asphalt shingles. They are more resistant to fire and may reduce the premium for your homeowner's insurance.
- *Laminated Fiberglass* shingles are thicker, heavier and project deeper shadows that appear more dramatic than the single layer type. Some designs resemble cedar shakes or slate.
- *Aluminum* shingles are very light and generally have a shake texture. They last indefinitely. Be sure to use aluminum nails for applying them to avoid any electrolytic reaction that could cause corrosion.
- *Wood* shingles are available in several species with cedar being the most popular. In wood, the term *shingle* indicates the material has been sawn, whereas the term *shake* means the material has been split. The shake is usually thicker and has a much more rustic appearance. The labor to install and the cost of the material can be four to five times that of standard asphalt or fiberglass shingles.
- *Clay Tile* shingles are very popular in the Sunbelt areas. They are an excellent shingle with a very long life. Tile shingles are very heavy, weighing from 800 to 1600 pounds per square. If your original plans are based on wood or asphalt shingles, have the structural design of the roof checked by an architect or engineer before making the decision to change from standard shingles to the much heavier clay tile.
- *Slate* is among the finest materials for roofing. It is also one of the most expensive. Again, if this is your choice, be certain that in your plan the structural design of the framing is based on a slate roof that can weigh from 700 to over 3,600 pounds per square.

Preventing Ice Buildup on the Roof

If you are building with a shingled roof in a cold climate you should consider special construction methods to eliminate ice buildup.

Ice dams are caused by heat from the attic space melting the underside of the snow on the roof, as shown in Figure 10.1. The water

FIGURE 10.1 Ice Buildup

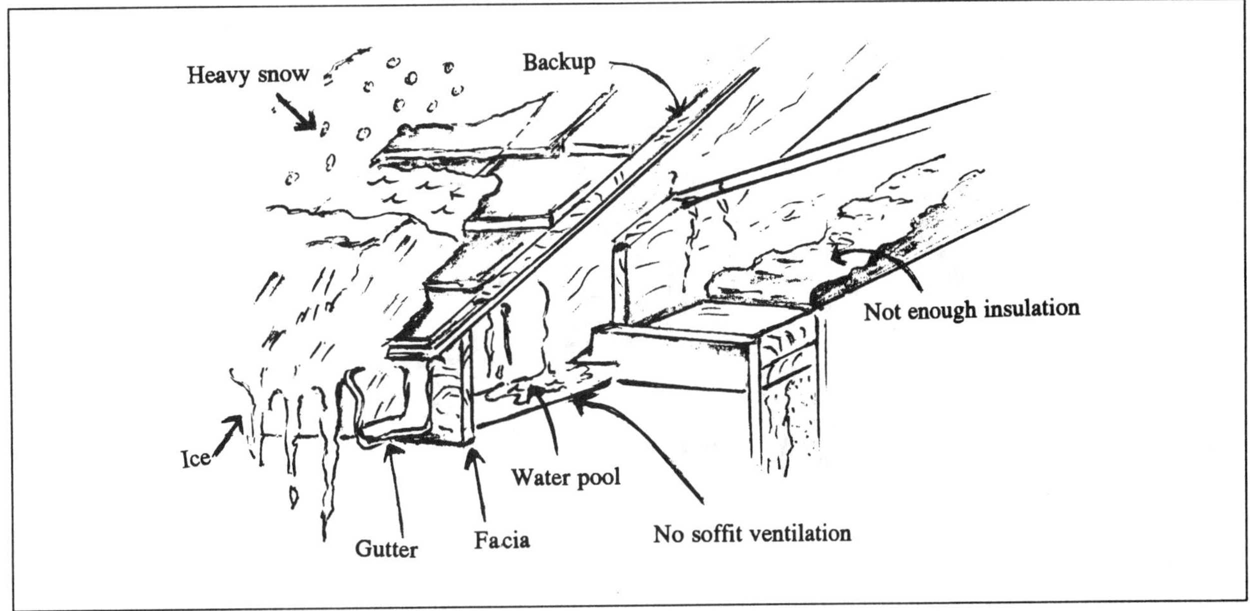

from the melted snow trickles down the shingles under the snow until it reaches that part of the roof surface over the eaves where interior heat does not warm that part of the roof. The water freezes and continues to build an ice dam that will move water up the roof slope underneath the shingles to leak into the house structure causing damage to the wood frame, ceiling and wall finishes, and other parts of the house interior.

The first preferred step to prevent this ice damage is to install rubberized asphalt ice and water shield roll roofing before the shingles are laid. Compare Figure 10.2 with Figure 10.1.

A second step is to increase the amount of insulation in the ceiling to reduce the movement of heated air from inside the house into the attic space. The insulation should extend to the top plate around the perimeter of the ceiling. Do not let the insulation block the movement of outside air through the soffit vents.

A third step, as a last resort, is to install thermostatically controlled electric heating strip cables outside along the edge of the roof and into the gutters to prevent the formation of the ice dam.

Metal Roofs Have Their Place

Among roofing materials, the following metals are worth considering:

- *Copper* sheeting can be a striking choice particularly on a contemporary home. In time, copper turns to a salmon color to brown to

FIGURE 10.2 Eliminating Ice Buildup

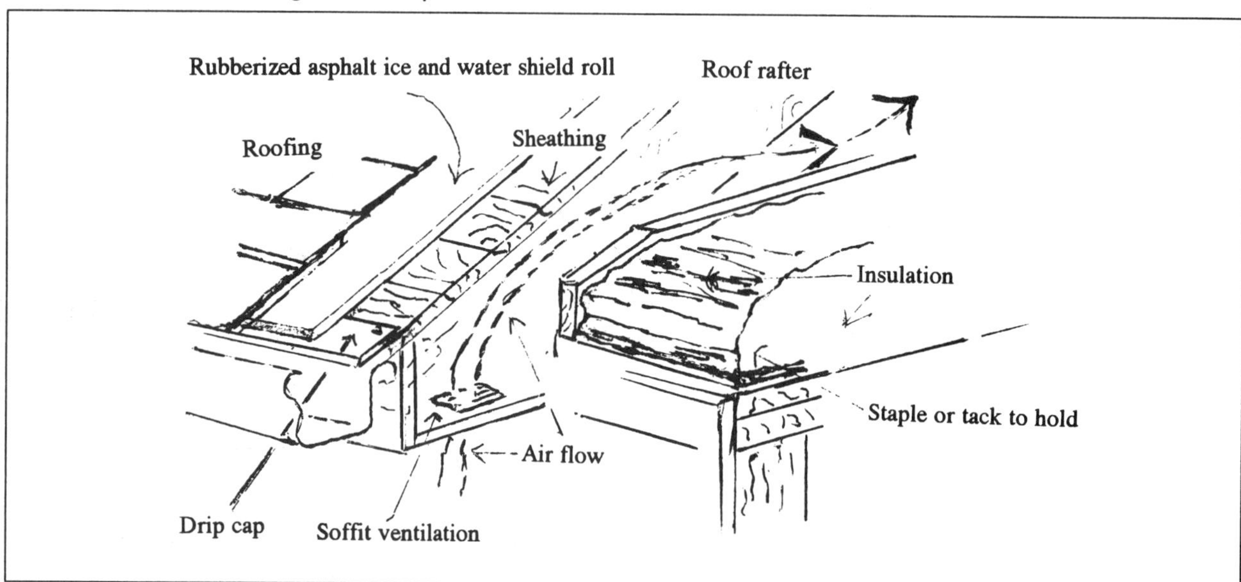

black and finally to a beautiful green patina. A copper roof can last up to 100 years.

- *Terne* sheeting has been used in America since the 1700s and can last as long as 50 years with proper maintenance. Terne consists of a lead-tin coating over a copper-bearing steel base. Typically, terne must be brush-painted with a linseed-oil primer when installed and repainted every 8 to 10 years. Terne takes and holds paint extremely well.
- *Terne-Coated Stainless (TCS)* sheets consist of stainless steel coated with terne alloy. It does not have to be painted, but it can be if its normal gray color is not desired. TCS lasts at least 30 years.

Sheet metal roofing is usually installed in a standing seam configuration (see Figure 10.3). Because roof sheeting should not be punctured or penetrated when put on, it is installed by using hold-down cleats that are formed into the standing seams.

Built-up Roofs Great for Some Situations

Figure 10.4 illustrates flat-roof construction consisting of several alternating layers of fiberglass felt with a coat of asphaltic cement in between and a finish coat of gravel on top.

FIGURE 10.3 Standing Seam

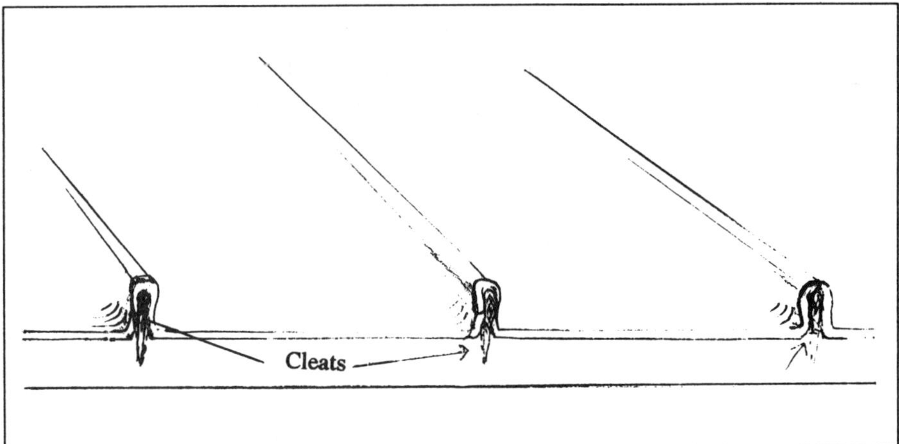

Another newer system uses a single, synthetic, rubberlike membrane that is less affected by the sun's rays and readily expands and contracts with the roof as the temperature changes. Most roofers are familiar with this product.

Avoid a built-up roof with no pitch at all unless your plans specifically call for the collection of water on the roof for heating and/or cooling purposes. Under these circumstances the roof must be specifically designed to hold the water because a built-up roof with no pitch will collect and hold water and tend to develop leaks.

FIGURE 10.4 Built-up Roof Construction

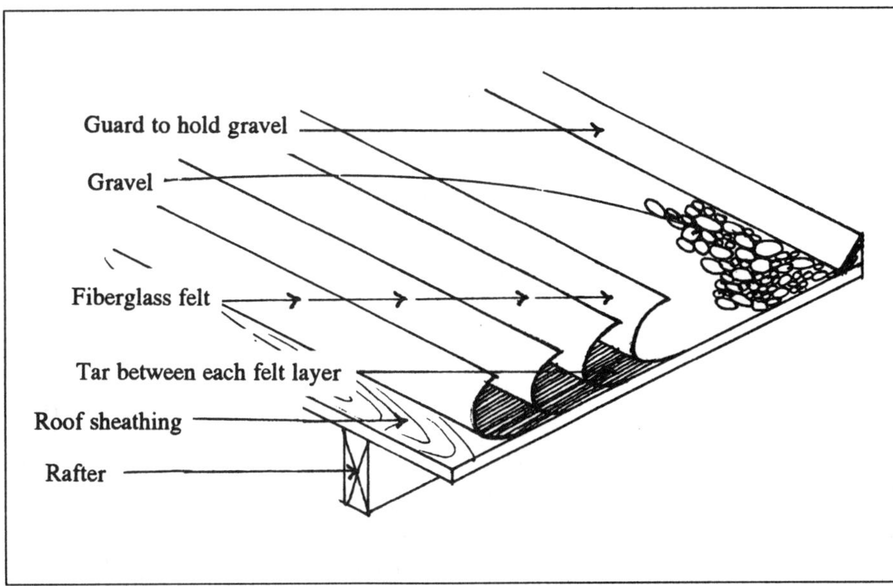

Flashing Helps Stop Roof Leaks

Flashing is the application of material at critical points—such as at the juncture of the shingles with the chimney or at the juncture of the siding of a dormer with the main roof—to prevent water and snow from leaking through the roof system. Figure 10.5 illustrates some flashing applications.

An excellent choice for the flashing material is copper. It seems to last forever and requires almost no maintenance, but it is expensive. A vinyl flashing material in various colors is now on the market. It is an excellent choice and costs less than copper. Aluminum can also be used, but its drawback is a shiny appearance unless painted, and aluminum does not hold paint well. Galvanized and tin-plated steel can be used, but they also must be painted.

Gutters and Downspouts Can Be Vital

Gutters and downspouts may be useful in preventing drainage problems. They may be a vital necessity, in certain cases, to carry water away from the house. They can be very troublesome in areas with many trees because they will require cleaning four or five times a year.

Cleaning gutters can be facilitated if you specify removable end caps. Then you can pop off the cap and flush the gutter with a garden hose. Also require that the gutters be mounted so that the back of the gutter is offset from the facia board. Without this air space, the paint will fail and the facia board will rot.

Your choices in guttering are copper, aluminum with baked-on paint, galvanized steel (must be painted) and vinyl. Considering both cost and long life with low maintenance, the best choices are vinyl or aluminum.

Underground Roof Drains Solve Special Problems

If, in your area, it will be necessary to clean out your gutters several times a year to remove large amounts of leaves, acorns, seeds and other yard debris, underground drains may be your best choice (see Figure 10.6).

The drain consists of a ditch about 12 inches deep from grade level and 18 inches wide centered directly under the roof edge where the rain and snow will run off.

Place a continuous 4-inch slotted plastic pipe in the center of the bottom of the ditch. Fill the remainder of the ditch with gravel. The size

FIGURE 10.5 Roof Flashing Details

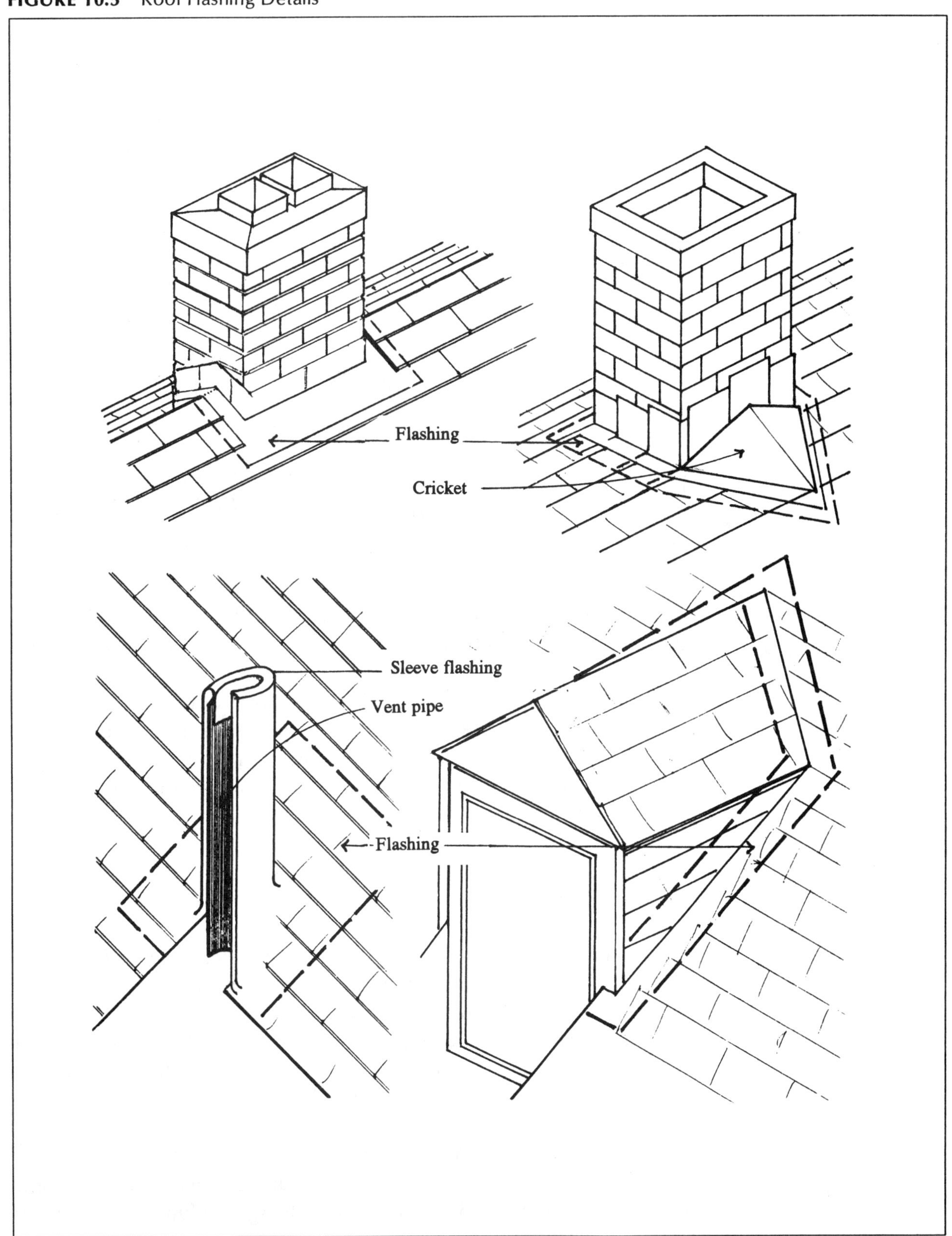

FIGURE 10.6 Underground Roof Drain

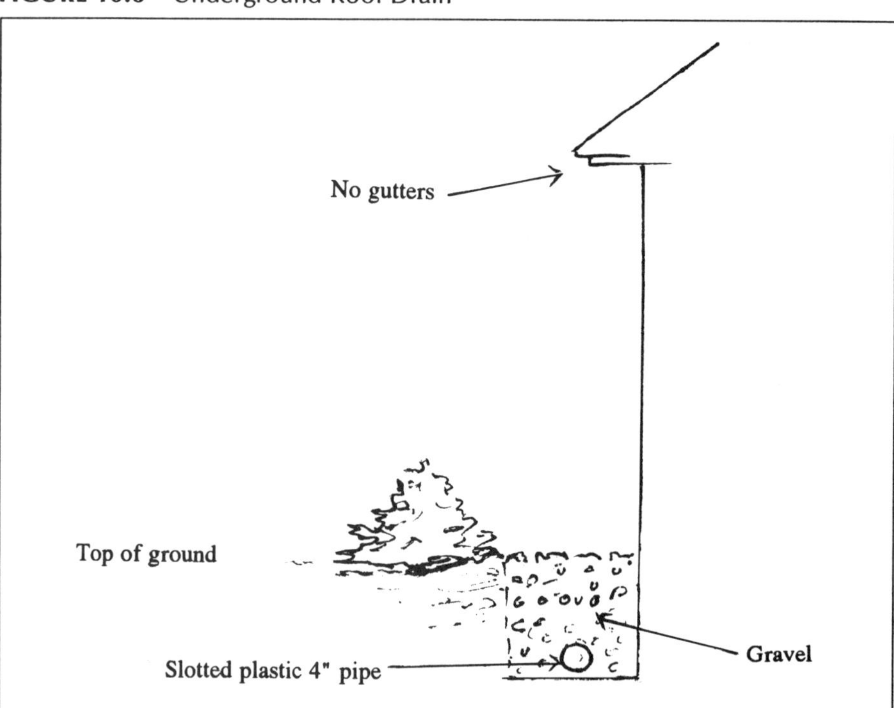

of the individual stones of the gravel should be large enough so that they will not move into the slots of the pipe and reduce the flow of the drain water.

With this system, the water falls from the roof edge down to the gravel in the ditch, then into the plastic pipe where it is carried away to a storm drain, stream, pond or other collection source.

This system will function even when the ditch is covered with leaves, twigs and other yard debris.

Costing

The cost of roofing labor is provided by the contractor. Either you or the contractor can furnish the shingles or other roofing material. Just be sure that this is made clear in your bidding.

Flashing material and labor to install it are usually provided by the roofer, but you must specify the type of material. The plumber will furnish and install flashing around the plumbing vent pipes penetrating the roof.

The roofer usually installs gutters and downspouts, providing both material and labor. Make sure that your plans indicate the actual length of downspouts required, including any changes to foundation height.

If you have built-up roofing, ask the roofing contractors to include both labor and materials in their bids.

Labor for installing an underground roof drain system can be provided by the contractor who put in the footings. The supplier can give you the cost of the pipe and gravel.

Management

Building a snug roof requires careful, timely management that includes the following:

- The shingles should be installed very soon after the application of the building paper on the roof by the framing crew. In rough, windy weather this paper will not last long. In addition, you should push to have the house weatherproof as soon as possible.
- If you are to furnish the shingles, make sure that they are on the job site, at the proper time. Also, have all flashing materials (aluminum rolls, plumbing vent stack collars, etc.) on site unless they are to be furnished by the roofer. Arrange with your roofer for a location for the supplier to place the shingles on site. Like most building material, shingles are heavy, and the contractor doesn't want to have to move them any farther than necessary.
- Avoid having shingles placed on the lot way ahead of the time they will be applied, particularly in hot weather. The mastic that seals the shingles after installation will sometimes, during open storage, soften and leak past its cover strip and stick to adjacent shingles. This leakage can also happen if the supplier has old stock, so make sure that your shingles are fairly new.
- The gutters and downspouts should not be installed until completion of the exterior painting. If you have selected galvanized gutter material and the painter is to paint them, have them on the site but not installed so it's easy do the job.
- Masonry and metal chimneys, plumbing vent stacks and skylights should be in place and completed before the roofer begins. It is not good practice to bring in the roofer before these items are finished because the roofing crew will have to make an extra trip to complete the shingles and install the flashing later. It will justify an extra charge.
- The underground roof drain system should be installed just before the final grading of your lot.

■ — CHAPTER 11 — ■

Pulling It Together with Masonry and Concrete

This chapter discusses those items of masonry and concrete that have not been included elsewhere, including some items that tend to be overlooked in the costing of a house.

■ THE BASICS OF FIREPLACE DESIGN

For centuries, the fireplace functioned as the principal means of heating a house and in the recent past as an auxiliary heating system. Unfortunately, it has not done either job very well. Depending on the use of room air for combustion, the fireplace can actually waste more heat than it generates. In modern homes, the room air used for fireplace combustion has already been heated by the primary heating system, but most of the heated air is lost up the fireplace chimney. Therefore, rather than assist it in its heating function, the fireplace increases the primary heating system's work load.

To be energy efficient and to provide a realistic addition to the primary heating system the fireplace must have

- a *combustion chamber* that is supplied with fresh air from outdoors, and
- a *heat chamber* that is warmed by the combustion but isolated from the outside air and the combustion chamber.

FIGURE 11.1 Energy-Efficient Fireplace Design

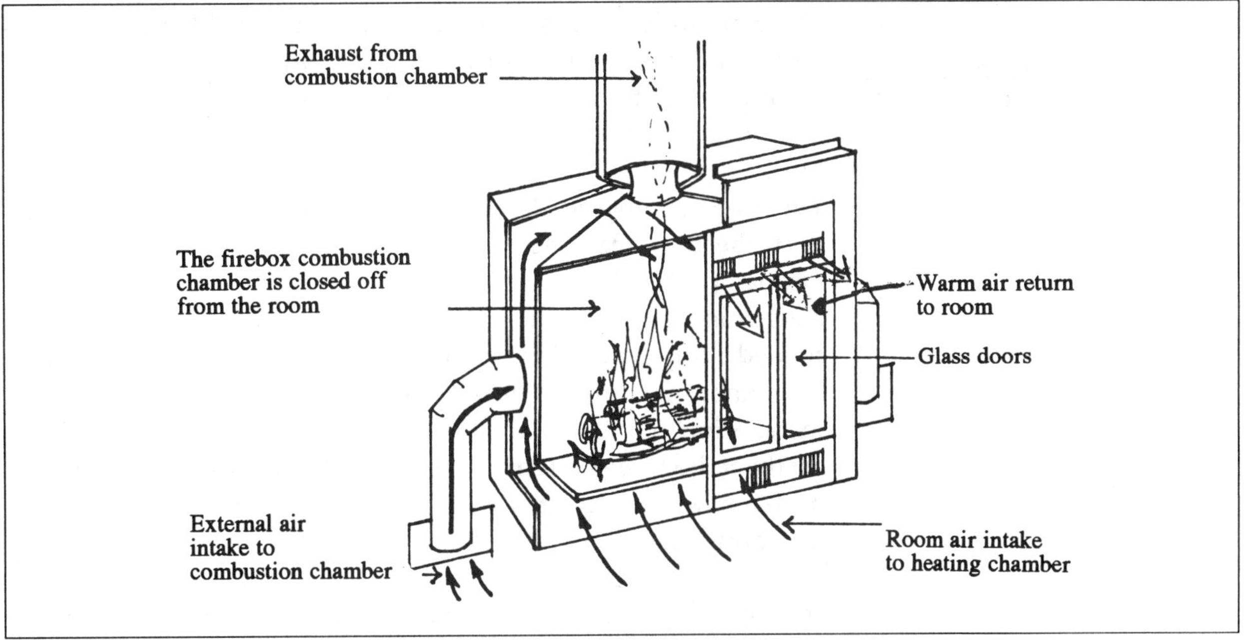

Air heated by the fireplace is blown or circulates from the heat chamber to the room and then back into the heat chamber for reheating. Air to support the combustion of the fuel is drawn from out of doors through special ducting into the combustion chamber (sealed from the room by glass doors), around the fuel, then out through the damper and up the chimney. With this design, heat from the room is not lost up the chimney, and the fireplace becomes an efficient heating system on its own or an efficient auxiliary system to the primary system (see Figure 11.1).

Different Fireplaces for Different Spaces

- *The All-Masonry Fireplace:* With a full-masonry firebox and chimney, this type can be designed and built to meet the energy efficiency requirements indicated above. Its construction requires a skill that may not be widespread because this technique has only recently been introduced into the construction business. While labor costs will be high, maintenance will be low, and the beauty of the brick work can enhance your room's overall appearance. If you choose this option, be certain that you have a good design and that your mason has had experience in building this type of fireplace.

- *The Masonry/Steel-Box Fireplace:* This type is similar to the all-masonry fireplace except that the firebox is prefabricated steel. The remainder of the system is all masonry. This type is less costly and retains most of the other architectural and aesthetic advantages of the all-masonry fireplace. Vents into and out of the combustion chamber can emerge from the front or side of the box.
- *The All-Steel Fireplace:* This fireplace is 90 percent prefabricated with the 10 percent being the assembly and installation of the various parts. The system includes the firebox, the parts of the steel chimney in lengths of 2, 3 or 4 feet, the chimney cap and related equipment. This type of fireplace has been on the market for some time, and most framing crews are experienced in its installation. The fireplace functions efficiently and is the least costly of the three systems. However, it may present one difficult problem: what to use to cover that portion of the metal chimney that protrudes through the roof.

If your house has exterior wood, aluminum or vinyl siding or stucco, even in part, one acceptable method to conceal the exposed metal chimney is the use of 2×4 framing, sized to complement the architecture of the house and covered with the same siding used on the rest of the house.

The top of the frame must be covered by a metal cap to prevent rain from getting inside the structure. This cap is not normally furnished by the supplier of the fireplace; it must be job made. Contact your roofing or heating contractor (both usually have sheet metal tools) and have them make it for you.

If your house is brick or stone veneer, its weight prohibits using it to hide the wood-framed metal chimney. You may use the factory-made artificial brick covers, but they do not always look very attractive. Your best choice is to select the all-masonry or the masonry/steel-box fireplace with its brick chimney built from top to bottom.

The room-side finish on steel fireboxes can be brick, tile, plaster, stucco or almost any material that does not create a fire hazard.

Most building codes require a minimum height of 3 feet for that part of the chimney above the roof. This is for flat roofs. If your roof has any pitch, this exposed chimney height could be several more feet depending upon the amount of the pitch. For most codes, the rule is that the chimney must be 2 feet higher than that point of the roof that is 10 feet away (measured horizontally) from the chimney. In Figure 11.2, note that the height of the exposed chimney not including the cap is almost 10 feet.

FIGURE 11.2 Chimney Height Requirements

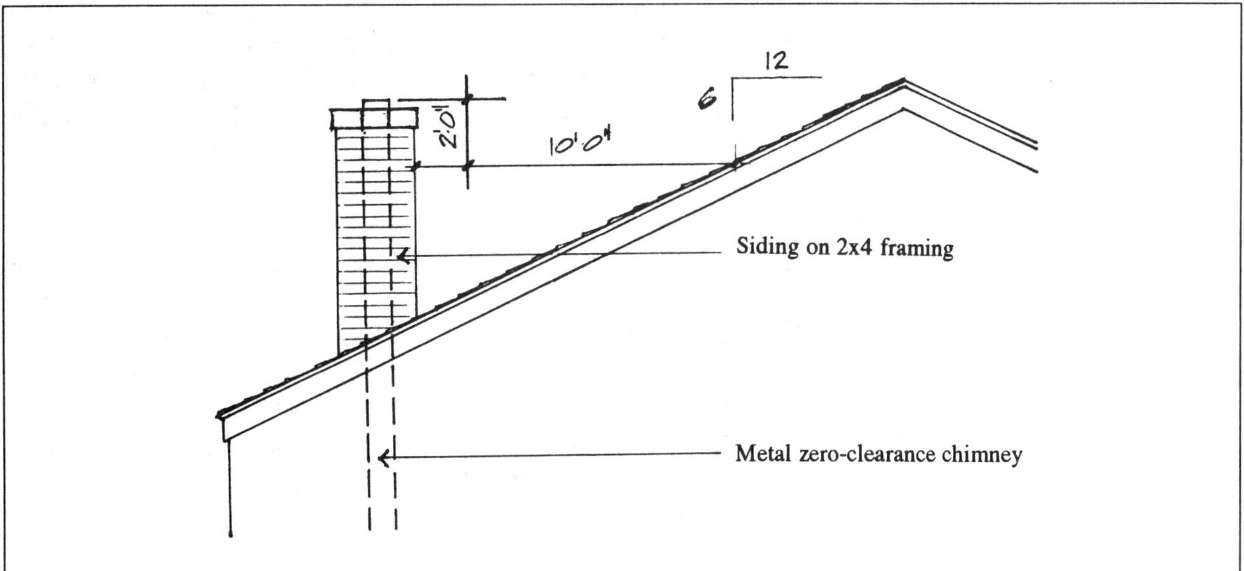

Electrical Requirements for the Fireplace

Practically all of the fireplaces discussed use electric blowers to circulate the heated air from the heat chamber to the room and then back into the heat chamber for reheating. Be sure your electrician is aware of the need to provide the electrical hookup. In addition, select a design that will allow easy access to the blower for periodic maintenance. Most blowers do produce some noise even when set on "low," so choose one that can be completely turned off while the fireplace is operating.

Masonry Hearths Need More Support

If your fireplace is built with a hearth of some form of masonry or tile at floor level, the weight of this material can normally be carried by the floor joists with some modest reinforcement. On the other hand, if your fireplace has a large raised hearth, the weight of the masonry can be considerable. It must be supported from the ground up beginning with a concrete pad 12 or more inches thick (usually part of the total fireplace footing) and then brought up to the subfloor level with concrete block. Failure to provide this type of support may cause separation of the heavy, large hearth from the firebox after the house is built.

Fireplace Mantels Must Meet Code

If your fireplace is to have a heavy timber mantel, check the local building code to see what limitations you must follow for its installation. Usually, as long as the timber mantel is placed 12 inches or more above the fireplace opening, the amount of the projection does not matter. Most milled-wood mantels are built to conform to these rules and present no installation problem.

Gas-Fired Fireplaces Come in Great Variety

Many styles of prefabricated efficient gas-fired fireplaces are available today, and they are easy to install and much easier to take care of than the wood burners. Many types can be installed directly against a plaster- or Sheetrock-covered wall or on top of an existing wood floor. Look for the "zero clearance" type. Most of these fireplaces need a very simple "chimney" consisting of a short 4-inch metal pipe installed horizontally through the exterior wall behind the fireplace into the outside air.

If public gas service is available in your area, you can hook up to it for the fuel supply. If not, butane or propane gas can be supplied from an exterior tank.

Gas-fired stoves with similar characteristics are also available.

■ MISCELLANEOUS MASONRY

Walks, patios and other exterior slab work should not be built until the final grade has been determined and preferably finished. Among the more popular materials used for this work are:

- *Brick* laid either in mortar on a concrete slab or laid without mortar on a level bed of crushed rock or sand. The mortarless system requires less skill and is therefore one task the homeowner may undertake himself. The preferred bricks for these jobs are called "pavers" and are supplied in thicknesses from 1½ inches to 2 inches. If you would rather use the brick matching that on the house, don't forget the problems of color and texture previously discussed in Chapter 9, Considering Exterior Finishes. Order solids to eliminate the problem of the holes in the brick.
- *Stone* or *Flagstone* can be laid in mortar or directly on a sand bed that has been tamped and leveled. If the work does not require mortar and concrete, consider doing it yourself.

FIGURE 11.3 Exposed Aggregate Concrete Patio

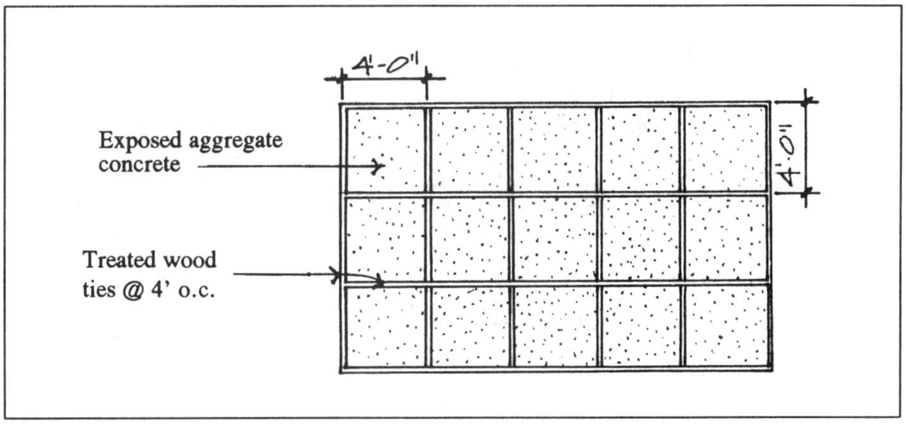

Exposed aggregate concrete

Treated wood ties @ 4' o.c.

4'-0"

4'-0"

- *Concrete* is an excellent material for patios and walks. Choose any of four selections: standard concrete, standard concrete with color added to the mix, exposed aggregate concrete and concrete stamped with a pattern.

The "aggregate" of exposed aggregate concrete (see Figure 11.3) consists mainly of brown smooth pebbles. Shortly after the concrete is poured and floated, a retardant is applied on the surface. This is a liquid that holds back the setting of the top film of the concrete. At the appropriate time (following the directions of the retardant manufacturer), the top layer is washed with water, thus removing the concrete binder and exposing the top of the brown pebbles. This process gives the concrete an attractive textured look.

Concrete stamping is the technique of using special tools to imprint designs into the top of the concrete to give the effect of tile, brick, cobblestone and so forth.

Another interesting method of laying concrete is the use of 1-inch or 2-inch boards (should be redwood, cedar or salt treated pine) as expansion joints (see Figure 11.3). The wood inserts also serve as forms for the concrete and facilitate screeding (leveling).

Concrete Porch Floors

Concrete porch floors should be supported by the masonry wall that contains the fill and not by the fill alone (see Figure 11.4). This design will prevent any dropping or cracking of the concrete floor due to further compaction or settling of the fill. Make sure that in each case the metal reinforcement in the concrete reaches over the corbeled brick or over the block wall.

FIGURE 11.4 Concrete-Slab Porch Floors

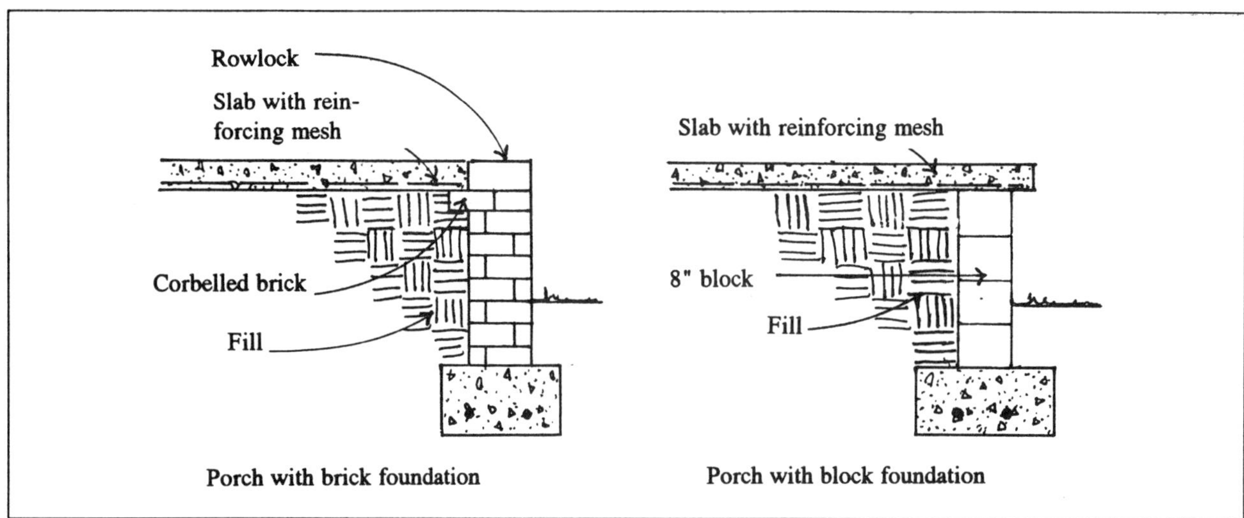

Porch floors may also be constructed of the different concrete options discussed earlier, or of earth stone, ceramic tile, or almost any other form of masonry.

Retaining Walls

Retaining walls can be made of most forms of masonry, landscape timber or railroad ties (see Figure 11.5).

The masonry must be laid on suitable footings. These walls must have provisions to drain water through them by the use of weep holes or by a plastic footing drainpipe to prevent pressure buildup behind. The types of walls illustrated are to be used only for jobs where the height of the wall does not exceed 4 feet.

Costing

Costing of the masonry and concrete for your house is fairly straightforward, as follows:

- In computing the cost of the all-masonry fireplace, have the mason give you the material requirements and the labor cost. Be sure the brick, block, mortar, firebrick, flue liners, damper and brick ties are included.
- In computing the cost of the combination masonry/steel fireplace, have the mason give you the material requirements and

FIGURE 11.5 Retaining Walls

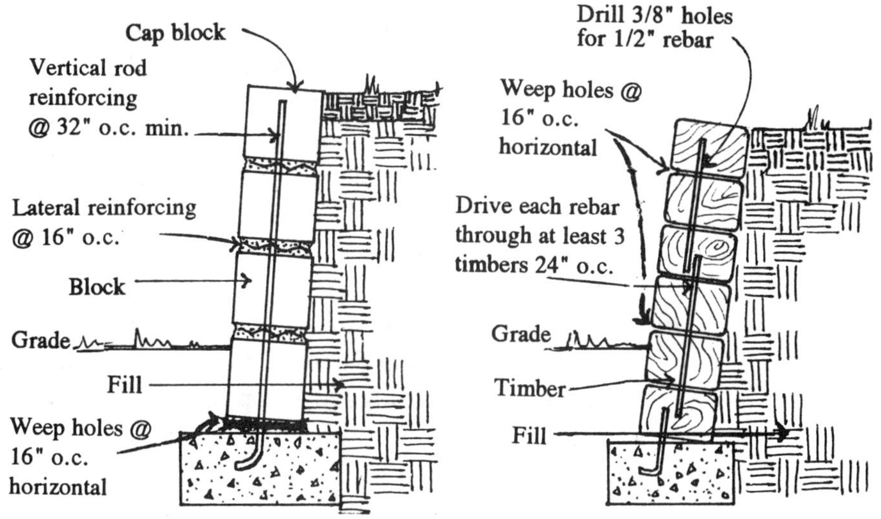

Cap block
Vertical rod reinforcing @ 32" o.c. min.
Lateral reinforcing @ 16" o.c.
Block
Grade
Fill
Weep holes @ 16" o.c. horizontal

Concrete block wall

Drill 3/8" holes for 1/2" rebar
Weep holes @ 16" o.c. horizontal
Drive each rebar through at least 3 timbers 24" o.c.
Grade
Timber
Fill

Timber wall

Note: Retaining walls slope back at 3 to 10 degrees.

the labor cost. The suppliers of the firebox and masonry will give you the cost of their materials.

- For the all-steel fireplace, the cost of the fireplace parts is provided by the supplier, the labor cost by the installer. Don't forget to include the labor and materials for whatever treatment you have chosen for the exposed chimney.
- Costs for other masonry, such as sidewalks and patios, is derived from the labor charged by the mason; the material cost is provided by the supplier.
- For wood retaining walls, the supplier will give you the cost of the materials, and the contractor the cost of labor.

Management

Management of the installation of masonry and concrete is also straightforward:

- Have the materials on hand at the proper site location before the work is to be done (except the concrete, of course, which should be ordered the day of the pour). If large quantities of heavy material are involved, have a plan for their delivery and site location as discussed in Chapter 5, The Importance of Footings.

- For the delivery of the prefabricated steel fireplace system, make sure that it includes placing it in the house. The system is very heavy and will require three people to unload and put in place. Check with the framing crew so that it does not arrive too early and thus interfere with the framing work.
- For the construction of the all-masonry or part-masonry fireplace, coordinate the work between the framing and masonry crew so that the two crews do not interfere with each other. The masonry crew should be brought on the job when the framing process has reached the point where the masonry work can be completed without interruption.
- Although the work should have been done at the time the footings were poured, check once again to make sure that adequate concrete footings are in place for fireplaces and masonry steps.

CHAPTER 12

Air Infiltration

SEALING A HOUSE CAN BE EASY AND INEXPENSIVE

One of the most important elements in producing an energy-efficient home is to reduce air infiltration to the minimum. If special sealing measures are not taken during construction, large quantities of air will move back and forth through cracks in the walls, floors and ceilings of the occupied house. Studies produced by the Department of Housing and Urban Development (HUD), the National Association of Home Builders (NAHB), the National Research Council of Canada (NRCC), and the National Applied Science Development Center (NASDC) indicate that the average loss of house energy through air infiltration is about 33 percent, with some test homes experiencing a loss as high as 60 percent.

During the heating season, warm indoor air holds more moisture than cold outdoor air. This creates vapor pressure, which constantly forces warm water vapor out through exterior walls, floors and ceiling.

Fortunately, sealing a home against air infiltration is a simple process *if done during construction,* and it is relatively inexpensive, particularly considering the energy fuel saved heating the house.

Most of the sealing is accomplished after the framing is complete and the electrical, plumbing and heating rough-ins have been finished and inspected. Hold off on the insulation until the sealing has been completed—with the exceptions discussed in the remainder of this chapter.

The sealing job should be performed by an experienced sealing contractor who will apply the proper sealant at each appropriate place. In most cases, the sealant is an expanding foam that is excellent for permanently filling large openings, such as the gap between the frame of the window and the stud framing of the house, and for caulking small cracks in selected areas most likely to leak.

Where To Seal

Figure 12.1 and 12.2 illustrate those areas to be sealed. The numbers 1 through 8 show in detail just where the sealant is applied:

1. Seal between the sill plate and the foundation wall. This sealing should be accomplished during the framing by the carpentry crew who install a special batt of insulation made for this purpose. Install this batt even if the inside of the foundation is ventilated crawl space, because it will reduce the wind effect in the winter months.
2. Seal around the window between the frame of the window and the frame of the house.
3. Seal around each exterior door frame in a similar manner.
4. Seal the seam at the sole plate–subfloor junction. Or have the framing crew seal this area by placing a double row of caulk on the subfloor before the sole plate is put in place. See Chapter 7, Framing Your Project.
5. Fill the openings of the corner studs and the T-junctions during the framing. By the nature of their construction, it is very difficult to get insulation into the voids of these pieces after the framing is complete.
6. If the house is to be built with finished drywall or plaster on the inside of the exterior walls and ceilings, it is not necessary to seal the top plates because the drywall and the plaster serve this purpose well. If, however, some of the inside of the exterior walls are to be finished with paneling instead, an air gap may exist unless special sealing steps are taken. After the drywall or plaster ceiling has been finished and the wall paneling installed by the trim carpenter, the gap between the top of the paneling and the ceiling should be sealed with an expanding sealant and covered with the crown molding.

   If your plans include a dropped ceiling in the kitchen or elsewhere, unless precautions are taken, a serious gap permitting air infiltration will remain above the dropped ceiling. The simplest solution to this problem is to install the drywall or plaster on the entire wall and ceiling just as if there were to be

FIGURE 12.1 Sealing for Air Infiltration

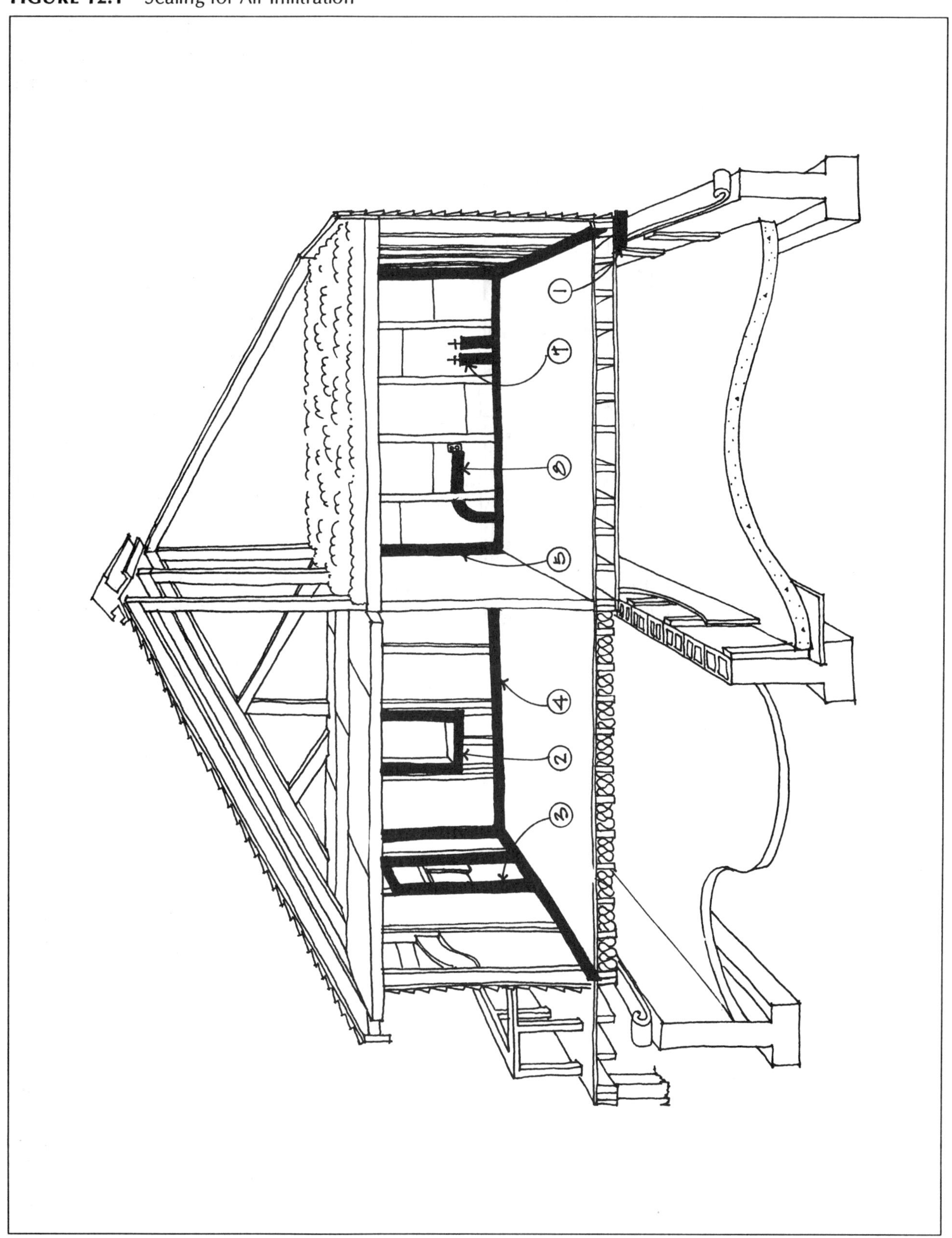

FIGURE 12.2 Sealing for Air Infiltration—Details

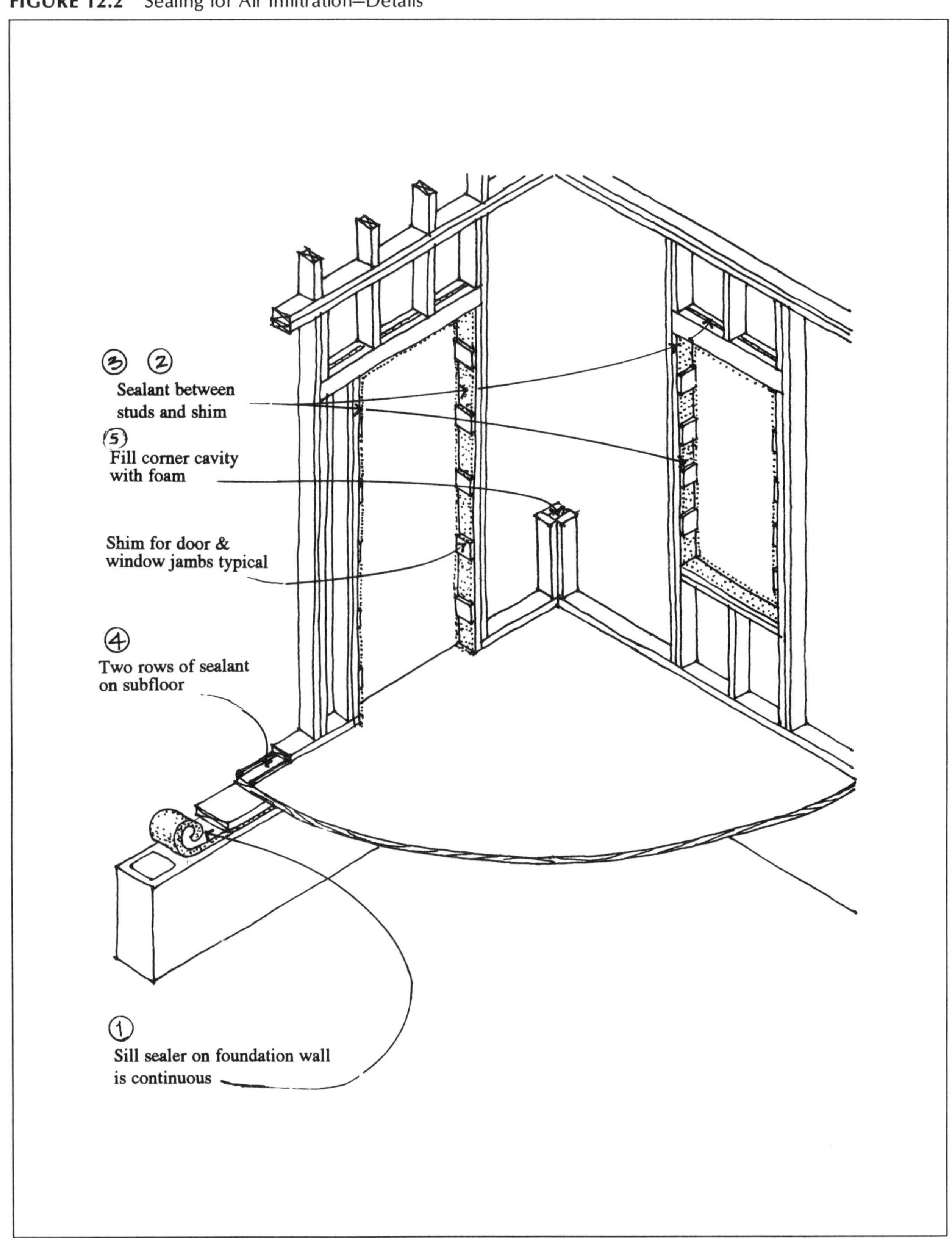

no dropped ceiling. Finish this drywall or plaster, then install the dropped ceiling. The small extra cost will be compensated for by the saving in energy from a tight house.

7. Seal where the pipes penetrate the sole and top plates.
8. Seal where electric, telephone and TV cables penetrate the sole and top plates.

Additional Sealing Measures

The most effective anti-air-infiltration measure is to wrap the entire exterior wall, over the sheathing before the siding is applied, with material such as DuPont's Tyvek. There are several other similar materials. These wrappings are paper thin, very strong and will prevent the passage of air through the exterior walls without trapping moisture within the walls. The cost for this installation is very low compared to the fuel savings for heating and cooling. Make certain that the framing crew repairs all damage to the sheathing before wrapping.

Seal around plumbing drains under the bathtubs by blocking large openings with pieces of construction sheathing and sealing the remaining cracks with expanding foam.

The object of this entire sealing process is to enclose the whole living area of the house to minimize the passage of air, heated and cooled, through the exterior walls, ceilings and floors and thus decrease the cost of heating and cooling the house.

Costing

The sealing contractor should provide the cost of both labor and materials in the bid.

Management

Management here is simple, but when done well results in substantial long-term savings and comfort.

- Schedule the contractor at the proper time.
- Following the guidelines discussed in this chapter, check the work to ensure that none of the areas to be sealed have been overlooked.

■ — CHAPTER 13 — ■

Energy-Saving Insulation Options

The basic principle of insulation is the capture of air space and the use of this air space as a barrier to the movement of heat. Consequently, the less dense the material (i.e., the greater the air space in the material), the greater its insulating value. For example, in Figure 13.1, the 2-inch polyurethane has the same insulating capacity as the 137½-inch thick concrete.

FIGURE 13.1 Thicknesses of Materials for Same Insulation

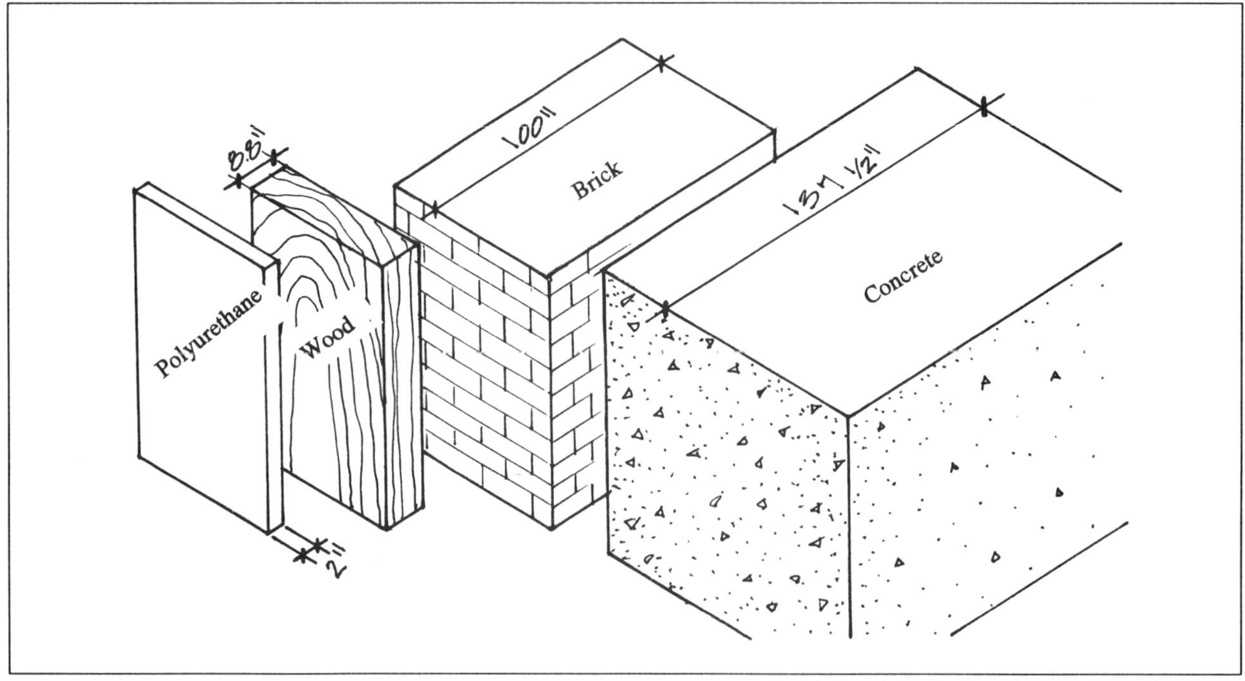

In house design, the living area (the area heated and/or air-conditioned) should be completely enclosed by the proper amount of insulation for the local environment. This process consists of the application of insulation in the exterior walls, ceilings and under the floor for both crawl space and concrete slab construction.

R-Value of Insulating Material

The ability of material to resist the passage of heat is expressed in terms of R. For example, a fiberglass batt 6 inches thick has an R-value of 19. The same material in batts 12 inches thick has an R-value of 38. The greater the R-value, the greater the material's resistance to the passage of heat.

R-Values of Various Insulating Materials

	BATTS		**LOOSE AND BLOWN FILL**		
R-value	*Fiber-Glass*	*Rock Wool*	*Fiber-Glass*	*Rock Wool*	*Cellulose Fiber*
R-11	3″–4″	3″–3½″	5″	4″	3″
R-19	6″–6½″	5″–6″	8½″	6½″	5½″
R-22	7″–7½″	6″–7″	10″	7½″	6″
R-30	9″–10″	8″–9½″	13″	10″	8½″
R-38	12″–13″	10″–12″	17″	13″	10½″

Note that the R-value per inch of thickness of the blown-in cellulose is higher than for blown-in fiberglass or rock wool. The blown-in process also seals the space from air infiltration better than the batts.

U-Value of Insulating Material

On occasion you will find the thermal quality of an insulating material expressed in terms of U. The U-value is the reciprocal of R and can be determined by dividing the R-value into 1. For example, the fiberglass batt with the R-value of 19 has a U-value of 1/19 or .053. The lower the U-value, the greater the thermal resistance of the material. U-values are used primarily by engineers, architects and heating contractors in determining the heating and cooling system needs for an entire structure.

Vapor Barrier Helps Insulation Work Better

In addition to insulation, the living area should also be sealed with appropriate vapor barrier material applied to the inside of the studs, ceiling and floor joists to prevent the movement of moisture from the living area into the insulation.

The vapor barrier serves two purposes: (1) insulation will lose some of its thermal properties if it becomes damp or wet, and (2) if the moisture is retained inside the living space, the occupants will be more comfortable with less heat. This second reason does not apply to the use of air-conditioning, particularly in humid climates, because one of the principal functions of an air-conditioning system is to remove moisture from the air.

There are three methods for applying a vapor barrier to exterior walls:

1. Install insulating batts with vapor barrier backing, such as treated kraft paper or aluminum foil, with the vapor barrier material on the living area side. If you use loose blown-in insulating material in the ceiling (usually less costly than batts), establish a vapor barrier as described in the following two paragraphs.
2. Use friction fit or other type of insulation without an integrated vapor barrier and install aluminum foil-backed drywall. This method provides a good vapor barrier and is simple to put up. In those rooms where gypsum paneling is not used as a wall finish, use either the system described above or below.
3. Use friction fit or other type of insulation without an integrated vapor barrier and glue, staple or nail polyethylene sheet material to the interior of the studs and ceiling joists. This is probably the most effective barrier. But experts disagree about whether or not the increased efficiency of this system when compared to the aluminum foil-backed drywall is worth the extra step of installation and the extra cost. In addition, if this system is used, drywall, wood or other paneling cannot be applied with adhesive (the best method for attaching these materials; see Chapter 18, Striking Interior Wall Finishes).

The usual procedure for installing an effective vapor barrier in floors over a crawl space is to place 15-pound building paper between the subfloor and the finished floor. In addition, apply batt insulation under the subfloor between the floor joists with an integrated vapor barrier face up against the subfloor.

FIGURE 13.2 Installing Insulation

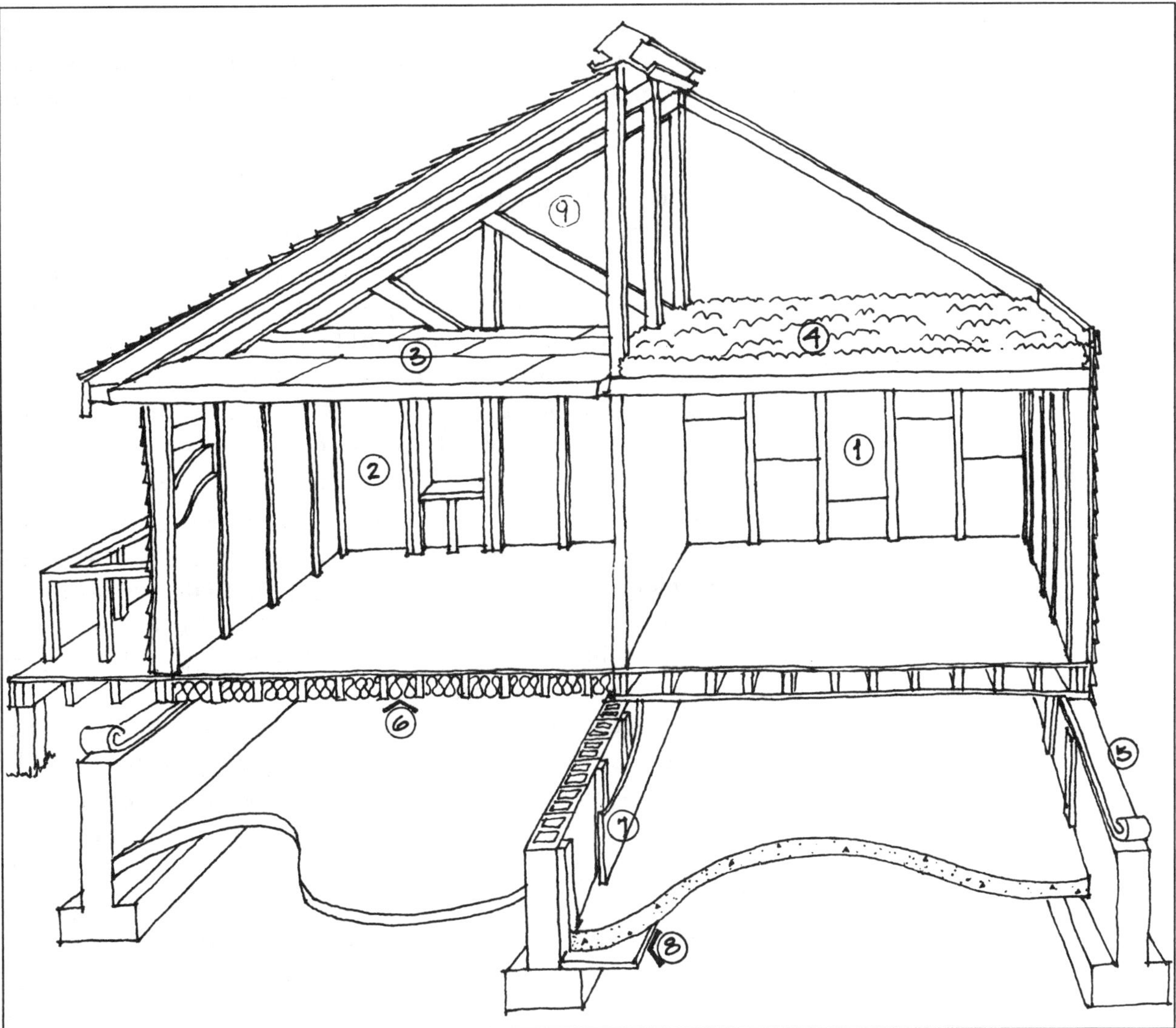

If your house is built on a crawl space foundation, make sure that a vapor barrier is placed over the soil after all construction operations using the crawl space have been completed. This measure prevents deterioration of floor framing because of high moisture levels.

Installing Insulation

A properly insulated house may use several types of insulation to isolate the heated living area from the outside atmosphere. Figure 13.2 shows examples of where the various types can be installed.

1. Shows the use of 3½-inch batts or 6-inch batts with kraft paper vapor barrier in stud walls. The vapor barrier faces the heated area.
2. Illustrates the installation of friction fit batts, unfaced (without vapor barrier). A vapor barrier of polyethylene film not less than 3 mils thick has been applied over the insulation on the heated side of the wall.
3. Shows ceiling using batts.
4. Shows blown-in loose ceiling insulation.
5. Points out insulation between foundation wall and sill plate. This serves the purpose of stopping air infiltration more than it insulates—which is what it should do.
6. Illustrates underfloor insulation. A vapor barrier must be placed on the side next to the heated space, or "up."
7. Shows the insulation of basement areas. This insulation, installed between the studs or furring, should be covered with drywall or paneling as with any interior wall. The studs or furring should be salt treated .25CCA lumber and be fastened to the block or concrete walls with case-hardened nails or nails driven by an explosive charge. Before the studs are put up, it is also a good idea to paint the exterior masonry walls, with two coats of a masonry waterproof paint.
8. Illustrates the installation of rigid insulation (about 2 inches thick) under the concrete floor. The entire floor need not be insulated—only the 2 feet horizontally around the perimeter. In addition, a vertical piece of the rigid insulation should be installed against the wall the same thickness as the concrete floor. This insulation is, of course, applied before the concrete floor is poured. Also, review Chapter 6, Foundations.
9. Points out where reflective foil (shiny aluminum foil with reinforcing layers or fibers is preferred) should be stapled—on the bottom of the roof joists to reduce the amount of heat entering the attic space. If your roof has a metal ridge vent, make sure that vent is not covered by the foil so air flow from the soffits to the ridge vent moves freely.

Insulating Cathedral Ceilings

In the construction of a cathedral ceiling, the ceiling joists associated with the normal 8-foot-high ceiling are eliminated so that the insulation cannot be placed between the joists over the drywall. There are two methods used to solve this problem.

FIGURE 13.3 Cathedral Ceiling with Drywall or Plaster Finish

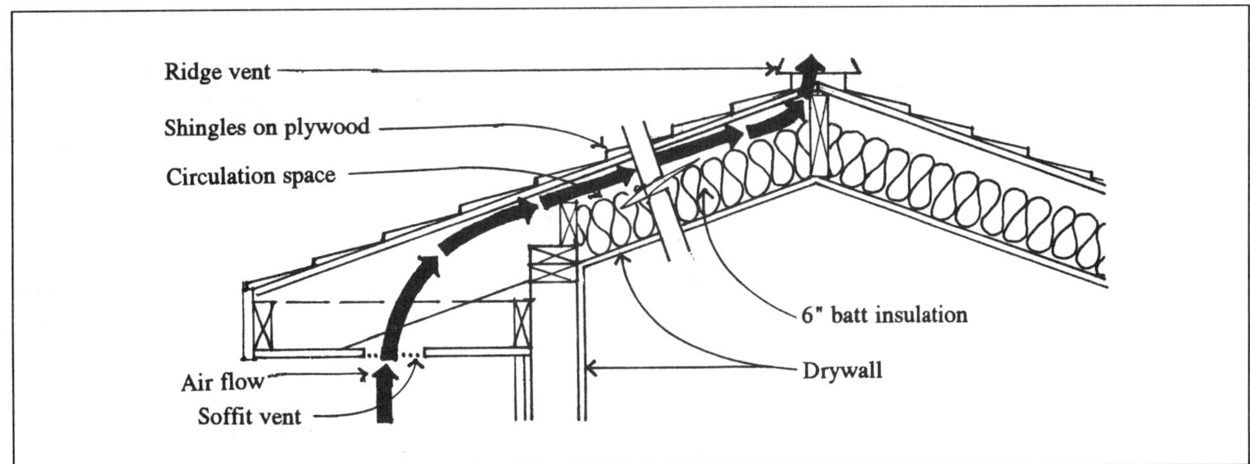

Figure 13.3 illustrates the construction of a cathedral ceiling in which the drywall is nailed to the underside of the roof rafters. False beams may be added under the Sheetrock for decorative purposes. In this type of ceiling, the insulation must consist of batt material that is nailed to the bottom of the roof rafters *before the installation of the drywall.* Note the air space between the top of the insulation and the underneath side of the roof sheathing. This air space is very important to ensure the proper ventilation of the area. To allow for this air space, the roof rafters must be sized larger than the required depth of the insulation. For example, if the roof insulation is to be 6-inch batts, (just about the minimum for most of the country), the roof rafters must be at least 2×8s to allow a 1½-inch air space. If the required insulation is 8-inch batts, then the roof rafters must be 2×10s, and so forth.

Figure 13.4 illustrates the type of cathedral ceiling associated with the post-and-beam framing found in many contemporary designs.

In this construction, the roof sheathing consists of tongue-and-groove lumber, 2 or more inches thick. This sheathing is nailed directly on top of the roof rafters (usually 3 inches or more thick material) with the underside of the sheathing and the rafters forming the finished ceiling. In this case the insulation will consist of rigid urethane nailed to the outer side of the sheathing with building paper, hard board for nailing and shingles installed on top. The ventilation problem does not exist because there is no confined air space.

R-Values of Rigid Urethane Board for Roof Insulation

1½″ thick board = R-7
2″ thick board = R-12
3″ thick board = R-21
4″ thick board = R-29

FIGURE 13.4 Cathedral Ceiling–Exposed Beam and Plank

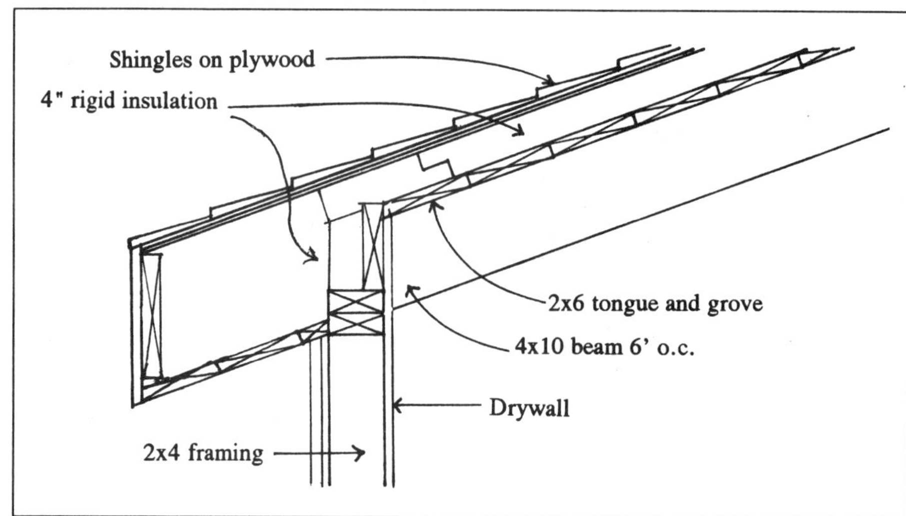

Higher R-values can be attained by combining various thicknesses of boards.

Figure 13.5 indicates the various recommended R-values for ceilings, walls and floors for different geographical areas of the United States. Those building in the higher-numbered (colder) areas and Alaska and Canada should check with local HVAC contractors for advice on special insulation steps warranted in these locations.

FIGURE 13.5 Recommended R-Values for Areas in the United States

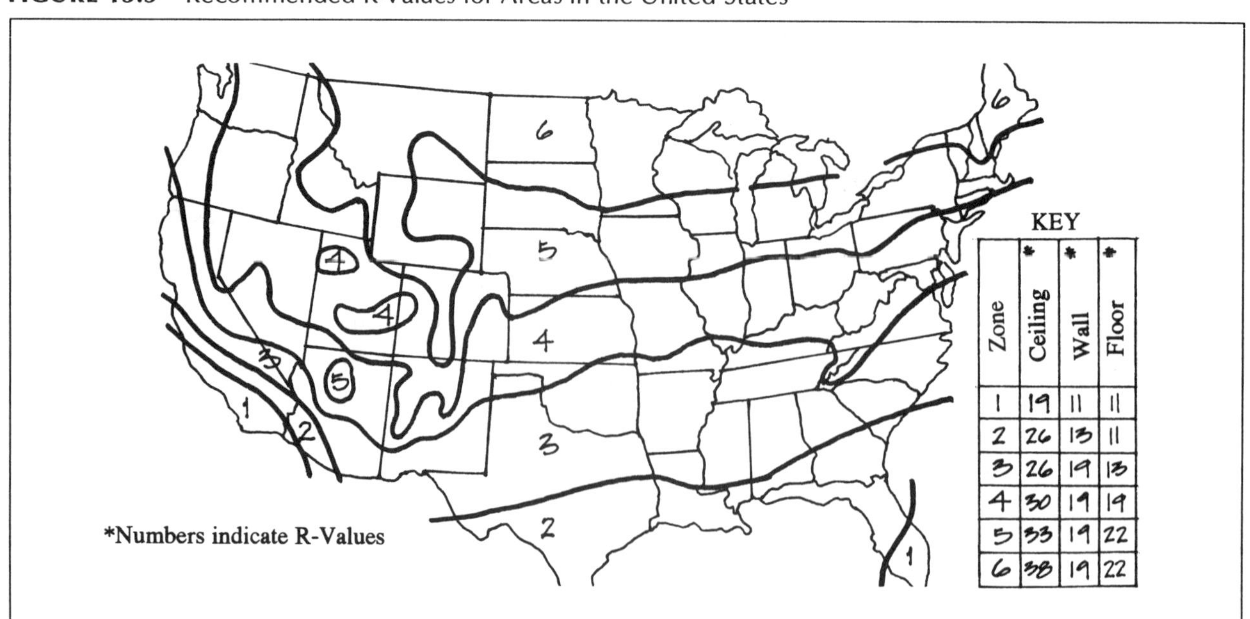

Zone	Ceiling*	Wall*	Floor*
1	19	11	11
2	26	13	11
3	26	19	13
4	30	19	19
5	33	19	22
6	38	19	22

FIGURE 13.6 Insulation for Pulldown Stairs

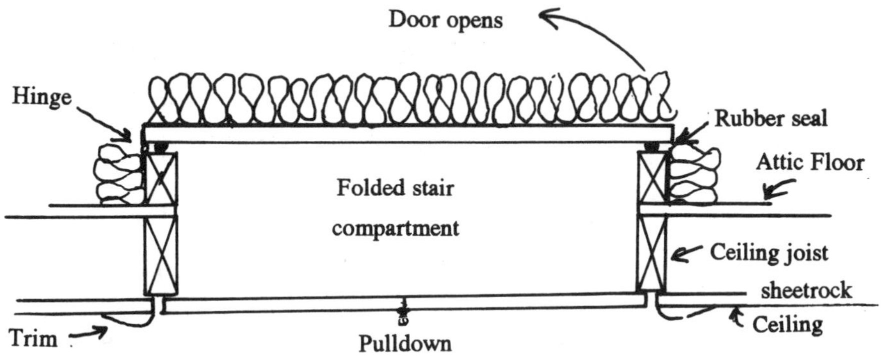

One of the most neglected areas for potential heat loss through both air infiltration and lack of insulation is the pulldown stairs to the attic space. To install these items properly requires special measures (see Figure 13.6).

The frame installed on top of the subfloor must be high enough to accept the pulldown stair in its folded position with about an inch of clearance. The door should be hinged on one side of the frame and equipped with screen door hooks so that when closed, the door can be snugly pulled against the rubber seal to stop air infiltration.

Insulation to match the other parts of the ceiling should be installed on top of the door and around the sides of the frame. Seal the seam at the juncture of the frame and the subfloor with caulking compound.

A similar installation should be built around the openings of ceiling-mounted attic fans used for house ventilation. The door is opened when the fan is in use.

Sound-Deadening Insulation for Walls

If your plans include special sound deadening in certain interior walls, such as between the bathroom and living room, two sound paths must be blocked. One is through the air space in the wall and the other is through the studs themselves.

Figure 13.7 illustrates construction techniques that will block both sound paths. Note that the wall is built with staggered studs of 2×4s on a 2×6 plate. This technique eliminates the touching of the drywall on both sides of the wall by any stud and thus reduces the passage of sound through the material itself. The air space voids are filled with 3½-

FIGURE 13.7 Sound-Deadening Insulation for Walls

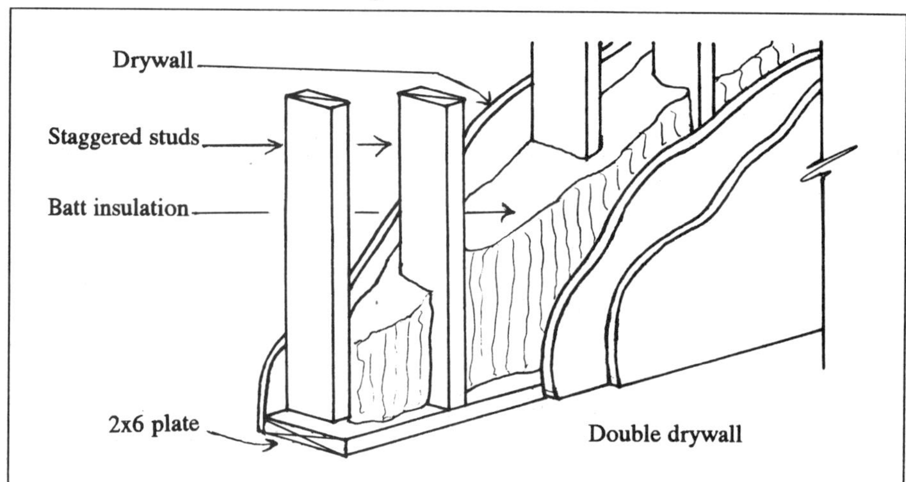

inch batts. Note that one side of the wall is finished with two layers of ½-inch drywall. All drywall should be the fire-rated type because it provides a better sound-deadening barrier. This combination gives a Sound Transmission Class (STC) of 53, which is excellent.

If your house is to use metal water supply pipes such as copper, reduce the noise of water flowing through these pipes by packing felt around the pipe where it goes through the framing or masonry walls, as shown in Figure 13.8.

FIGURE 13.8 Sound-Deadening Insulation for Metal Pipes

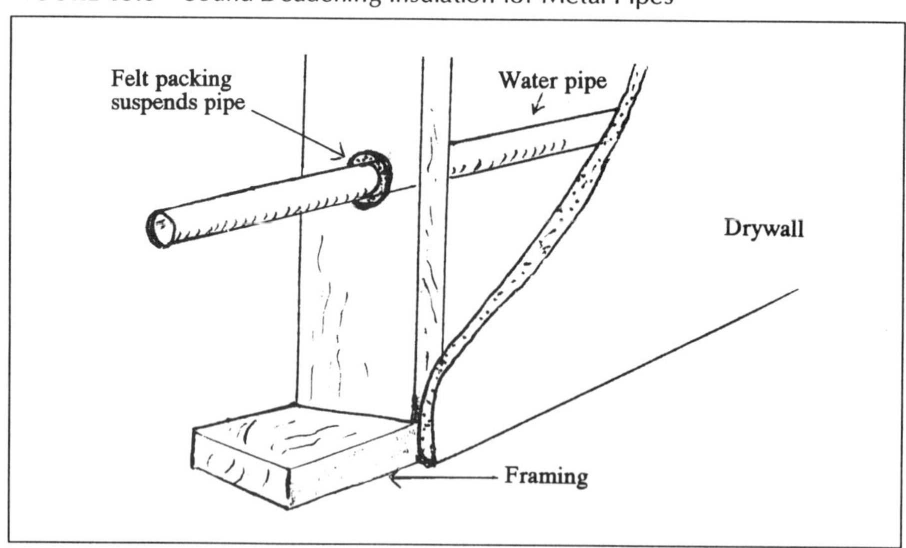

FIGURE 13.9 Sound-Deadening Insulation for Floors

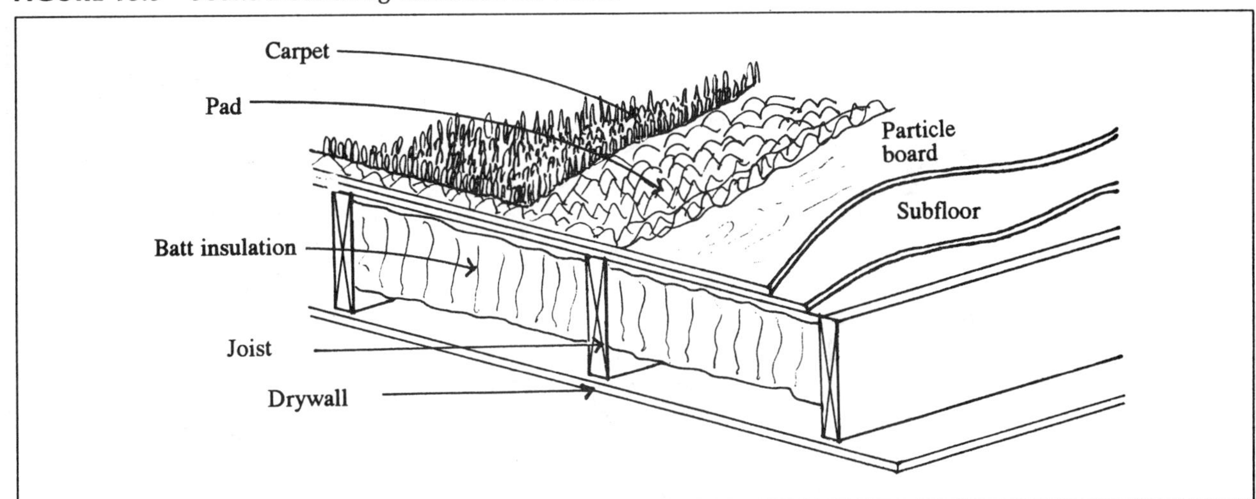

Sound-Deadening Insulation for Floors

Passage of sound through floors is not usually a problem for single-family ranchers without basements; it is more typically a requirement for apartments and multifloor houses. If your plans call for a noise barrier, Figure 13.9 illustrates a method of accomplishing it.

Starting at the top is a layer of carpeting followed by its pad, a particleboard underlayment of ⅝ inch, the subfloor of ½-inch plywood, 3½-inch batts of insulation without vapor barrier and finally a layer of ½-inch drywall installed by nailing it to a special resilient channel. The drywall should be fire rated because this type provides better sound insulation. The resilient channel is a narrow steel form nailed to the ceiling joists and parallel to them. The drywall is nailed or screwed to the channel on one side only. Your drywall contractor should be familiar with this process. Installed in this manner, the resilient channel will tend to dampen the sound and deter its transmission between floors. This system will give a Sound Transmission Class of 53, which is excellent.

Insulating Block Walls

If your plans require block walls or block walls with brick or stucco exteriors that need to be insulated, the methods shown in Figure 13.10 can be used.

In method 1, use lightweight concrete block and fill the cavities in the block with loose insulating fill.

FIGURE 13.10 Insulating Block Walls

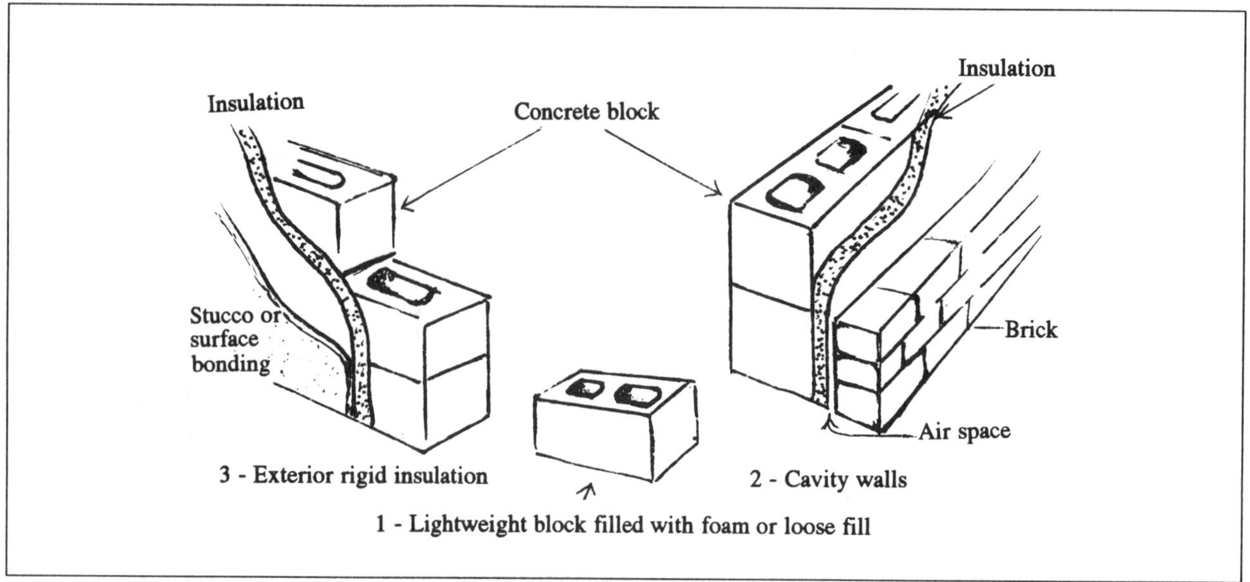

In method 2, construct the block wall as described in 1, install rigid insulation, then an air space and brick veneer.

Method 3 is designed to accommodate stucco or surface bonding. Construct the concrete block wall with rigid insulation as in 1, and then apply the stucco or surface bonding directly to the rigid insulation.

Costing

Insulation installation follows routine costing procedures:

- The cost of both labor and materials for the insulation work is provided by the contractor.
- The roofing contractor should provide the labor and materials for the installation of rigid insulation on the outside of the wood roof sheathing because this work is usually done as part of the shingle job.
- The cost of labor and materials for the drywall is discussed in Chapter 18, Striking Interior Wall Finishes. Be sure to point out the special requirements for sound insulation if there are any.
- If you have decided to use the vapor barrier system based on the installation of polyethylene sheet material over insulation batts installed in the walls, make certain that your contractors understand this requirement in their bidding. If not understood, this could be one of those extra-cost items that appear from time to

time despite the best-laid plans. There is additional labor in this process, and the material costs more.

Management

Take extra care when managing the installation of insulation to reap immediate and long-term benefits.

- Make sure that you select an experienced insulating contractor. There are skills and know-how required to do a good insulation job that may not be readily apparent.
- Schedule the contractor to begin work just after the sealing has been completed. And once again, *be sure that the rough-in inspections of the framing, electrical, plumbing and heating have been completed and approved.*
- At this stage of the job, the insulating contractor will only install the wall insulation. Until the ceiling drywall is applied, the insulation for standard ceilings should not be put up.
- If you have cathedral ceilings of the type shown in Figure 13.3, the insulation must be installed at this stage. Insulation for the type of cathedral ceiling shown in Figure 13.4 should be installed by the roofer at the point where the job is ready for the shingle work. Because the roof insulation is part of the overall roof system, it is best to have one contractor do the whole job. In case trouble should develop later, you have to deal with only one contractor.
- The insulation under the floor in the crawl space should not be applied until most all of the crawl space work, such as final inspections for electrical, plumbing and heating, have been completed. This scheduling prevents damage to the insulation by other contractors.
- Because they tend to be trouble spots, you should personally check the following four areas (illustrated in Figure 13.11):
  1. Look for gaps, breaks and voids in insulated areas. In particular, make sure that the insulation for the cathedral ceiling has no gaps. After the ceiling drywall has been installed, this insulation is completely covered and very difficult to check.
  2. Check to see that the soffit to attic ventilation has not been blocked.
  3. After the underfloor insulation has been installed, check to ensure that the headers (band boards) around the exterior walls have been covered.

FIGURE 13.11 Attic Ventilation, Sill Plate, Cantilever Insulation

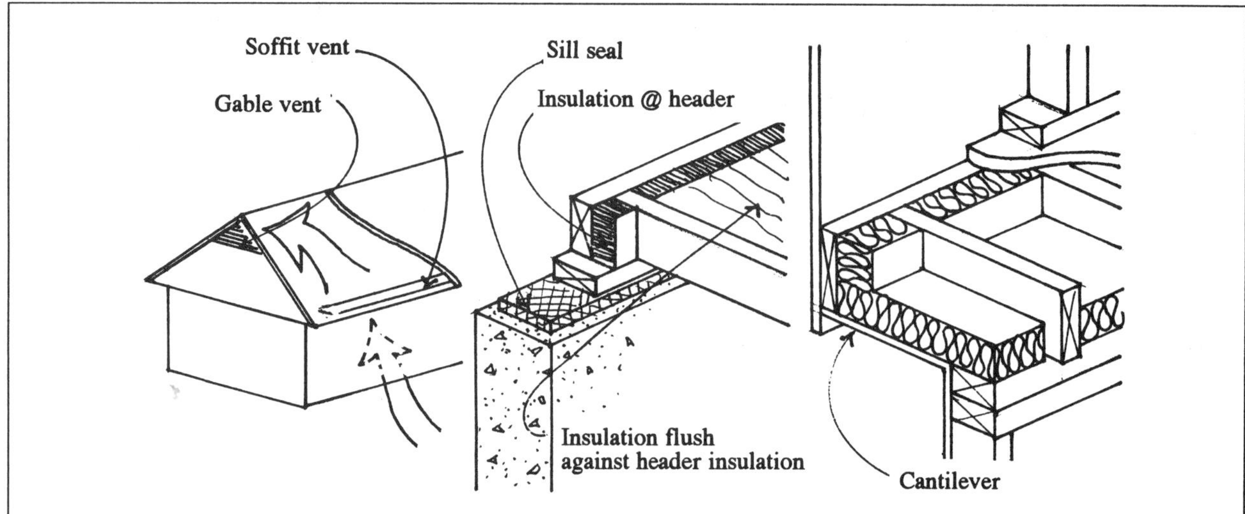

4. If your plans have cantilevered overhangs, such as the second floor jutting out beyond the first or bay windows jutting out from exterior walls, be certain that insulation has not been omitted from the underside of these areas.

- Management of the drywall installation is discussed in Chapter 18, Striking Interior Wall Finishes.
- For those who are building in the cold areas of Alaska, Canada, and the northern parts of the United States, check with local HVAC contractors for advice on special insulation steps warranted in these locations.

CHAPTER 14

Heating with Sunshine (Solar Energy)

Solar energy is free. Therefore, any time you can use it for efficient heating and cooling, do so. In the present state of the art, solar energy has its limitations; it does not produce economic and efficient heating in all its forms and in all geographical areas of the country. In most situations, a back-up heating system is required.

THE WAY HEAT MOVES

It is important to understand that heat moves in the following three ways:

1. *Conduction* is the way heat moves through a solid, such as metal or wood or masonry. If you place a metal spoon in a cup of hot coffee, the heat will move up the handle. This is conduction.
2. *Convection* is the way heat moves through the air, water and other liquids. Warm air rises because it is lighter than cold air. This causes heat to accumulate at the ceilings and in the second floor of a house.
3. *Radiation* is the movement of heat as a wave similar to light. For example, a bathroom electric resistance heater mounted in the wall will emit heat radiation that travels toward the cooler areas of the room.

TAKE ADVANTAGE OF PASSIVE SOLAR HEAT

A passive solar heating system uses the natural processes of conduction, convection and radiation to move collected heat. Its successful functioning is based primarily on the proper structural design of the house. With the exception of the occasional use of low-powered electric fans to assist in air distribution, it does not use mechanical equipment. It is the most practical use of solar energy in the house. To function efficiently, however, the house must be designed specifically to use this type of heat in your area. Any passive solar heating system should have the following components:

- A *collector:* Usually consists of large glass or plastic window areas facing generally south or at least within 30° of south. During the heating season, the collector should not be shaded by other structures or trees from about 9 AM to 3 PM.
- An *absorber:* Usually consists of a masonry wall or floor or a water tank. The absorber, a storage element, receives the heat that has passed through the collector and holds it for later distribution.
- A *distribution system:* Takes the heat from the storage element and circulates it throughout the living area. A strictly passive system would use all three methods of heat transfer. Some passive solar heating systems require the addition of electric fans to help circulate the warm air.
- A *control* or *regulation device:* Prevents the loss of heat from inside the house to the outside during sunless periods. Most heat regulators consist of movable insulating curtains. A control system may also include electronic sensing devices to signal a fan to turn on or to open or close vents and dampers that restrict the flow of heat.

Direct Gain: Solar Heating at Its Simplest

Figure 14.1 illustrates the simplest form of passive solar heat—direct gain. Sunlight enters the house through the large window area, the collector, striking the walls and floor where it is absorbed and stored. At night, as the room cools, the heat stored in the walls and floors radiates into the room. Note also that the insulation curtain should be closed at night and during sunless days to prevent the loss of heat back through the collector. This is one of the drawbacks of the direct gain passive solar heating system. It gives the owner two poor choices: either lose the heat through the collector or draw the curtain and lose the pleasure of daylight on a cloudy, sunless day.

FIGURE 14.1 Direct Gain

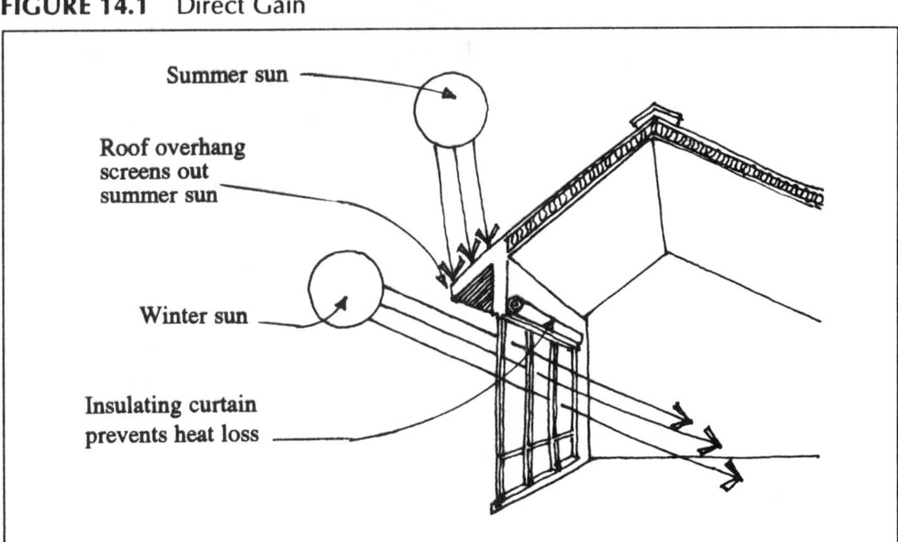

There are other passive systems that are more efficient than direct gain, but they usually require such items as large above-floor water tanks or upright concrete walls, both installed inside the house, that inhibit the pleasant use of the living space. If you wish to investigate these systems, consult with an engineer or architect skilled in these areas.

■ ACTIVE SOLAR HEATING IS MORE COMPLICATED

An active solar heating system uses mechanical equipment such as pumps and fans to collect and distribute heat. There are two types: liquid based and air based, designating the medium used to transfer the heat through the system.

The design of an effective active solar heating system for a particular plan is much more complicated than the application of passive solar principles. Such a design should be tackled only by an architect, engineer or other person who has had extensive experience in this field. The practical application of active solar heating systems usually does not have the widespread usage as does the passive solar system.

Like passive systems, in those periods when the solar heat source is not available, a back-up system is needed.

Active Solar Heat for Hot Water

Independent active solar heating systems are available for your hot water. In most cases a back-up heating system will be needed. As with the active solar heating for the house, the problem is one of the cost (see below) that can easily exceed $3,000 plus the back-up system. On the other hand, local conditions may permit the installation of solar hot water heating systems at costs that can be recouped in about five years. Get some expert advice to determine whether the cost of the solar system for hot water makes this choice practical in your area.

Does Zoning Law Protect Against Sun Stealing?

If your plan depends substantially upon passive and/or active solar heating, check the zoning laws for your area to ensure that further construction on adjacent property cannot block the sunshine from your lot and eliminate or reduce the capacity of your solar system.

Costs of Solar Heat

The cost of installing passive solar heating measures in a house varies considerably. For example, if the only passive measure used is to face the side of the house with the most windows and doors to the south, the direct cost is about zero. If more efficient but modest measures are adopted, the cost of these measures could run several thousand dollars. This is not an exorbitant price to pay for the one-time construction of these features, particularly if the fuel savings is high.

The expense of installing a complex active solar heating system can exceed $20,000 not including any back-up system.

In any case, investigate the cost trade-offs before adopting any solar heating measure, particularly the active solar systems.

CHAPTER 15

Heating and Cooling Considerations

This chapter provides information to assist the reader select a heating and cooling system for new construction. It describes conventional central and auxiliary heating and cooling systems and suggests combinations to meet various requirements throughout the country.

FUELS

The standard fuels available for house heating include the following:

- *Electricity* is readily available almost anywhere. It is clean, leaves no residue and will not contaminate the atmosphere. It requires no chimney. Its cost will probably go up or down along with the cost of fuels used to generate it. One of the greatest advantages of electricity as a fuel for the future is that it can be produced from almost any other type of energy—solar, nuclear, oil, gas, coal and geothermal. For the future, relying on electricity for house energy appears to be less risky than other fuels.
- *Oil,* today, is readily available. It is relatively clean if the burner is regularly serviced. Storage, usually an underground tank, is needed. It does require a chimney.
- *Gas* is available in two forms, natural and liquid propane. Natural gas comes from the ground in a gaseous state; propane gas is manufactured from crude oil. Natural gas is not available

in many areas. Liquid gas is available in most areas but its cost is higher. Gas is clean, requires no storage (except bottled gas), but it does require a chimney. It can be used to operate both heating and air-conditioning equipment.

- *Coal* was widely used for central home heating systems during the first part of the twentieth century. Most localities then had efficient delivery systems, and most homes were designed and built with a local bin for storage and a coal chute to get the coal from the truck or wagon. Because most of that system has disappeared, the problems with using coal to fuel central house heating systems are so great that this fuel should not be considered for this purpose. Coal also requires a chimney; it is dirty before and during burning and leaves relatively large amounts of ashes that must be disposed of. Depending upon availability in your area, coal might be a good choice for fueling auxiliary or back-up heating systems such as a fireplace or free-standing stove.
- *Wood,* like coal, is best used for back-up systems. If quantities of the hard woods such as oak, locust, birch, beech, elm and ash are available at reasonable prices, the use of wood in an energy-efficient fireplace or stove as a back-up for other systems may be a good choice. The homeowner should realize, however, that substantial labor is required to place the unburned wood in storage, to move it to the stove or fireplace as needed and then to remove the ashes after combustion.

FORCED-WARM-AIR HEATING SYSTEMS

These systems, *with the exception of the heat pump,* are based on the provision of heat by burning fuel to create a supply of warm air that is then blown by a fan through a duct system to the various parts of the house. The spent air is returned to the furnace through a return duct system for reheating and redistribution.

Before making the final selection of your heating and cooling system, check with the local power company for available rebates that are often given for heat pumps, ground-coupled heat pumps and dual-fueled systems such as a heat pump for cooling and heating when outside temperatures are modest combined with a gas furnace for heating in more severe weather.

FIGURE 15.1 The Heat Pump

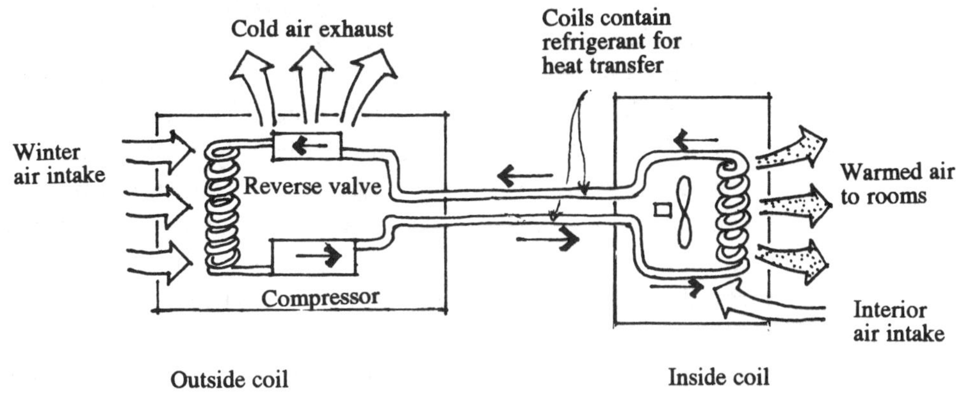

How the Heat Pump Works

The heat pump is one of the most innovative heating and cooling systems available today. It is also highly efficient.

The heat pump is the only heating system that does not make heat; it moves the heat already existing from the outside of the house to the inside when in the heating mode and from inside the house to the outside when in the cooling mode (see Figure 15.1).

In the heating mode, liquid refrigerant moves into the outside coil, where it evaporates (expands) and absorbs heat from the outside air. The heated vapor then moves into the compressor, where it is squeezed, gets hotter and is pumped into the inside coil. There the vapor condenses and gives off heat that is picked up by the blower, added to the house air flowing through the return duct and redistributed throughout the house. For air-conditioning, the cycle is reversed so that the refrigerant picks up heat from the air inside the house and deposits it into the outside air.

Air-Source Heat Pump

The air-source system works in the manner described above, taking heat from the outside air in the winter and bringing it inside the house through the use of a refrigerant as a transfer medium. It can operate very effectively with outside temperatures of 25°F and above. Below that temperature range its efficiency is reduced, and it will need auxiliary heat to maintain a comfortable level in the house. This auxiliary heat usually consists of electric resistance heat strips built into the fan coil unit. When signaled by an outdoor thermostat, these strips come on and reinforce the heat brought into the house by the refrigerant. Auxiliary heat may also consist of an oil or gas furnace installed as an integrated system with the heat pump (see page 155).

It's difficult to visualize the extraction of heat from outside air that has reached a temperature of 25°F, but all cold air contains some heat. For example, the air at 0°F has 89 percent as much heat as air at 100°F. Heat is completely absent from the air only at absolute zero or 460°F below zero, which can only be approached in the laboratory. As the temperature goes down in cold winters, however, the air-source heat pump begins to lose its ability to replace the heat lost from the house through its exterior skin at the same rate as the loss. When this "balance point" is reached (and it will differ because of the variations in house construction, heat pump machinery, etc.), auxiliary heat must be brought into the system.

The Underground-Water-Source Heat Pump

The underground-water-source heat pump is more efficient than the air-source pump. It works very much like the air-source pump with one very important exception: The water-source heat pump requires water such as an underground well or perhaps a lake that does not freeze during the winter. To be highly efficient, the temperature of the water source should not drop below 45°F all year round. In the United States, even in the coldest parts of the country, the temperature of underground water at depths of 40 feet or more rarely drops below 45°F.

Instead of working with the outside air as a source of heat, the water-source heat pump works with the ground water through a condenser that brings together the refrigerant in its pipe and the ground water. The net result is that the water-source pump does not lose efficiency in cold winters because it is extracting heat from 45°F to 60°F water instead of from 20°F to 35°F cold winter air. Rarely is there a need for back-up or auxiliary heat. *Depending on the local conditions, the underground-water-source heat pump can do the job completely by itself.* It may be useful, however, to install auxiliary electric resistance heat strips to provide temporary heat should the water supply system break down.

In the summer, while air-conditioning, the water-source heat pump is putting heat from the house into water at 50°F to 60°F instead of into hot outside air at 85°F to 95°F. This is another bonus for the water-source heat pump since less energy is needed to provide air-conditioning.

FIGURE 15.2 A Water-Source Heat Pump

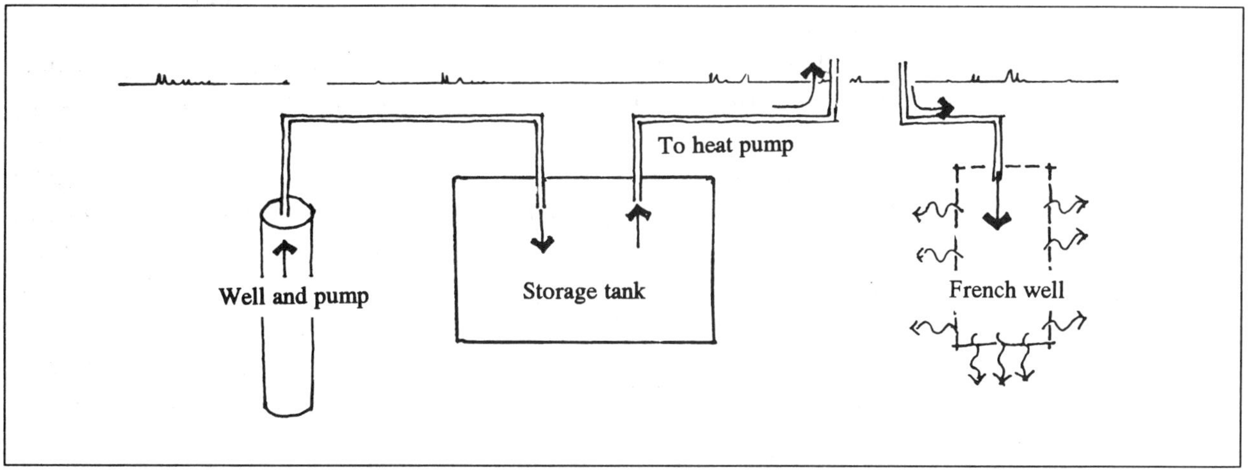

Water-Source Heat Pump Requirements

The water requirements for a water-source heat pump average three gallons per minute per ton of heat pump capacity. In developing a source of water for the heat pump, care must be taken to ensure that the water discharged from the heat pump after use does not change the temperature of the water at the source point (where the fresh supply is drawn) to such a degree that efficiency is lost. You can prevent this by establishing the discharge point of the used water 100 or more feet from the point where water is drawn into the heat pump. This solution could be very expensive, particularly if the water is drawn from a well, because it could require the drilling of two lines into the well water. An alternate and, in many cases, a less costly and more efficient system is to provide an auxiliary underground storage facility using a tank (see Figure 15.2). A new or unused concrete septic tank with the proper capacity is a good choice. Water is drawn from the well and held in the tank until drawn out by the heat pump system. After use, the water is discharged into a French well (large hole in the ground filled with rock and gravel) or a similar device that will put the water back into the ground. If you elect to go with the water-source heat pump, consult with a local contractor to determine which water supply and discharge system is best for your location and the capacities needed.

The Ground-Coupled Heat Pump

The closed-loop, ground-coupled heat pump is a version of the water-source heat pump. It can be installed almost anywhere. It has operated successfully in Canada, Germany, France, Italy, Denmark and

Sweden. The major difference between this system and the water-source heat pump discussed above is that in the ground-coupled system a water/glycol mixture circulates through plastic pipe underground, absorbing heat from the ground in the winter and giving off heat to the ground when operating in the summer as an air conditioner. Rather than continually pumping water from a well through the heat pump and then discharging it after use, the ground-coupled heat system uses the same water/glycol mixture over and over again and thus eliminates the problem of the large amount of water required by the water-source system and the problem of getting rid of the water after passing through the system only once.

Figure 15.3 illustrates three different forms for the ground coupling. The horizontal method places the pipe several feet underground in a horizontal plane. This is the least expensive method because the trenching for the pipe is shallow. But it also requires the most land. If you are installing a septic system, consider laying the closed-loop pipe for the heat pump in the same trenches dug for the drain field of the septic system. Moist ground gives up and extracts heat better than dry soil.

Where lots are too small for the horizontal method, there are two other choices. The deep vertical layout uses the least land of all types. Because it plunges deep, it is in contact with more stable ground temperatures and usually requires less pipe.

Where drilling is a problem (for example, when faced with layers of rock) in conjunction with little land, the multiple vertical system may be the answer. With this method several vertical pipe loops are installed at less depth than the single vertical loop.

Here are some of the details the homeowner/contractor should be aware of:

- The pipe for the closed loops should be polyethylene (PE3408 type) or polybutylene (PB2110). In most cases, diameters of 1½ inches to 2 inches are needed. Underground joints should be heat fused to give a life of 50 years or more to the underground closed loop.
- In the sun belt, horizontal loops are buried from 4 feet to 6 feet—the 6-foot depth preferred. In the north, the loop depth is 3 feet to 4 feet so that the sun may thaw the ground around it during the summer. If the loop remains in frozen ground throughout the year, it will lose some of its effectiveness.
- The length of pipe required and of the size of the area needed for it are based on the size of the heat pump, climate, soil type, burial depth and operating cycle pattern of the system. For horizontal systems, 400 feet to 600 feet are needed for each ton of heat

FIGURE 15.3 Ground-Coupled Heat-Pump Systems

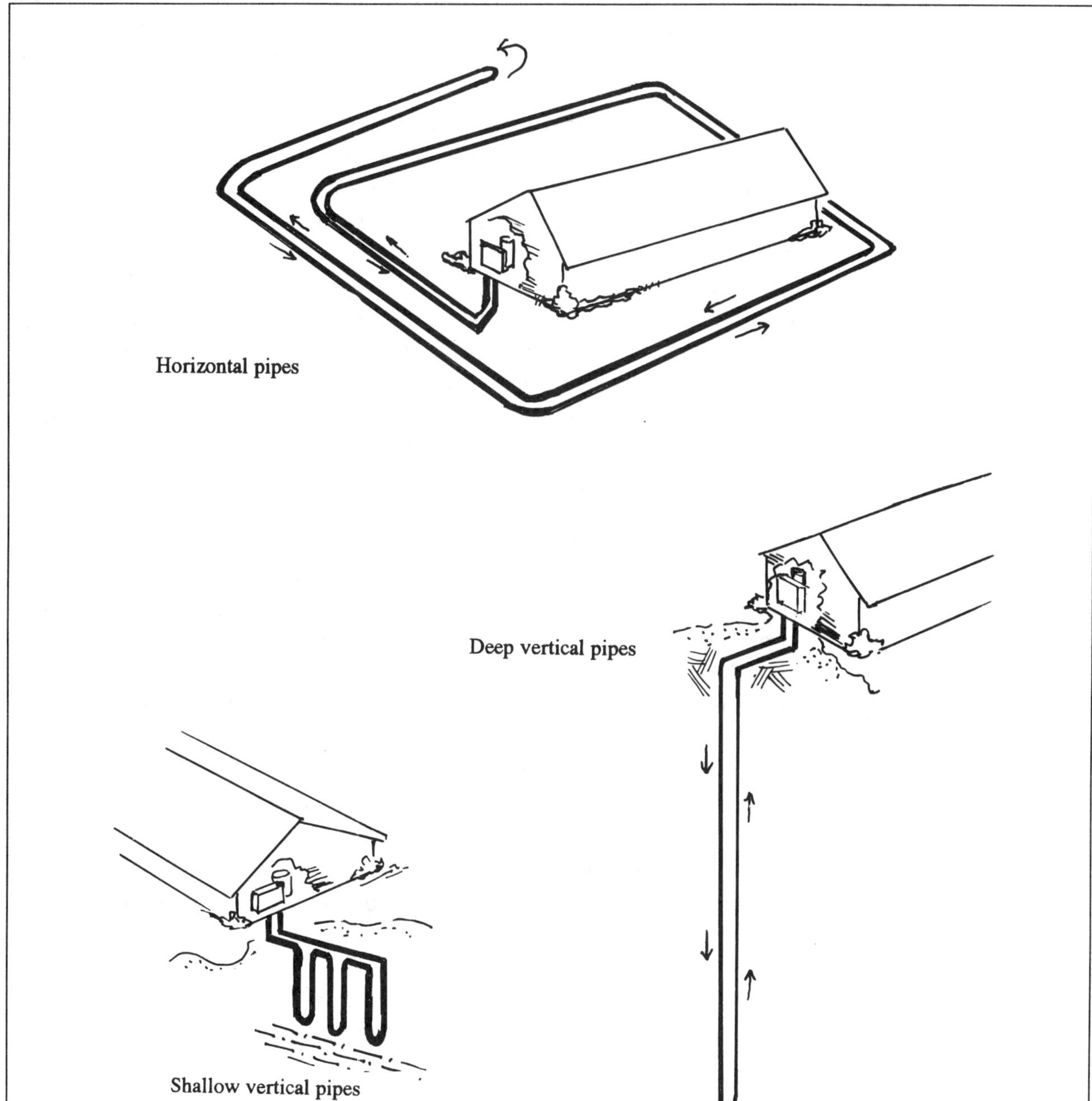

pump capacity. Vertical systems will need 150 feet to 200 feet of bore hole per ton of heat pump capacity and generally will have smaller diameter pipe.

- Lateral distances between the pipe are 4 feet to 5 feet for horizontal systems and 15 feet to 20 feet for vertical systems.

You can expect up to 35 percent savings in fuel consumption cost compared to the more conventional electric baseboard and oil-burning forced-warm-air systems.

The Heat Pump and Hot Water

Several heat pump manufacturers have developed an add-on device that permits the central heat pump to heat the hot water as well as the house.

In addition, some manufacturers market a small heat pump to be used solely for making hot water. It gathers heat from the basement or other area in the house and uses it to heat water in the tank. It does not reverse into the cooling cycle. Check with a contractor about the cost of this device and compare it with the cost of an electric hot water heater. Include operating costs to determine the best system for you.

Determining the Efficiency of Heat Pumps

In judging the relative efficiency of different heat pump systems from various manufacturers, compare the SEER (Seasonal Energy Efficient Ratio) and the HSPF (Heating Seasonal Performance Factor). For a high-efficiency model, the SEER should be at least 10.0 and the HSPF should be at least 6.5.

With some early designs of the heat pump, during the cold season the hot air pumped into the house was below body temperature (98.6°F) and thus felt cold and perhaps uncomfortable to some (although the temperature of the hot air was well above the thermostat setting of 68°F to 72°F). The designs now available have largely eliminated this problem by providing warmer air (up to 113°F) at greater efficiency during the heating season.

The newer high-efficiency heat pump with its two-speed compressor or variable-speed compressor operates more efficiently because it tailors the speed of air flow to meet the heating/cooling requirements at any particular time. The unit runs longer at lower speed reducing the on/off cycling and greatly increasing comfort by providing even, continuous heat in the winter and improving the level of humidity in the summer.

Other Forced-Warm-Air Heating Systems

Other fuel options in your choice for forced-warm-air heating systems are the oil-fired or gas-fired (both natural and liquid) furnace and the electric resistance-heat furnace. All three are proven and effective heating systems, and each can be combined with central air-conditioning. Like the heat pump, they use a duct system to transport the heated or cooled air throughout the house.

Increases in the efficiency of the oil-fired or gas-fired furnace can be obtained by the application of the following:

- *Flue dampers,* particularly if the furnace is installed in a heated area of the house with an outside supply of air for combustion
- Pilotless ignition, in gas-burning furnaces, that uses an electrical spark generated only at the moment the fuel begins to flow

Gas- and oil-burning forced-warm-air furnaces are now available with AFVE (Annual Fuel Utilization Efficiency) in excess of 90 percent.

Combination of Forced-Warm-Air Systems

In many situations, a combination of a heat pump with a gas or oil furnace provides a more efficient central heating system than the single gas or oil furnace by itself. This is particularly true in the colder climates.

This improvement is the result of using the gas or oil furnace only at outside temperatures below 28°F to 32°F, where most efficient. In addition, the heat pump will provide air-conditioning in the summer at no additional equipment installation cost.

The initial cost of installing gas- or oil-fired systems in combination with the heat pump will be higher than either the gas or oil system with air-conditioning alone. To be economically sound, the annual savings in fuel costs should pay back this additional cost in not over seven to ten years.

Because this combination system has a low operating cost, this payback requirement should be easily met in most cases, particularly if the house is properly insulated (see Chapter 13, Energy-Saving Insulation Options) and if anti-air-infiltration measures have been applied during construction (see Chapter 12, Air Infiltration).

If you have gas available, ask your HVAC contractor about a newly developed combination of hot water and space heating system (see Figure 15.4) that is very efficient and inexpensive to install. As heat for living space is required, natural water pressure or a pump pushes the hot water from the hot water heater through the coils of the air heater. Air is blown over the coils, extracting heat from the water, and is then forced through the duct system throughout the house. After the heat is removed, the water is cycled back into the hot water heater where it is reheated and then recycled into the air heater.

FIGURE 15.4 Combination Hot Water and Space Heating System

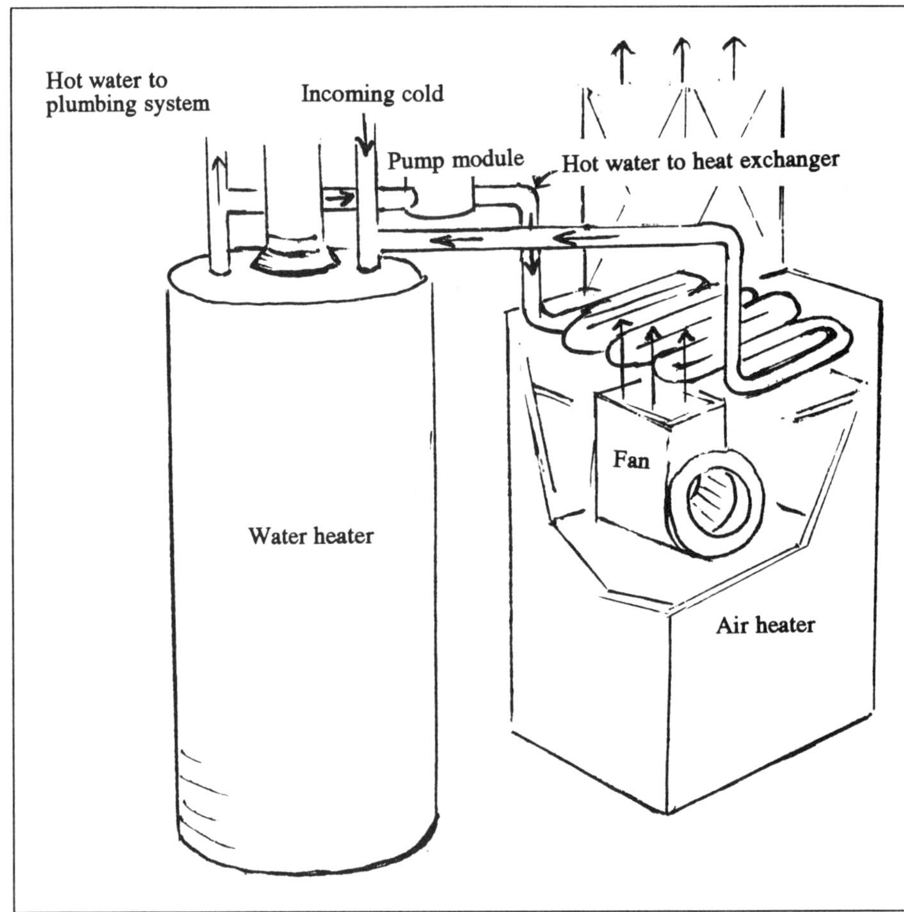

This system is easy to install, economical to operate and occupies less space than most other systems. It was originally developed for apartments, townhouses and small houses, but units are now available to heat much larger homes.

Similar systems have been developed for oil burners but they are not as efficient as the gas burners.

Duct Work

Two materials are generally used to make the ducts for forced-warm-air heating or independent air-conditioning:

- *Fiberglass Duct Board* makes a quiet system. It is usually fabricated in the shop and assembled at the job site using staples and tape. This duct is not as rigid nor as rugged as one built of galvanized sheet metal. The fiberglass duct board should cost about the same as the galvanized sheet metal wrapped with insulation. This duct board is available with an aluminum foil jacket on the outside and with or without a coating on the inside fiberglass. The inside coating is best because it reduces the amount of airborne fibers throughout the system. Some reports indicate that fiberglass fibers may be just as cancer causing as asbestos. However, some fiberglass batt manufacturers now enclose their batts in plastic envelope to drastically reduce or eliminate the flow of fiberglass fibers.

- *Galvanized Sheet Metal* is also made up in the sheet metal shop then brought to the job site, for final installation. Sheet metal ducts are put together using more durable means of fastening than staples and tape.

Some contractors use spiral-reinforced flexible ducts for branches to the rooms. This type of duct is not recommended because it can sag between hangers and partially collapse.

By itself, a sheet metal duct tends to be noisy. This noise can be substantially reduced, however, by lining the inside of the duct with insulation material that also provides thermal insulation. The most noise is eliminated by lining all of the duct system. In the interest of economy, costs may be reduced by lining only selected sections that produce the most noise. Listed below in order of priority (most important are first) are the four areas that should be lined:

1. First 6 feet to 10 feet of return duct from return air grille toward furnace
2. All of the return duct system
3. Supply ducts from furnace through the first "tee"
4. All corners

Duct Work Design and Installation Tips

A poorly designed and installed duct system will reduce the efficiency and comfort of your heating and cooling system. Consider the following:

- Where practical, run the whole duct system within the heated area. This will improve the insulation because the duct then uses the house envelope insulation rather than its own (usually less thick) and reduces heat losses through leaks in the system.
- The plan for the location of supply registers and return diffusers (entry points where the heated or cooled air enters and leaves the

heated or cooled area) for any heating/cooling combination is a compromise.

- The best location of the supply registers and return diffusers in a one-story house is in the floor or low in the walls to get the most out of the heating system. Unfortunately because cold air sinks, to maximize the air-conditioning system, both the supply registers and the return diffusers should be placed in the ceiling or high on the wall. The solution requires a compromise. Locate the supply registers in the floor along the exterior walls and in front of windows and doors. Mount the return diffusers in the ceiling or high up on the wall in the interior of the house. With this system, the air enters the room low on the outside wall and is drawn by the duct to leave the room high and on the inside wall (or an interior hallway), thus the entire room is cooled or heated.
- For a two-story house, install the supply registers and return diffusers on the second floor to maximize air-conditioning (i.e., install both high on the wall or in the ceiling). For the first floor, maximize the installation for heating with the supply registers and return diffusers on the floor or low in the wall.
- Floor-mounted supply registers are more efficient than the baseboard type. It is a good idea, however, to use the baseboard register in rooms such as the bath, kitchen and laundry to prevent wax, water and other material from getting into the duct system.
- After the completion of the rough-in, require the heating contractor to install temporary covers over the outlets, both supply and return, to prevent debris, dust and other material from getting into the duct system during the remainder of the construction period.
- When installing registers in front of windows, if heavy drapes are planned for the window, mount the register in the floor far enough away from the wall so that the closed drapes will not interfere with the flow of the air supply into the room.
- When mounted outside the heated space of the house (such as in the unheated attic or crawl space), both heat output and return cold air ducts should be insulated with at least 2 inches of duct insulation.

Multiple Forced-Warm-Air Heating Systems

If your house is very large, you should consider a multiple system, that is, two completely independent systems with separate duct work, separate heating elements and separate cooling elements. Each of the parts of a multiple system would have less capacity than an overall single system.

Multiple systems are particularly effective in large two- or three-story houses or long ranchers. Under these circumstances, the efficient distribution of the warm or cooled air from a single system is difficult to obtain. A multiple system solves most of these distribution problems and saves energy. It also provides the basis for a zoned system whereby the bedroom area, for instance, can be maintained at a lower temperature than the rest of the house. Even though the initial costs are higher, you will have a much more comfortable house and one that is more energy efficient.

Air Cleaners

Because of their duct network, forced-warm-air heating and air-conditioning systems are ideal for electrostatic air cleaners. They can be installed as an integral part of the system. They not only clean the air but tend to make it smell fresher. That is important now because houses are sealed tighter, which reduces the fresh air moving into the house through cracks in the outer shell.

Humidifiers

If your house has been constructed with little or no anti-air-infiltration measures, the air inside may be dry because of the loss of the moisture through the gaps in the exterior walls, floors and ceilings. If so, higher temperatures will be needed to gain the same comfort as with moister air. Should this be the case, consider the use of humidifiers.

A humidifier can be installed directly into the duct system and hooked up to a water supply so that it will continually and automatically put the needed moisture into the air.

For houses heated with systems other than forced warm air, small portable humidifiers can be placed in appropriate areas throughout the house to accomplish the same thing.

Ventilation

With the advent of efficient methods of sealing a house (see Chapter 12, Air Infiltration), the inside air may have too much moisture. Under these circumstances, rather than move through the exterior walls, floors and ceilings, the moisture generated by normal living activities (showering, clothes washing, cooking, etc.) will remain in the house. This lack of fresh air may make living uncomfortable. In addition, the

FIGURE 15.5 Schematic of the Air-to-Air Heat Exchanger

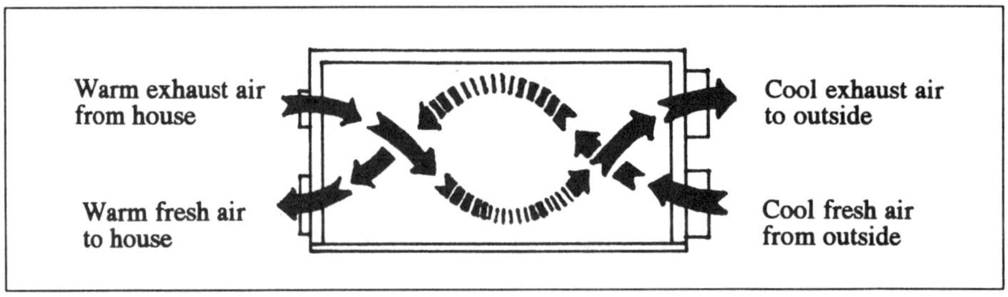

high moisture content of the inside air may cause condensation on the inside of even dual-glazed windows and doors. This problem can be solved by installing a dehumidifier in the heating and cooling system or independent of the system.

The Air-to-Air Heat Exchanger

The heat exchanger, Figure 15.5, uses electric-powered blowers to bring outside fresh, dry air into the house while moving stale, moist air out and exchanging the heat from the stale air to the fresh air in the process. Heat exchangers are about 75 percent to 85 percent efficient.

The heat exchanger should be installed in the basement or in the mechanical room along with the furnace and hot water heater. It should not be installed in an unheated crawl space because the moisture from the stale air will freeze and the exchanger will not operate properly.

Figure 15.6 illustrates the installation of a heat exchanger system in a house that does not have a forced-air ducted heating system. Note that to operate efficiently, the exchanger must have its own duct system that extracts the stale air (black arrows) from the rooms that usually generate the moisture (baths, laundry and kitchen) and brings fresh air into the other parts of the house.

In houses with central forced-warm-air heating systems, the fresh air supplied by the exchanger should be ducted to a room where it can mix with air in the room and then be picked up by the return air ducts of the heating system. *There should be no positive connection between the ducts of the heat exchanger and the ducts of the central heating system.*

The heat exchanger can be installed in a heated crawl space, usually by suspending it from the floor joists. Use a flexible type of suspension to minimize the transfer of the operating vibrations of the exchanger to the floor system.

The rated hourly cubic capacity of the heat exchanger should be large enough to change the air inside the house once every two hours.

FIGURE 15.6 Fully Ducted Air-Exchanger System

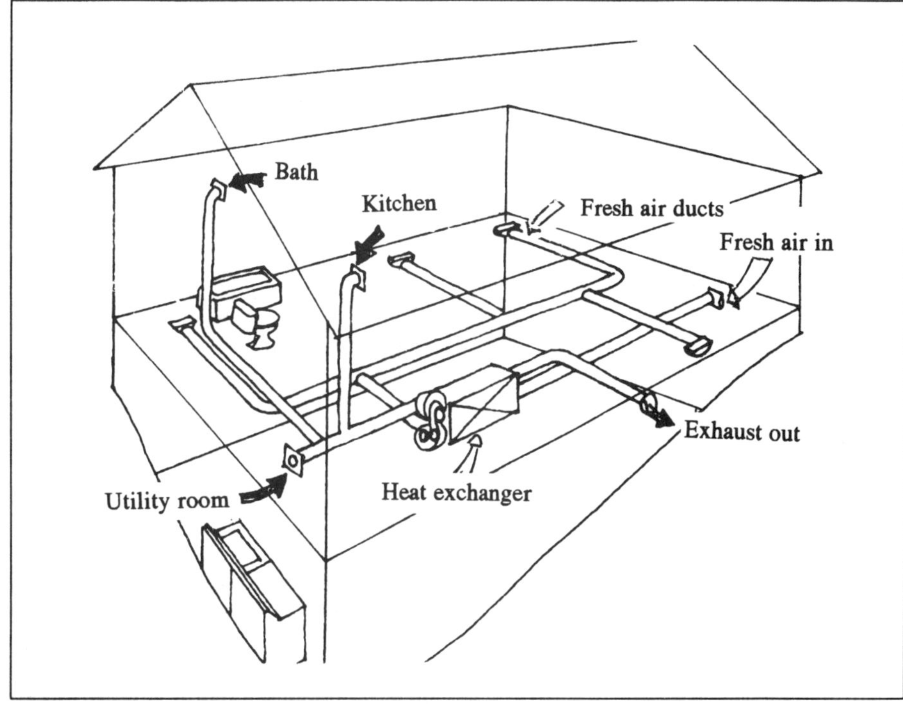

In very cold climates, water and ice may build up in the discharge duct of the exchanger. To monitor this problem, locate the discharge duct where it can be easily inspected and drained.

OTHER HEATING SYSTEMS

Hot-Water Heating Systems

Although they are largely being replaced by the heating systems discussed previously, you may want to consider installing an oil- or gas-fired hot water heating system. In this design, water is heated in a boiler by the gas or oil burner and is pumped all over the house through a pipe system equipped with radiators that distribute the heat into the rooms.

Figure 15.7 illustrates the two-pipe system (preferred over the single-pipe system) where the supply of hot water and return of the cooler water travel in separate pipes.

Note that two types of radiators are shown. One is the familiar under-the-window style modernized with an attractive grilled cover, and the other is the baseboard radiator. The disadvantage of the under-

FIGURE 15.7 Forced-Hot-Water Heating System

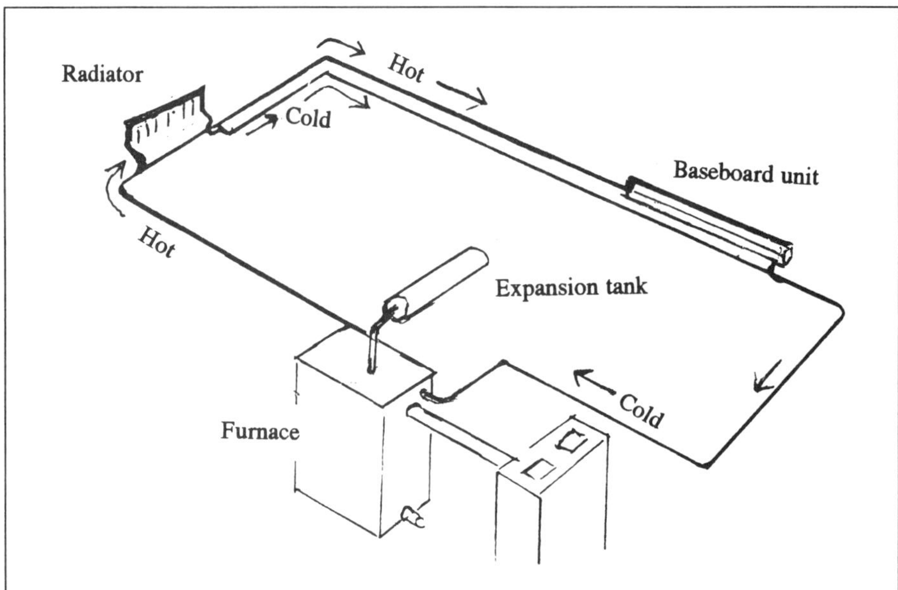

window type is that it juts into the room and may interfere with furniture placement and the drapes. If it is recessed into the wall, the remaining space available for the insulation of the exterior wall is inadequate. Because the baseboard system gives more outside wall coverage and is thus more efficient, it is the preferred system.

The forced-hot-water system is a good one, operating with little temperature difference between the floor and ceiling. Be sure that your system is a closed-loop type with an expansion tank partly filled with air that allows the pressure to build up and raise the boiling point of the water. This permits operation of the system at higher temperatures without generating steam. Also, smaller radiators can be used.

Radiant-Panel Heating

Radiant heating may be attained by installing panels of hot water coils or electric resistance wiring in the ceiling, floors or walls. Design of these systems can be very tricky and should be undertaken only by professionals experienced in this field.

These systems depend primarily on radiation for the passage of heat. Because radiant heat striking the person reduces body heat loss and increases comfort, the person will be more comfortable at lower temperatures than with other systems.

Electric Baseboard Heat

Electric baseboard heat is one of the simplest and least expensive heating systems to install. Its operating costs are high, however. It is unobtrusive, noiseless and, depending upon the circumstances of its use, can be somewhat efficient. Each room has its own control permitting variations in the amount of heat provided. If these controls are properly used and if the house has been well insulated (including interior walls between rooms) and properly sealed against air passage, the cost of operation can be low. Maintenance costs are the lowest of any heating system.

Fuel Savings with Set-back Thermostats

Substantial savings in fuel can be realized by the use of a thermostat that automatically lowers the heat (sets back the temperature) when occupants of the house are away or asleep. For example, a working father and mother with two school-aged children could have an arrangement whereby the temperature automatically turns up to about 68°F a half hour or so before rising, then turns down to 63°F a half hour after the last person has left the house, then sets back up to 68°F just before the first child returns from school, and then once more sets back down 63°F at the preset time for the night.

Figure 15.8 shows the savings from heating setbacks (thermostat setting moved *down* 5°F or 10°F) from 68°F; and from cooling setbacks (thermostat setting moved *up* by 5°F or 10°F) from 75°F.

FIGURE 15.8 Fuel Saved by Thermostat* Setbacks

City	*Heating*			*Cooling*	
	A	B	C	D	E
ATLANTA	15%	22%	38%	10%	16%
DALLAS	15%	24%	39%	9%	16%
HOUSTON	18%	25%	39%	9%	13%
JACKSONVILLE	24%	30%	40%	9%	21%
LOS ANGELES	25%	30%	38%	11%	16%
LOUISVILLE	11%	16%	30%	10%	17%
MINNEAPOLIS	6%	10%	20%	11%	19%
PHOENIX	19%	27%	38%	8%	21%

A = 5°F single setback (8 hours/day)
B = 10°F single setback (8 hours/day)
C = 10°F dual setback (8 hours twice/day)
D = 5°F single setback (8 hours/day)
E = 10°F single setback (8 hours/day)

*Figures are based on a Carrier "Pro-Stat" thermostat.

Savings can also be attained when air-conditioning is in operation by raising the temperature on the thermostat for those hours the house is not occupied.

Special thermostats are available for air-source heat pumps with electric resistance back-up heat. They minimize use of the electric back-up and produce substantial energy savings.

Mechanical Air-Conditioning

All of the forced-warm-air-heating systems are readily adaptable at modest additional cost to include mechanical air-conditioning. The heat pump automatically includes it because the same machinery is used for both operations. The other forced-warm-air systems are designed to accept machinery for air-conditioning using the same duct system for cool air distribution.

If your primary heating system is not one requiring a duct system and you want central air-conditioning, it will have to be a separate system.

Do not excessively oversize the system in hopes of getting quick cooling. If oversizing is much greater than 15 percent, air cool-down will be fast but will lack sufficient moisture removal. The result will be cold, clammy, very uncomfortable air.

The suggestions on good duct work discussed on pages 157 and 158 apply to the separate air-conditioning system as well.

If possible, locate the outdoor section of the compressor (some manufacturers make a two-section compressor) away from decks, patios, bedroom windows and dryer vents. Also avoid interior corners that tend to accentuate the noise of the compressor. Locate the compressor in a shaded area because direct sunlight on the coils will unnecessarily increase the workload.

Auxiliary Heating and Cooling

Up to this point, the discussion of heating and cooling has been of central systems for the whole house. Many auxiliary systems are now available that may be ideal for solving special heating and cooling problems.

Through-the-wall air conditioners, heaters and heat pumps may be the best solution for heating and cooling an isolated part of the house or a part that is only occasionally used. If the design of the house allows the mounting of this equipment through the wall, the appearance is improved and no loss of the use of windows is experienced. The unit is only turned on when the room is in use.

Small wall-mounted electric heaters with blowers are very effective for giving quick heat to a room, such as a bath, for short-time occupancy and as a supplement to the main heating system. Electric heat lamps provide similar heating.

Water-evaporation coolers are very effective in hot, dry climates. They require less energy to operate than the conventional air conditioner and are much less expensive. They need a more-or-less constant source of water.

Ceiling fans may be used to provide summer comfort where high humidity is not a problem. They are also useful in helping circulate air heated by a fireplace or stove in the winter. In houses designed with a cathedral ceiling, the ceiling fan can be used to move the warm air that may accumulate in a pocket at the apex of the ceiling.

Whole-house ceiling exhaust fans are also useful in providing comfort where humidity is low. They should not be used to circulate heated air in the winter, however, because they discharge the heated air to the outside. These fans are noisier than ceiling fans that run almost silently at the lower speeds in quality models.

EXAMPLES OF MIXTURES OF HEATING AND COOLING SYSTEMS

In many cases, the best heating and cooling is provided by a mixture of more than one source. The following sample cases illustrate this point.

Simple Passive Solar Heat Plus Simple Cooling System

Case 1 House designed along contemporary lines with lots of free open space. More-than-average sunshine throughout the year. Hot and dry summers. Winter cold spells with temperatures below freezing on a few occasions. Fire-wood in ample quantities at modest cost.

For Heating Passive solar heat (see Chapter 14, Heating with Sunshine (Solar Energy), is maximized by efficient design. Back-up heating provided by an energy-efficient wood-burning or gas-fired fireplace. Wall-mounted electric heaters with blowers in each bathroom.

For Cooling Ceiling fans plus through-the-wall or window water evaporation coolers.

Combination provides a very inexpensive heating and cooling system. The savings enjoyed, in comparison to other more elaborate systems, will very quickly make up for any extra cost of the construction to provide the passive solar heat. In addition to giving greater comfort during the summer, the ceiling fans will assist in the distribution of the warm air from the solar storage areas and the fireplace.

More Complex Passive Solar Heat Plus a Simple Cooling System

Case 2 The house design is such that distribution of heat from a fireplace would be a problem. Above-average sunshine, dry hot summers and mild winters. Wood not available. Local costs of electricity relatively low.

For Heating Passive solar heat with electric baseboard heat as backup.

For Cooling Same as Case One.

The electric baseboard heat is used to provide good distribution. The baseboard heat should be adjusted in each room to fit the pattern of family living. In those rooms used very little, the controls should be set at relatively low temperatures.

Ground-Coupled Water-Source Heat Pump Plus Fireplace

Case 3 Below-average sunshine. Wood is not readily available in quantities at reasonable cost. Very cold winters and hot muggy summers. Ground water available.

For Heating Ground-coupled water-source heat pump with an energy-efficient gas-fired fireplace as supplement. Bathrooms equipped with supplemental wall-mounted electric heaters with blowers.

For Cooling Heat pump. Ceiling or whole-house exhaust fans.

The ground-coupled water-source heat pump will provide plenty of heat by itself, but with the fireplace operating, the thermostat for the pump mounted in the hallway of the bedroom area could be kept around 65°F. In this situation, the whole house is on the cool side with the fireplace boosting the warmth in those high-use areas during the day. Bathrooms have electric heaters to quickly increase the heat when they are turned on. The ceiling fans will improve the distribution of the heat from the fireplace.

During those periods when some cooling is desired, the ceiling or exhaust fans used alone will improve comfort before the real heat of the summer sets in, when the heat pump can be turned on.

Air-Source Heat Pump Plus Fuel-Burning Furnace

Case 4 Below-average sunshine, very cold winters, no ground water, ground not suitable for ground-coupled heat pump, hot summers, and wood not readily available.

For Heating Air-source heat pump integrated with an oil- or gas-burning forced-warm-air system. Electric wall-mounted heaters with blowers in each bathroom.

For Cooling Heat pump with ceiling or exhaust fans.

The integrated system permits both the heat pump and the oil- or gas-fired furnace to operate at their most efficient temperatures.

Passive Solar Heat Plus Heat Pump

Case 5 Average sunshine, underground water source available, wood scarce and expensive, cold winters and hot muggy summers.

For Heating Passive solar heat with water-source heat pump as back-up. Bathroom wall-mounted electric heaters with blowers.

For Cooling Heat pump and ceiling fans.

The purpose of presenting these different cases is to encourage the homeowner to think in terms of integrated systems for heating and cooling rather than only one system. With this approach, the various methods can be used to provide heating and cooling in their most efficient mode.

An additional but very important factor to consider in designing the heating and cooling system is your particular living requirements. For instance, a family with four children living in a three-bedroom house with living, dining and family rooms will need more heating and cooling throughout the house than a retired couple without children at home living in the same house. In the latter case, large parts of the house will not habitually be used and can be maintained at lower temperatures than would be the case with the large family.

Costing

Different systems, of course, have different costing requirements, but watch the following in any case:

Mechanical Heating/Cooling Systems Labor and material costs are provided by the bidding contractors. Again, specify the details so that you can be assured all contractors are bidding on the same items. (See Appendix A, Sample Specifications.)

Auxiliary Heating and Cooling Equipment Labor and other costs may be overlooked unless the requirement for this equipment is reviewed carefully. Most items are electrical, so the cost for labor and material should be provided by the electric contractor.

Management

In house construction, the installation of plumbing, central heating and cooling systems and the electrical work are all accomplished in at least two phases. If your house is to be built on a concrete slab, the installation of these services may require three phases: (1) work performed before the slab is poured (such as the installation of under-slab ducts), (2) work done after the framing has been completed and (3) the final work after the wall finishes have been applied.

If your house is built over a crawl space, the entire rough-in is done after the completion of the framing but before the wall insulation, sealing and drywall are applied.

For heating systems, the rough-in consists of the installation of the duct work (or piping for hot water systems) and the control wiring. The wiring to supply the power to the system is installed by the electrician.

To avoid possible conflicts in the use of space, you should arrange for a meeting on the site with your heating, plumbing and electrical contractors to go over the plans. In most cases, the plumber has the least flexibility because the waste-pipe system must conform to certain minimum grades for proper flow. Should conflicts arise, it is far easier to reach a solution before work begins. This meeting also gives you the opportunity to ensure coordination among these contractors. For example, to make sure that the electrician installs the power supply wiring for the hot water heater (installed by the plumber) and the electric power to the heating and cooling system.

If some of your duct work lies inside the heated area of the house (which is a good idea) and requires carpentry work after installation (e.g., framing to provide a base for the drywall and/or plaster lathing), check with the carpentry crew so they can get the work done without having to make a special trip for only a two- or three-hour job. This can be costly because you may be billed for a full day's work unless the work has been clearly stated in the specifications.

If you are using a high-efficiency (85+ percent) gas- or-oil burning heating system, make certain that your contractor is following the chimney/ventilating requirements specified by the manufacturer.

Check the duct work to ensure the following are done:

- The duct work has been properly hung from the framing. This is a matter of judgment. Be wary of long spans between hangers that permit sagging of the duct.
- If ducts are installed within the heated space, the drywall or plaster lathing has been hung with seams sealed on the top and sides of the duct chase area. The object is to eliminate cracks through which heat from the duct can flow and be lost into unheated areas.
- The ducts have been completely hooked up. Surprisingly, contractors do on occasion overlook the complete hookup of all sections of the duct system.
- The electrician has roughed-in service to provide electric power to heating and cooling systems including, auxiliary heating and cooling such as ceiling fans. These fans can weigh over 50 pounds, so make sure that the electrical outlet can carry this weight.
- *Get inspections done on time. In most areas, local building codes require an inspection of rough-in of plumbing, heating and electrical work.* The scheduling of these inspections is usually done by the appropriate trade contractor. Verify completion of these inspections yourself. It can be very costly to have to rip out drywall to expose work for an inspection that someone forgot to schedule. And you can be assured that the drywall contractor will charge for the extra work.

CHAPTER 16

Planning for Your Plumbing

The house plumbing system consists of the following parts:

- A source of water, usually a public system or a private well
- The pipeline connecting the water supply to the house
- A system of supply pipes within the house to provide hot and cold water to the various fixtures
- A waste and vent piping system to carry the waste water away from the fixtures
- A waste outlet to dispose of the waste, usually into a public sewer or into an on-site septic system provided by the owner

Figure 16.1 illustrates, in part, a typical house plumbing system.

Types of Water Supply Pipes

The homeowner has several choices, within the building codes, of the type of pipe to use in the water supply system:

- *Copper* makes an excellent pipe. It has a very long life, is generally not affected by corrosion and can be used to supply hot and cold water. It does have disadvantages, however. It is expensive compared to other pipe and the labor to install it is costly. Although somewhat flexible in the smaller sizes, it cannot bend to the same radius as polybutylene pipe. It can be ruptured by water freezing inside, and it requires special pressure

FIGURE 16.1 Residential Plumbing System

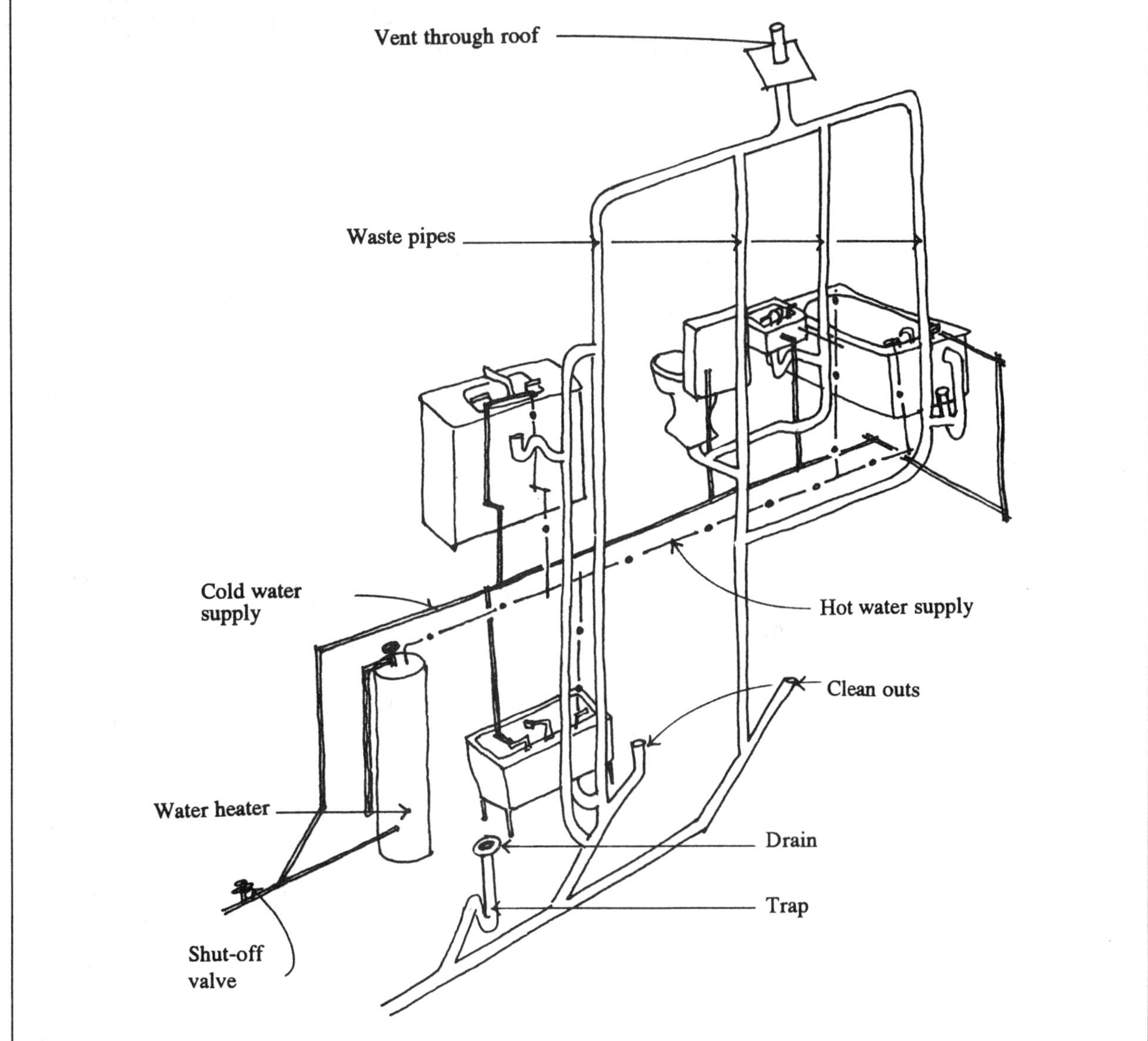

chambers to eliminate water hammer (noise created by the sudden turning off of the water).

- *PVC (polyvinyl chloride)* for cold water and *CPVC (chlorinated polyvinyl chloride)* for hot water are two of the modern vinyl-based pipes. These pipes are much less costly in both material and labor to install than copper pipe. They are chemically inert and therefore unaffected by corrosive material. They are rigid and do not have the bending capability of copper. This shows up as a disadvantage when it is installed under or within a concrete slab where it is most desirable to have pipe runs with no splices.

With PVC and CPVC, each time a bend is required, an elbow joint must be installed, providing a potential source of leaks under the slab that would be costly to repair. Like copper, PVC and CPVC are subject to bursting when the water within the pipe freezes. Freezing of any pipe can be substantially reduced by installing it within interior walls.

- *PB (polybutylene)* pipe has all of the advantages of PVC, CPVC and copper, plus some additional ones. It is no more costly than PVC, is much more flexible than copper, has fewer joints due to its flexibility, does not need pressure chambers to eliminate water hammer, and it will expand and not burst when the water inside freezes. When the water thaws, the pipe returns to its normal size without any loss of strength. In addition, PB can be used for both hot and cold water. Unlike PVC and CPVC whose joints must be cemented, the fittings and their rings of PB are made by mechanical means, thus reducing labor costs and saving time. *It is important that only brass fittings and rings be used with PB pipe.*

There are other kinds of supply pipe available, but any house plumbing requirement can be effectively solved with the selection based on the pipe material discussed above. Galvanized steel pipe for the supply of water in homes has generally fallen into disuse because of its many disadvantages, the most important of which is short life due to rust and corrosion.

Waste Pipe Distinction

In the language of the plumber, *waste pipe* carries the waste material away from the fixtures, but if the waste pipe happens to be connected to a water closet (toilet), it's called a *soil pipe.*

The materials available for waste pipe are the same as those listed for supply pipe, with the exception of PB. Cast iron waste pipe is also still in general use. PB is not yet manufactured in large enough sizes for this purpose. Cast iron is less expensive than copper but more costly in both labor and material than plastic pipe.

Compared to the plastic pipe, cast iron has two advantages. It delivers the waste with much less noise. Therefore, if you cannot avoid running a waste or soil pipe through a wall adjacent to the living or dining room, consider the use of cast iron pipe for quietness. In addition, cast iron pipe is more durable in withstanding the rigors of mechanical pipe-cleaning equipment.

Take Care in Selecting Plumbing Fixtures

Except for the fixtures, most of the plumbing system is buried inside the walls and floor of the house or in the soil. The fixtures are the items you see and use every day. Their proper selection, therefore, is very important. As a general rule, try to select your fixtures from the same manufacturer. Very often you will get a better price from the plumber who enjoys a professional discount, and if you want color in your fixtures, you are assured of getting a better color match.

To select your fixtures, go to one or more plumbing supply houses and take your time looking over the various types on display. Ask questions about their features. Remember, you are going to be using these fixtures for a long time.

Tubs, Showers and Tub/Shower Combinations

Your choices for tubs are a steel or cast-iron base coated with porcelain, fiberglass or other plastic. Avoid the steel tub. It chips very easily and sometimes it will distort after installation, working the ceramic tile loose on a tub with tiled shower combination.

The fiberglass tub, particularly when done in a one-piece tub/shower combination, has many advantages. It is easier to clean and it tends to resist mildew more than the ceramic tile. Fiberglass tubs and tub/showers have drawbacks that are relatively easy to correct. They will bend under the weight of the body. And when the water is turned on and strikes the bottom of the fiberglass unit, they are noisy. Both of these faults can be largely eliminated by installing a material like dry sand (usually available in ample quantities at all construction sites) on top of the plywood subfloor then placing the tub unit on top of the sand. There should be just enough sand so that the voids in the bottom of the fiberglass unit are filled snugly.

Another choice is a combination of a cast-iron or fiberglass tub with large wall panels of patterned fiberglass or ceramic tile.

In making a choice among the above, consider the ease of cleaning the fiberglass versus the greater array of colors available in the ceramic tile.

Full showers without tubs again offer the choice of the fiberglass unit versus the ceramic unit. Ceramic tile has a greater selection of design and an unlimited choice in size and shape. The size and shape of the ceramic-tiled shower, however, is only limited by the space available in the bathroom.

Specify that the plumbing plan include the installation of a lead or PVC pan underneath the stand-alone shower as a protection against leaks.

Two methods are used in applying ceramic tile to walls. One is the "quickset" method, where the tile is attached by a mastic to Sheetrock that has been nailed to the stud walls. The other method is to place the tile in a bed of "mud" or cement that has been laid over metal lathing. The "mud" system is preferred for longer life.

Water Closets (Toilets)

Most manufacturers make water closets that vary in price from low to very high. The best buy is usually in the middle of the range. Water closets are also available that operate with less water than the standard. If you are ecologically concerned or water supply is a problem in your area, install this type.

Lavatories

A lavatory is a wash basin. They are made of many different materials and in various sizes and shapes. The most popular are the china lavatory mounted on or dropped in a plastic-laminated vanity top, the marbleized integrated bowl and top, and the Corian® bowl (bowl and integrated top) made by the DuPont Company. Although the porcelain-finished cast-iron lavatory is still available, it is not very popular because it requires a metal mounting ring and is very heavy and difficult to work with.

The one-piece marbleized bowl and countertop is very popular because of its appearance, ease of cleaning and low cost. The exterior coating, however is very thin and a heavy scratch can penetrate this coating and expose the white material beneath it. This damage is difficult to repair. On the other hand, solid plastics, such as Corian or Nevamar®, are made with the color all the way through the material. If scratched, there is no color change and the scratch mark can be removed easily with steel wool or fine sandpaper. Solid plastics can be sawed and filed for an accurate fit. They are more expensive than marbleized material.

Kitchen Sinks and Laundry Tubs

Kitchen sinks are available in various sizes and are made of either stainless steel, solid plastic or porcelain-finished cast iron. The selection is one of personal preference with the option of one, two or three sections or bowls.

The more expensive line of the stainless steel sinks have more chrome alloy that provides a better look and a reduced tendency to water spot. Otherwise, for home use there is little difference.

Porcelain sinks tend to chip when given hard usage.

Most laundry tubs are now made of fiberglass. They have a deep bowl to hold more water than the average kitchen sink. If, however, the size and shape of a kitchen sink is acceptable for laundry use, it will give you an extra, more versatile sink for doing other chores. One side of this second kitchen sink may be a deep bowl with the other shallow.

Faucets, Shower Heads and Related Hardware

The selection of these items is a matter of personal choice, with quality ones lasting longer.

Because it means less work for the plumber, it is to your advantage to select all of this hardware from the line of a single manufacturer. The plumbing supply house will usually help you in this regard.

Sill Cocks

A sill cock is an outside cold water tap for lawn watering and other outdoor uses. You should have at least two and, for a very large house, as many as four so that your garden hose need not be excessively long and hard to handle.

In cold areas where freezing is a problem, sill cocks should be the freeze-proof variety.

Hot Water Heaters

Hot water heaters are available that are fueled by either gas, oil, electricity, heat pump or the sun.

A standard 52-gallon water heater is normally sufficient capacity for a family of four living in a 2½-bath house. If you feel a need for additional capacity, then either go to a larger heater or change to a quick-recovery type if your fuel is electricity. The quick recovery model has higher wattage heating elements, giving faster heating capacity.

Have the hot water heater hooked up with a timer set so that the heat comes on late at night to properly meet the demand for the following day. This arrangement will save fuel because the heater will not automatically turn itself on every time the temperature drops a few degrees.

Hot water heaters should be located near the area of major demand to reduce the energy waste in running the heated water long distances. If your house has two major demand areas, install two smaller hot water heaters with one near each of these areas. The additional cost for the material will be made up by the energy saved in a few years. You will also have a hot water system that is not only more convenient to use but requires less water.

If you locate the hot water heater in an unheated area, add an additional layer of insulation to the sides and top (if fueled by gas heat, do not insulate the top).

Each hot water heater should have a drain line to the outside to take away water from leaks or other mishaps.

Clothes Washers

As part of your contract, have the plumber install an in-the-wall box for the hookup faucets and drain. This box will dress up the installation and provide protection to the plaster or drywall. It is worth the additional cost.

Plumbing Plans

It is most likely that your plans contain only the location of the various fixtures. Actually this is not a problem, because most good plumbing contractors can and will design the supply and waste pipe systems. Your plans should contain at least the following four items:

1. Location and type of each fixture including the manufacturer and model number for fixtures and hardware (faucet, shower head, etc.)
2. Location of water supply tap-in. If the water supply is a private well, show the location of the well. If it is a public water system, show the location of the tap-in. Utility companies can supply this information.
3. Location of the sewer-tap in. If the sewer system is to be a septic tank system on your lot, indicate the location of the tank. In most cases, the local codes require that the hookup to the septic tank be made by a master plumber. If the sewer is a public system, show the location of the tap-in so that the contractor can determine the distance to lay the pipe.
4. Your preference for pipe material

Costing

The total cost for both labor and material should be provided to you by the plumbing contractors who are bidding.

Do not attempt to keep the costs down by buying fixtures yourself and asking for bids from plumbing contractors for labor and the rest of the material. By supplying the showers, tubs, lavatories and water closets you are cutting out some of the profit the plumber normally expects to get. Under these circumstances, he may increase his price for the labor and the remaining material, with the result that your overall costs may be greater than if you did not furnish the fixtures.

Then, there is another, perhaps even more serious, problem. If you furnish the fixtures and the plumber the labor, and something doesn't work properly, who is responsible for making the correction? Is it the fault of the plumber's labor or did you furnish defective material? If the material is defective and has to be replaced, you have the additional problem of making the exchange and paying the plumber for removing the defective material and installing the replacement as an extra cost to the contract. On the other hand, if your contract calls for the plumber to furnish all material and labor, should anything go wrong with the system, the plumber is obliged to make the necessary corrections regardless of the cause at no change in his contract price.

In your bidding process you may have to divide the plumbing task into three parts. The first is the septic system; it should be installed by a contractor who specializes in this work. Second is the plumbing system in the house; it must include hookup to the septic system and the water supply pipe 5 feet out from the foundation. The third part would be the laying of the supply pipe and the final hookup to the main. The reason for going to a specialist for the third part is that hooking up the water supply to the water main requires special equipment because the main is under pressure. Some plumbing contractors do not have the necessary equipment and prefer not to do this work. If you can get one contractor to do the entire job, however, it will make your management task easier.

The design and specifications for a septic system are usually provided by the local public health department. This information should be the basis for the septic system contractor bid.

Management

Plumbing installation is a complex procedure that requires careful attention to details such as the following:

- Coordinate the work of the plumbing, electrical and heating contractors as previously discussed in this chapter and keep them informed when you would like to have them on the job.
- Any site work that includes excavations, such as the ditch for the water supply and the septic system, should be scheduled so that at least six weeks remain (to allow the excavations to settle) before the final grade is done. Failure to do this may result in settling of the soil after the final grading, requiring a redo of the job.
- If your lot is restrictive to the extent that machinery for the septic system cannot get to the septic area after the foundation has been laid, install the septic system right after the lot has been cleared and the driveway base established.
- To avoid marring the appearance of the front of the house, require that all waste and soil pipe vents exit through the roof at the rear of the house.
- To protect them from freezing, run water supply pipes through interior walls if possible. Where this cannot be done, check to ensure that the pipe has been run at the interior edge of the stud to allow as much room as possible for the insulation. This insulation must be installed between the pipe and the exterior wall.
- Most building codes require that after rough-in, the supply pipe system must be tested under pressure for leaks, either at the pressure of the local water system or as high as 100 pounds per square inch. The waste pipe system, not under pressure, is usually tested for leakage by applying a 10-foot head. A *head* is the hydraulic term for a vertical column of water. For example, a 10-foot head would apply pressure to the waste pipe equal to the weight of a column of water 10 feet high. If the local codes do not require this or similar testing, include it as part of your plumbing contract to be sure it is done.
- During and after the installation of the rough-in of the supply and waste pipe systems, inspect the framing and look for places where the plumber has made major cuts into the structural framing. Require reinforcement as indicated in Figure 16.2.
- The Building Officials Code Administration (BOCA) National Building Code specifies that notches or cuts into beams, joists, rafters or studs shall not exceed 1/6 the depth of the members and shall not be located in the middle 1/3 of the span.
- Your best indication of quality workmanship in plumbing is neatness. Vertical pipes should be vertical and horizontal supply pipes should be horizontal. Horizontal waste pipe, on the other hand, must have a slope of about 1/4 inch for each horizontal running foot. If your plumber is using PB pipe, however, this material should run directly from one point to the next, not necessarily vertical or horizontal.

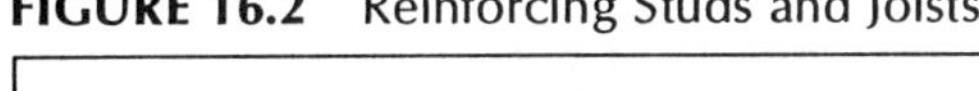

FIGURE 16.2 Reinforcing Studs and Joists

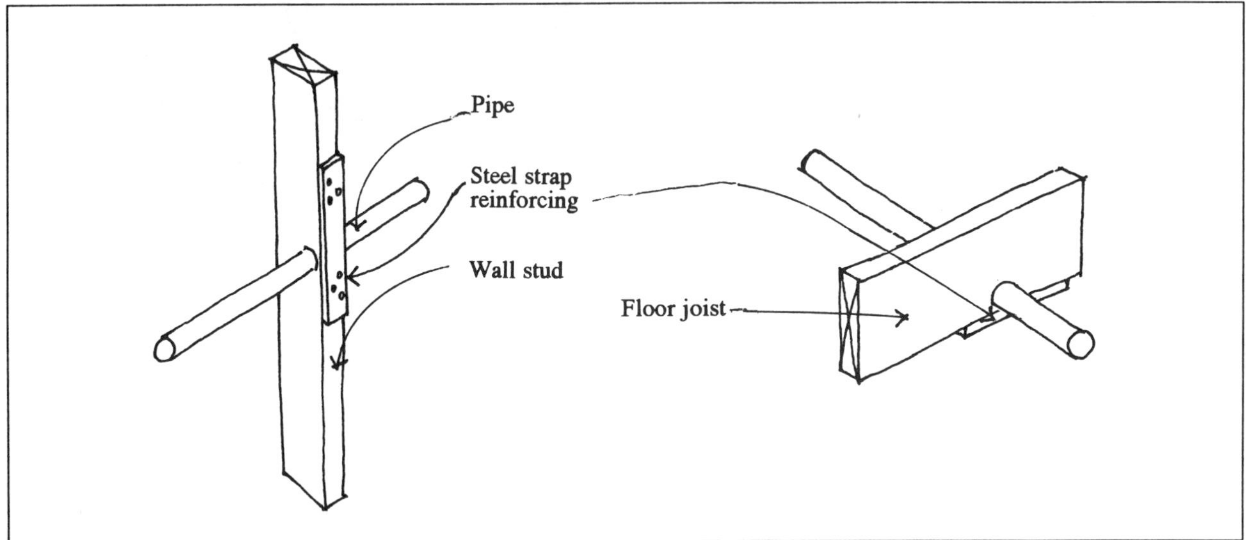

- Joints should be clean and neat.
- If you are not using PB pipe, require shock-arrester pressure chambers at all quick cut-off fixtures (faucets).
- Before scheduling the plumber for his final inspection, be sure that the following four tasks have been accomplished:
  1. Vinyl, ceramic tile and wood flooring should be installed in those rooms that will receive plumbing fixtures. You will have a much neater-looking floor if these types of flooring are put down first. If carpet is the selected floor covering, the underlayment should be laid, but the carpet itself should be installed after the fixtures have been set. The wood floor should not be finished.
  2. All kitchen cabinets and vanities and their tops that are to receive plumbing fixtures should be installed, with the cutouts of the proper size already made.
  3. Make sure appliances not furnished by but to be hooked up by the plumber are on hand, such as clothes washers or refrigerators with ice-making hookup.
  4. All ceramic tile for showers and tub/shower combinations should be installed.

CHAPTER 17

Safely Installing Your Electrical System

GENERAL BASICS YOU SHOULD KNOW

To understand the discussion in this chapter and to communicate with electrical contractors, you should be familiar with a few technical terms and their use.

An *ampere* is a measure of the quantity of electricity flowing through a circuit (a wire). A *volt* is the measure of the force pushing the ampere through the circuit. A *watt* is a measure of the power in a circuit and is a result of multiplying the amperes by the voltage (for resistance-loaded equipment such as toasters, light bulbs, etc.). A circuit designed for 20 amperes working with a voltage of 110 (normal house voltage) is capable of handling 110×20 = 2,200 watts (resistance load). The call for power in this circuit cannot exceed this wattage or the circuit breaker protecting it will open and break the circuit.

The number of amperes that a circuit can normally carry depends upon the size of the wire cable. The size of cable used in house construction is expressed in gauge numbers. The smaller the gauge number, the larger the wire in the cable and thus the greater the capacity of the cable to provide wattage. The actual design of each circuit should be done by your electrical contractor who is a licensed master electrician.

Electrical Capacity of the House

The electrical capacity of the house is based on the input (power source), the size of the service panel, and the size, number and layout of the circuits within the house.

Don't Skimp on the Service Panel

The selection of the size of the service panel should provide for future circuit and load growth. The capacity of the panel is expressed in amperes. For an average house this rating should be at least 150 amperes, and 200 is even a better choice because it should be sufficient to provide extra circuitry for the future at less cost than it would be to add auxiliary panels at the time of need later. Get some help on this selection from your electrical contractor.

Choose the circuit breaker type of panel rather than one using old-fashioned fuses because it is much less trouble and can be reset quickly by merely throwing a lever. It will "break" again, however, if the fault in the circuit has not been corrected.

Don't "Underbuild" House Circuits

The time to install house circuits is, of course, during construction when the structure of the house is exposed and labor costs are lower. Do not underbuild in this area. The small amount of savings could very easily be lost by having to add new circuits soon after the house is built.

Representative House Circuit Design

A typical three-bedroom, two-bath, full-basement house with circuits properly designed would have about the following (the number represents the number of the circuit in the panel):

- General Purpose Circuits*
  1. Two bedrooms and bath
  2. Master bedroom and bath
  3. Living room outlets and kitchen lights
  4. Dining room lights and hall outlets
  5. Basement lights

  *The above are not sufficient for electric wall heaters.

- 20-Ampere Kitchen and Appliance Circuits
  6. Kitchen receptacles
  7. Some kitchen and all dining room outlets
- Special Circuits
  8. 20-ampere laundry appliance (irons, etc.)
  9. 15-ampere circuit for fuel-fired furnace
  10. and 12. 240-volt circuit for central air-conditioning or heat pump (Note that the 240-volt requirements take up two circuits in the service panel.)
  11. 20-ampere workshop circuit
  13. and 15. 120–240-volt range circuit
  14. and 16. 240-volt hot water heater circuit
  17. and 19. 240-volt circuit for clothes dryer
  21. 20-ampere circuit for dishwasher
  22. 20-ampere circuit for garbage disposal

  18, 20, 23 and 24. Spare circuits for future use

This listing of circuits is not an attempt to design the electrical circuitry for your house. Rather, it is an attempt to show you the large number of circuits needed in a typical house so you are able to judge whether or not your electrical circuitry plan is adequate.

Review the Electrical Plan Carefully

The blueprints for your house may not have a complete electrical plan or the plan may not suit your needs. As in plumbing, however, this is not a serious problem. You should review the plan and be sure it includes the following four areas:

1. Location, identification and power requirements for each major appliance such as dishwasher, clothes dryer, clothes washer, stove and so forth. You should select these appliances by model number and manufacturer from the appliance supplier who can provide the necessary electrical data.
2. Location on the blueprint all of the wall receptacles, wall switches and overhead lighting that you want. If your plans already include a more-or-less complete electrical plan, make the changes to satisfy your preference.
3. The size of the service panel. You will probably have to get some professional help from an electrician for this.
4. Manufacturer's name and model number of all electrical fixtures you expect the electrician to supply as part of his bid. In this regard, see the discussion in Chapter 16, Planning for Your Plumbing, about the problems arising when the owner supplies

part of the electrical material. It is usually expected, however, that the owner will provide the appliances (dishwasher, clothes washer, etc.) through a supplier other than the electrical contractor.

With electrical fixtures, it is common practice to include a dollar allowance in the specifications instead of the selection of the actual fixtures. This system will ensure that all electrical contractors are bidding on the same specifications, but it leaves unsolved other problems. First, you will not know the real cost of the fixtures until after they have been chosen. If this is done after the awarding of the contract, it leaves you wide open as to the actual cost of your total electrical contract. Second, it could cause installation problems. For example, let's assume that your final selection of the chandelier for the dining room is not made until after the completion of the electrical rough-in and the application of the drywall. You may find that if you have chosen a very heavy chandelier, the base installed by the electrician cannot support its weight. Again you are faced with extra costs for rework.

Basic Electric Symbols You Must Know

To properly review your plans and to make changes, you should be familiar with the following symbols:

- *Duplex wall outlet with two receptacles*—Supplies power to lamps, vacuum cleaner and other household items.
- S *Single-pole switch*—Provides on and off control to outlets from one position.
- S_2 *Double-pole switch*—Provides on and off control from two locations. (For example, lets you turn off the lights in the kitchen from either of two doors on opposite sides of the room.)
- *Ceiling light fixture*
- T.V. *Television antenna and telephone outlets*

Figure 17.1 illustrates the application of these symbols.

Note that in the kitchen there are two double-pole wall switches that permit the overhead light fixture to be turned on or off at each door. The dining room, on the other hand, has only one door so the wall switch is only a single pole.

In the family room, the sketch shows no overhead fixture. Therefore, one of the wall outlets is wired to a double-pole switch so that a lamp may be plugged into this wall outlet and be turned on and

FIGURE 17.1 Electrical Switching

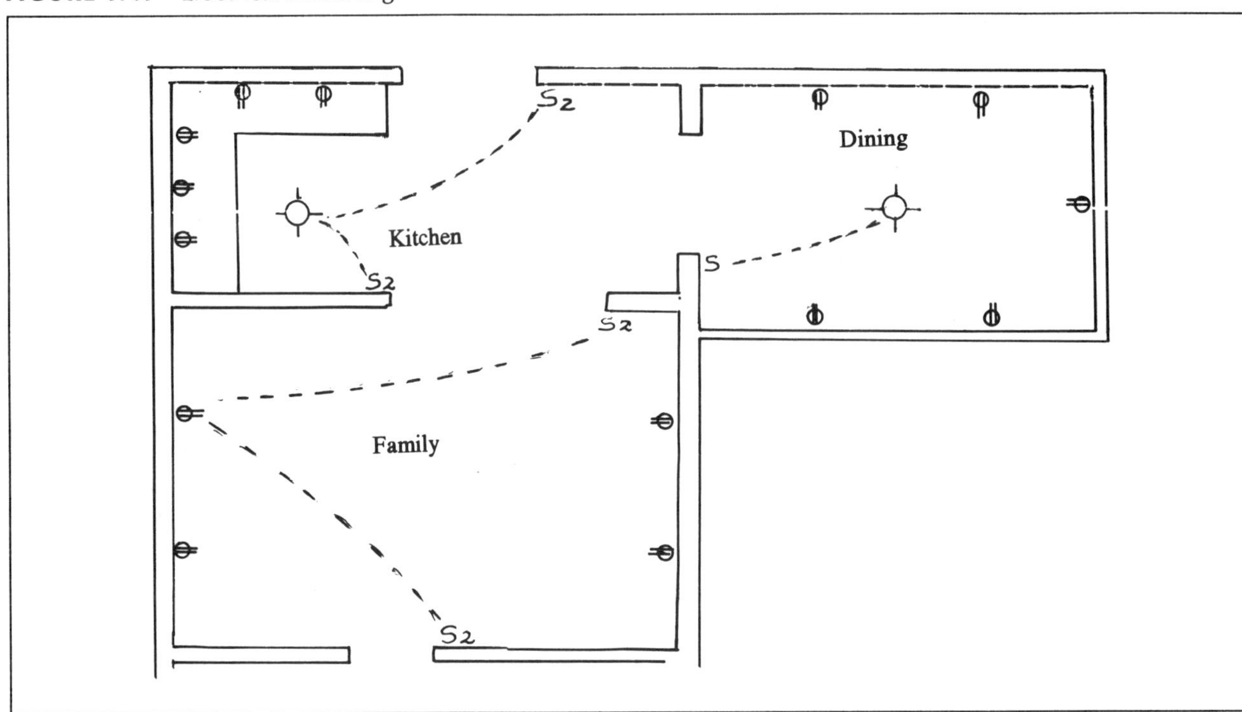

off at either entry to the room. An alternate solution is to wire all duplex wall outlets so that the top receptacle is operated by a wall switch and the bottom receptacle is always "hot."

Suggestions for Electrical Planning

- Place one duplex wall outlet for every 12 linear feet of wall for every room in the house. In the kitchen, have a duplex wall outlet for every 4 linear feet of counter space.
- Include an overhead light over the kitchen sink.
- Install wall switches to control overhead lighting. If the room has more than one entry, install double-pole or triple-pole switches so that the overhead light can be turned on or off at each entry.
- If the room has no overhead lighting, wire at least one duplex outlet so that the top receptacle is operated by the wall switch and the bottom receptacle is always "hot." Then plug the lamp into the top receptacle.
- Include exhaust fans in all bathrooms.
- Include electrical wall-mounted heaters with blowers or a similar auxiliary heating device in each bathroom. They will provide a quick source of heat for rooms that are seldom used throughout the day and permit the overall temperature in the

bedroom part of the house to be kept low with a resultant savings in fuel.

- Specify 20-ampere circuits as a minimum for most outlets.
- Wall switches located at the room entry should consist of the switch itself plus an outlet for plugging in vacuum cleaners, floor waxers and other house cleaning equipment. This arrangement avoids the problem of locating a low wall switch (usually behind furniture) to power electrical equipment for temporary use.
- Avoid recessed lights in ceilings with unheated space above. They cannot be properly insulated and leak air badly. If recessed lights are an important part of your design, consider installing a dropped ceiling (one that is suspended a foot or so below the regular foot ceiling). With this arrangement, ample insulation and anti-air-infiltration sealing can be accomplished above the regular ceiling.
- Include lights in all closets controlled by a wall switch mounted on the room side. Even shallow closets with bifold doors will need lighting on occasion. Pull-chain lights often malfunction.
- Specify that in all exterior walls, cables installed horizontally will run along the top of the bottom plate. This will give the least interference with the effectiveness of the wall insulation. Most electric cable is sufficiently flexible so that this requirement should pose no problem.
- Include some outside electrical outlets—at least two and up to four for large ranchers. They should be equipped with ground-fault circuit interrupters for additional protection from the hazard of wet ground.
- Consider some outside spotlights or floods to provide lighting for use of the yard and provision of some security.
- Install a ceiling outlet in the garage for an automatic garage door opener, whether or not you have this device now. You will probably want to add it later, and installing the outlet now will be less costly.
- Don't forget the following six items:
  1. Television antenna wiring
  2. Wiring for central vacuum systems
  3. Wiring for smoke and fire alarms
  4. Burglar alarm system wiring
  5. Intercom wiring
  6. Telephone wiring—a liberal number of outlets

Is Copper or Aluminum Wiring Safer?

Copper and aluminum are both efficient conductors of electricity. Unfortunately, a few years ago, aluminum wiring got a very bad reputation for causing fires and other hazards in homes. If the hardware—such as connectors, lugs and terminal blocks—are those designed specifically for aluminum wiring and are properly installed, there is no reason why aluminum wiring should not be used.

Although aluminum wiring is less expensive than copper, the savings is relatively small. Therefore, it is recommended that copper wiring be used instead of aluminum. For the greater capacity circuits requiring #8 cable or larger, aluminum is used as a common practice.

■ LIGHTING CAN'T JUST BE TAKEN FOR GRANTED

According to the Department of Energy, 20 percent of all the electrical energy produced in this country is used for the purpose of lighting homes and businesses. Furthermore, a reduction of 20 percent to 50 percent of this power use could be made primarily through the use of more efficient lamps (bulbs) available on the market today.

Interior House Lighting for Beauty and Economy

In selecting the bulbs for lighting your house, consider the following:

- Incandescent bulbs are by far the most widely used. *They are also the most inefficient.* About 90 percent of the energy consumed by an incandescent bulb is dissipated in the form of heat. The efficiency of bulbs increases as the wattage increases. For example, a 100-watt incandescent bulb produces the same amount of light as two 60-watt bulbs but uses less electricity.
- Incandescent bulbs have a short life span, and near the end of this span the light output will decrease as much as 20 percent.
- "Long Life" incandescent bulbs are the least efficient. They should be used only in those areas where an incandescent bulb must be used and replacement of a burnt-out bulb is difficult.
- Most devices on the market designed to prolong the life of an incandescent bulb reduce both the light output and the efficiency of the bulb.
- A tinted bulb has a lower light output than a standard incandescent.

- Fluorescent bulbs are up to five times more efficient than incandescent bulbs.
- Fluorescent bulbs are available as long narrow, U-shaped and circular tubes.
- Adapters are available to convert the incandescent socket to take the fluorescent bulb.
- Although the initial cost of fluorescent bulbs is higher than incandescent, this additional cost is made up by the greater efficiency and longer life of the fluorescent.
- Fluorescent bulbs are available in several shades of white and some will blend with incandescent bulbs.
- A 40-watt fluorescent bulb is more efficient than smaller ones.
- Straight fluorescent bulbs are more efficient than circular ones.
- Contrary to popular belief, to save electricity, fluorescent bulbs should be turned off when not in use, even for only a few minutes.

Outdoor Lighting for Beauty and Safety

Exterior lighting used to light wall surfaces, doorways, shrubbery and walkways can be accomplished with low-wattage incandescent bulbs. If your plans call for the lighting of large yard areas, however, consider the use of the very efficient mercury lamp. It is available in sizes ranging from 40 watts to 1,000 watts, with the 175-watt size being equivalent to about 300 watts of incandescent lighting. This lamp has one drawback in that it has a start-up delay of from one to seven minutes from the time it is turned on until full illumination has been reached. In designing your outdoor lighting system, ensure that it doesn't infringe upon your neighbor's privacy. Also, position exterior lights so they do not shine in your face as you go out the door. This is a dangerous situation that may cause anyone using the doorway to trip or fall.

Buy Inexpensive Light Fixtures at First

Light fixtures are available in a wide variety of prices and, unless you have a well-thought-out plan for their installation, it is best to lean toward the inexpensive fixtures with the idea of replacing them sometime in the future when you have had time to decide exactly what you want. As a suggestion, select good quality fixtures for the entrance foyer, dining room and baths. Most other fixtures, especially those in the bedrooms, are very seldom noticed and inexpensive fixtures would probably be satisfactory. Final selection can then be more easily made after the house has been furnished and lived in for a while.

The "Smart" House

In recent years, electrical techniques have been developed that can greatly increase the convenience for control of the house electrical system, appliances and other features. Several industrial organizations are now promoting different versions of this new technology. Basically, these systems are control systems that can be programmed to do things ordinarily controlled manually by the house occupants throughout the house such as control of lights, appliances, equipment and the home security system. For example, the HVAC system may be made "smart" by responding to changing weather to conserve energy while no one is at home, or one may telephone the house while away to actuate the thermostat, have the lights turned on before returning, or to be sure that the stove is off after you have left the house.

Another example replaces the function of many different cables presently installed to provide service for power, television cable, audio systems, intercoms, telephones, and security systems. A single multiwire cable is installed that allows you to hook up any or all of these devices at any wall socket. Each device will have its own "smart" module that ensures that only the correct connections are made.

Most of these systems have a feedback system to indicate what is working. In addition, the system can be designed to provide controls as to the timing of the operation of individual elements. For instance, you can set up the system to turn on the coffee pot 20 minutes before you get up and turn the radio or television on to wake you up.

The capabilities of the developing technology are numerous. If this interests you, consult with the local power company, an electrical engineer, architect or electrical contractor who has experience in this area for help in determining what elements and type of system you might want in your house.

Costing

Remember the following:

- The provision of all labor and material, including electrical fixtures, is normally included in the bid of the electrician. In addition, he will include the labor and materials for the electrical hookup of plumbing, heating and air-conditioning units requiring electric power. If your plans call for electric baseboard heat, the electrician will furnish the material and labor rather than the heating contractor. In any event, be clear in your specifications as to exactly what the electrician is bidding on. Usually the electrical contractor does not provide appliances but will hook them up.

- One easily forgotten electrical item is the kitchen exhaust fan. If it consists of a through-the-wall fan only, the electrician should furnish the material and the labor. If it is a range hood, the material is normally provided by the appliance supplier, with the electrician doing installation. If duct work is necessary to the outside for the fan, most electricians will do this work, but make sure to detail it in the specifications.
- The electrical contractor furnishes all labor and materials for the temporary electrical service.
- In the preparation of their bids for the electrical work, ask each bidder to give you information on the number and type of circuits he intends to provide. You can make a rough comparison and determine which is the better bid from the standpoint of circuitry.

Management

Management headaches can be avoided by observing the following:

- Arrange for the installation of temporary electric service early. The service is needed by the carpentry crew, and getting the approvals from the power company and the local authorities may take some time. Without this power in place, the framing work will be delayed.
- Have the telephone wiring installed at the same time as the electrical rough-in. Most electricians will do this work.
- Coordinate the work with the plumbing and heating contractors.
- Inspect the rough-in for completion of the following eight tasks:
    1. Junction boxes for all switches, outlets and fixtures have been installed according to plan.
    2. Power has been provided for all major appliances and plumbing and heating elements.
    3. Lateral cable runs in exterior walls are along the top of the bottom plate, where practical, so as not to interfere with the wall insulation.
    4. The electrical inspection of the rough-in has been made before the insulation and drywall are installed.
    5. Ceiling outlets will hold the weight of fixtures.

6. Select your electrical fixtures early. (Some of them may take several weeks or months to arrive. Check this with the supplier, and if unusually long lead times exist, select substitute items.)
7. The locations of the junction boxes for wall switches near doors have enough clearance to install the door trim without interfering with the switch cover plate.
8. The swing of the doors and box locations are such that the switch will not end up behind the door when open (unacceptable in most codes).

- Schedule the electrical contractor for his final installation when the following five jobs have been completed:
  1. Interior trim has been completed and all cabinets installed.
  2. Plumber has installed all plumbing equipment that must be hooked to electrical power by the electrician.
  3. The heating contractor has installed all of his equipment that requires electrical power.
  4. All major appliances requiring electrical hookup are on hand and have been installed by the plumber where required.
  5. All electrical fixtures are on hand. (In the event that one or two are missing and will not arrive shortly, the electrical final inspection may be scheduled by using temporary fixtures in place of those that have not arrived. This will permit the issuance of an occupancy permit, assuming that all other work is satisfactory, and you can move into the house without waiting for many days because of a couple of light fixtures.)
- If your plans include a central vacuum cleaning system, ensure that the rough-in for this system, including the tubing, is installed by either the electrical contractor or a separate vacuum cleaner contractor before the wall is covered with the drywall or other finish.

■ CHAPTER 18 ■

Striking Interior Wall Finishes

Traditional, Elegant, Conventional Plaster

There are two conventional plaster systems, two coat and three coat. The two-coat system can be applied over plaster board lathing or masonry, but not metal lathing. It consists of a base coat, doubled back for additional thickness and strength, followed by the finish coat applied after the base coat has thoroughly set. The finish coat may be smooth or textured. The minimum total plaster thickness should be ½ inch over gypsum lath and ⅝ inch over masonry.

The three-coat system can be applied over metal lathing, plaster board lathing or masonry with a minimum plaster thickness of ⅝ inch. It consists of a first or scratch coat, followed by a brown coat, and then the finish coat (either smooth or textured).

Either of these systems provides a fine white wall finish, but the three-coat is preferred because it produces a stronger wall. It is also the most expensive. Although it is the intent of the manufacturer of the plaster materials that finished walls be decorated, neither of these two plaster finishes need be painted or papered.

Compared to other wall finishes discussed in this chapter, conventional plaster is costly in time and labor. Its application requires highly skilled craftsman, and on a large house it can take as long as two or three days just to apply the scratch coat and to allow drying time before the brown or second coat can be put on. During the entire plastering process, because of the large array of saw horses and work platforms needed, almost no other interior work can be done.

Practical, Versatile Drywall

The most widely used wall finish is drywall (also called Sheetrock and gypsum board). It is also the least expensive.

Drywall must be painted because its finished appearance is not uniform. All joints are more or less white, whereas the rest of the area is buff, the color of the surface paper.

The three attachment devices used in hanging drywall panels to the wall studs and the ceiling joists are adhesive, drywall screws and annular ring drywall nails. The principal problem to avoid is the popping of the nails caused by the shrinking of the studs and joists as they begin to dry out. For this reason avoid using nails.

Although the drywall screw is the most widely used method of hanging, the best system is to apply adhesive made for this purpose to the studs and the joists with the use of enough screws to hold the drywall panel in place until the adhesive bonds. Screws on the side wall are put around the edges of the drywall and will either be covered with the wood baseboard, crown molding or a taped finished seam. In the ceiling, additional support is needed in the center of the drywall panel, so screws are temporarily used down the middle of the panel at every other joist. Once the adhesive has bonded, these screws are removed and the holes filled during the finishing process.

Panel adhesive cannot be used as a method of hanging exterior walls or ceilings if the vapor barrier consists of polyethylene sheet material nailed to the studs and joists (see Chapter 13, Energy-Saving Insulation Options). The polyethylene will prevent the adhesive bonding to the studs. An excellent alternate is to install foil-backed drywall panels with the adhesive. The foil provides a very good vapor barrier and you save on labor costs because the labor to apply the polyethylene has been eliminated.

The taping and finishing of the joints of the drywall are accomplished in three phases. In the first phase, joint reinforcement tape is set in joint compound over each joint. A second and wider coat of joint compound is applied after the first has dried. Finally a third, still wider, coat is put on. This process requires at least three days. More time may be needed if the air has a high moisture content and the drying is slow.

Drywall panels are manufactured in sizes of 4 feet by either 8 feet, 10 feet, or 12 feet long. Most work is done using the 4×12 size hung horizontally on the walls and perpendicular to the joists on the ceiling. Although the larger sizes are heavier and more cumbersome, their use will eliminate joints created if the smaller sizes are used.

Except for fire-rated drywall mentioned below, the normal thickness is ½ inch. It offers the best compromise for sound-proofing, fire resistance, rigidity of walls, ease of installation and cost.

If you intend to finish the ceiling by spraying textured material on the gypsum panels, to avoid their sagging, use ⅝-inch ceiling panels if the joists are installed 24 inches OC (the usual case when prefabricated roof trusses are used in the framing). If the ceiling joists are installed 16 inches OC, the ½-inch-thick panel will provide adequate strength to hold the extra weight of the heavy textured finishing material.

For rooms such as baths, kitchens and laundries, a special water-resistant drywall should be used. It is called "green board" because of the green color of the face paper. It is finished in the same manner as standard drywall paneling, but *make sure that the end joints are sealed with water-resistant sealer,* a process often overlooked in installing this type of material. In addition, a cement board is available in 4 foot × 4 foot sheets and makes an excellent waterproof backing for ceramic tile in showers and for tile on the wall at tubs.

Building codes usually require a ⅝-inch-thick fire-resistant drywall panel on those walls adjacent to potential fire hazard areas such as attached garages and furnace rooms. Even if not required by the local code, its use is warranted for the safety gained at very little additional cost.

Fiberboard, a Viable Alternative

An alternative to drywall is fiber-board. It is made from gypsum ore and recycled paper, mainly newsprint. Fiberboard is stronger, easier to install, more fire resistant and controls sound and moisture better than drywall. It is also heavier, harder to score (cut for breaking the board so it will fit) and may cost more than drywall.

Durable, Economical Plaster Veneer

Plaster veneer is available in either a one-coat or two-coat system. Both are applied over a gypsum base or plaster type lathing. Joints are taped with a fiberglass mesh tape and stapled to the ends and the edges of the gypsum before the plaster is put on.

The one-coat system consists of a special finish plaster applied as a thin base coat and then immediately "doubled back" for increased strength. The total thickness of the plaster is about 1/16 inch. The finish is rough like sand and white in color.

The two-coat system consists of the application of a thin base coat 1/16 inch to 3/32 inch, with the immediate addition of a finish coat for a full plaster thickness of ⅛ inch. The texture of the finish can be rough floated or smooth troweled. The color is white.

Both of these plaster systems provide a very hard finish that is much less susceptible to damage than drywall paneling and conventional plaster and with greater strength than the drywall. They can be applied in a matter of two or three days compared to the much longer time to complete conventional plaster.

In comparing the cost of labor, the time to do the job and the finished product, plaster veneer offers an excellent choice for interior wall finishes. If you pick this system, it is very important to make sure that the contractor has the experience and skills to do the job properly. Plaster veneer should not be attempted by amateurs.

Don't Skimp on Closet and Garage Finishes

In some areas of the country it is common practice to finish the interior of garages and closets (assuming a drywall selection) with only one coat of the joint compound instead of the usual three. This small savings is of doubtful value and the outcome is a very poor-looking finish.

Paneling from Plain to Palatial

You can choose from many different varieties of wood paneling, either real or artificial (see Figure 18.1). One line of prefinished paneling even looks like wallpaper. Though paneling has the advantage of low maintenance, it has little flexibility later in changing the decorating scheme of a room.

Paneling should be installed over a base of finished or unfinished drywall to give better soundproofing. If the framing of the wall consists of studs 24 inches OC or if the paneling is thin, it is even more important to apply the paneling over a drywall base to give needed strength.

Paneling requires its own matching trim and material for inside corners, outside corners and crown molding at the juncture of the paneling and the ceiling. The base used at the juncture of the paneling and the floor may also be matching trim or it can be the same baseboard used throughout the house. The paneling supplier usually carries all the trim needed to match.

Paneling is best installed by using adhesives and a few matching nails to hold the panel in place while the adhesive sets. These nails can be found at the paneling supplier.

FIGURE 18.1 Wood Paneling and Trim

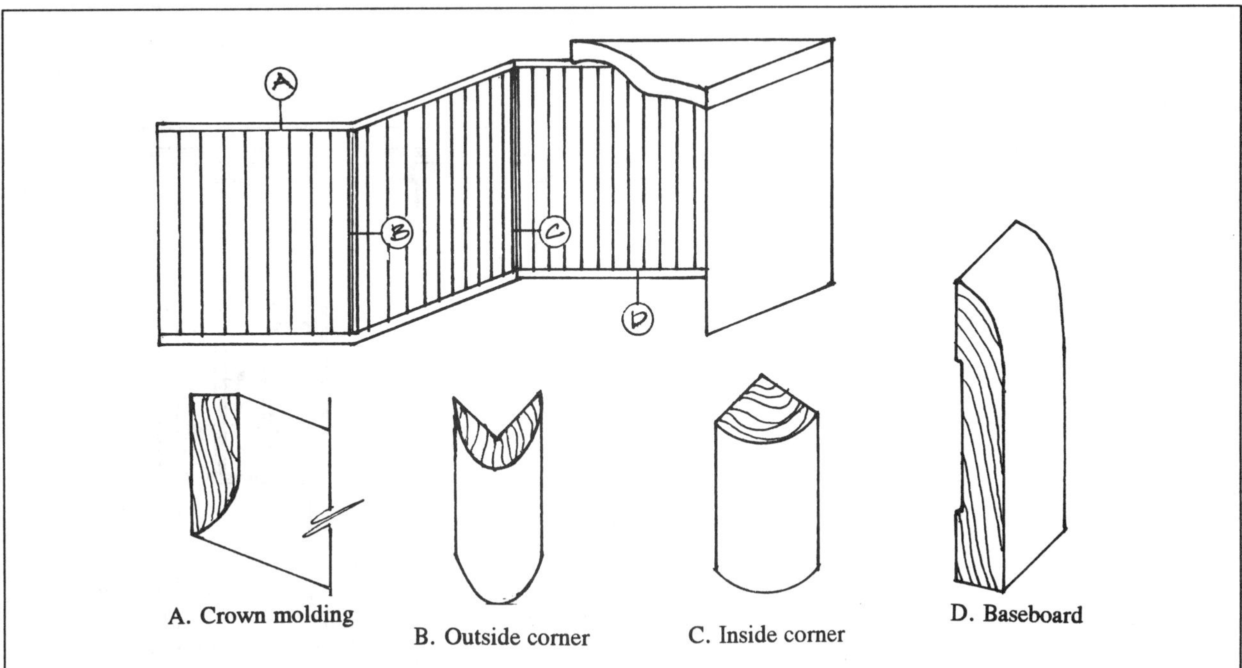

Good Interior Wood Trim Adds Finish

Wood trim gives the interior of the house a finished appearance. Its selection and installation is important because it is one of the items that is constantly in view and thus contributes to the quality of the house (or lack of it, if done poorly).

Figure 18.2 illustrates the various types of interior trim and the application of each.

- *Crown Molding* is applied at the juncture of the ceiling and the walls. It is made in several sizes with the larger ones being used in larger rooms or in rooms with higher-than-standard ceilings (more than 8 feet) or both. Crown molding can also be made up by using two or more pieces of trim to give a more massive appearance.
- *Casing* is the molding applied around the doors and windows to cover the juncture of the door or window frame and wall finish. It is available in several sizes and styles, with the ranch style normally being used in contemporary houses. In addition to casing, the window trim also requires a sill or stool and trim beneath the stool (an apron) or the window may be trimmed with the picture-frame technique where the casing is also used in place of the stool and apron.

FIGURE 18.2 Typical Wood Trim

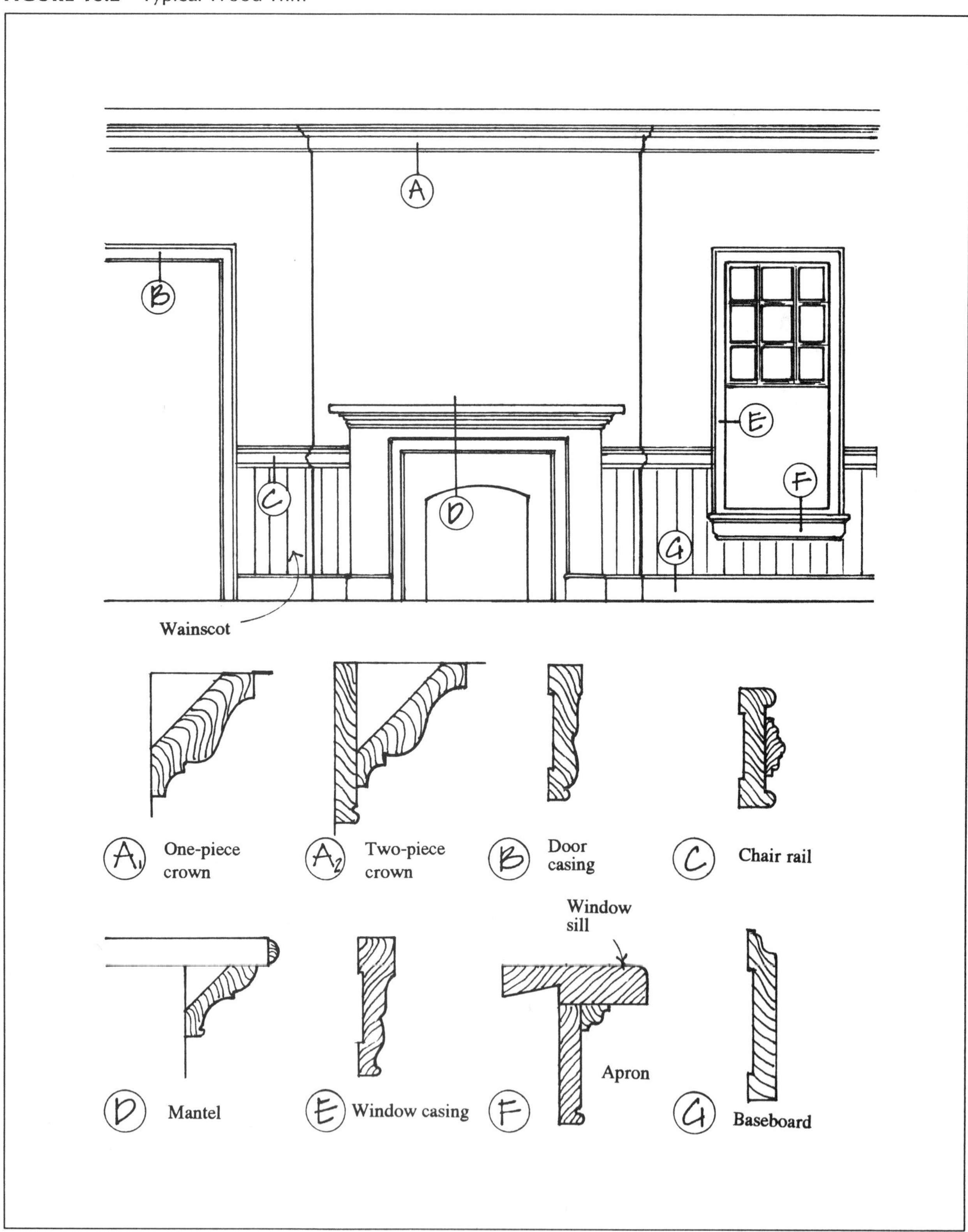

- *Base or Baseboard* trim covers the gap between the floor and the wall finish. Its style is usually the same as the door and window casing but larger in size. Plasterers and drywall finishers will assume that the baseboard is at least 2½ inches high and will leave unfinished that part of the wall that is less than that distance from the floor. If your base is less than 2½ inches, check with the drywall or plaster contractor to ensure that the wall is finished far enough down to the floor so that no unfinished wall will show above the baseboard.
- *Chair Railing* is a decorative trim installed about 32 inches above the finished floor. It can be one- or two-piece trim.
- *Wainscoting* is the application of wood planks with tongue and V-groove, or other similar material, between the baseboard and the chair rail. The vertical rails are installed first and the chair rail and base are applied over the ends of the vertical boards.
- *Shoe Molding* is applied between the floor and the baseboard. It is very flexible and can fit snugly both the floor and the base despite any irregularities of the structure that are always present even in the best of wood construction. Shoe molding is not normally used if the finish floor is carpeting.

Ceramic Tile Is Beautiful and Useful

Ceramic tile is often used on the walls of baths in the form of wainscoting (to a height of about 38 inches to 48 inches) and on the walls and ceilings of showers or over tubs that are a tub/shower combination.

As discussed in Chapter 16, Planning for Your Plumbing, of the two methods of applying tile, the preferred system is the application of the tile in a bed of cement over metal lathing that is nailed to the studs.

Costing

You may have a bit more work to do when costing the interior finishing:

- Most plastering and drywall contractors prefer that the owner/general contractor furnish the plaster lathing, drywall paneling and plaster material, with the contractor furnishing the labor and all other material such as adhesive, joint compound, etc. Ask one of the contractors or the supplier to compute the number of sheets of drywall or plaster lathing needed.

- The cost of paneling is provided by the supplier, with the trim crew doing the labor. Do not forget the special trim material to match the paneling.
- The cost of the interior wood trim is computed by the supplier. The labor cost is provided by the trim carpentry crew.
- The cost of all material and labor for the ceramic tile is included in the tile contractor's bid. Be sure the contractor understands the method of tile application you want.

Management

Interior finishing requires care to coordinate supplies and labor, especially the following:

- As mentioned in Chapter 7, Framing Your Project, you may need to remove or delay the installation of a window so that the drywall or plaster lathing can be put into the house with the least additional labor for spreading it around the rooms. Ask the supplier to visit the job site and give you suggestions as to the best method to use.
- Be certain that if the drywall is moved into the house before the completion of all required inspections (framing and electrical, plumbing and heating rough-in), the material does not block the view of the inspectors. Or, better yet, don't order the drywall or lathing delivered until all inspections have been completed.
- Do not schedule any other work inside the house until the drywall or plaster work has been completed.
- Wood paneling should be installed after the plaster or drywall work has been finished. It is part of the trim carpentry job.
- If you are not sure as to exactly what features of trim work you want other than the required window and door casing and the base molding, ask the trim carpenter to show you a sample of chair rail, crown molding or features you might like.
- If you have long runs of trim, for example in crown molding, that require splicing, the spliced joint should be cut on an angle and glued as well as nailed. Corner joints should be made so that the wood can expand and contract without resulting in the parting of the joint in clear view. Most trim carpenters will know how to use the coping saw to accomplish this.
- One of the first jobs the trim crew will do is to hang the interior doors. Make certain that this material (including hardware: hinges, knobs, etc.) as well as the rest of the trim material is on hand at the proper time so that once the trim carpentry begins,

the crew can work straight through with no stops due to your failure to order the material on time.

- Your doors can be prehung or not. Because prehung doors require less labor by the trim carpenters, make sure that this point is listed in your bidding information.
- The trim job includes the installation of towel racks, medicine chests, paper holders and other similar items. Be sure that they are on hand.
- Check your plans carefully to be certain that the doors of the medicine cabinets swing properly, that is, left-hand or right-hand hinge, depending on placement of the cabinet.

■ — CHAPTER 19 — ■

Choosing Your Cabinets

Manufacturing Methods Help Set Quality and Cost

Most cabinets are manufactured in one of three ways:

1. *Custom* made in a local cabinet shop according to your exact plans. This method offers almost unlimited selection as to material, design and finish. These cabinets are also the most expensive. If your needs are unusual, this may be your best choice. If possible, get bids from several cabinetmakers before making your final selection.
2. *Factory* made to the specifications of the lines the factory carries. Your choices are limited in the selection of design, material and finish by these standard factory lines. Cabinets are made up in advance and stocked by the factory or by outlets for the factory. Costs range from very expensive to least expensive of any line depending on the individual manufacturer.
3. *Custom factory* made at a centralized plant. Your cabinets are not built until your order has been received by the plant. You can expect a much greater choice in design, material and finish than in most factory-made cabinets. Prices are usually less than custom-made cabinets and more than the medium and lower lines of the factory-made cabinet.

Sources of Cabinets To Fit Your Needs

The cabinet store usually offers the greatest selection of cabinets. Because this supplier usually has contacts with several factory lines, including custom factory, and connections with one or more custom cabinet shops, he therefore can supply the entire gamut of cabinet selection. This supplier is usually skilled in offering good advice as to the design of your kitchen.

The custom-cabinet shop can supply cabinets made in its shop built to your specifications. Some of these shops may also have sidelines for various types of factory cabinets.

The building supply store usually sells the factory-made cabinet, with you providing the installation. Most carpenters who are qualified for interior trim work are also capable of installing cabinets and countertops. If you buy cabinets from a supplier who does not install them, be certain that your trim carpenter has the experience to do so and that the cost of this labor is included in the bid.

Choose from Many Cabinet Finishes

Unfinished wood cabinets can be bought at a very good price. Most painters can do a good job of finishing these cabinets either before or after installation. Check their experience before selecting this option.

Stained wood cabinets are finished at the shop or factory in an environment that ensures an excellent application and curing of the finish. There are many choices of stains.

Painted wood cabinets can be finished at the factory or finished on the job. If color in the kitchen is important, this may be your best choice.

Plastic laminate cabinets are made of wood or wood products and then covered with a plastic laminate. In some cases, the laminate is cemented to the inside and outside of the cabinet; in others, only the door (all sides) and the front of the cabinet are covered and the interior is painted. The plastic laminate offers a wide variety of colors and patterns and is easily cleaned.

With some paneled-door cabinets, the panels are removable and reversible with different finishes on each side.

Do You Want Soffits above Your Cabinets?

One question often arises: Should kitchen cabinets run all the way up to the ceiling? That top foot of the normal 8-foot ceiling usually requires some sort of stool or ladder to reach, but it is additional storage space that comes in handy for those seldom-used items.

FIGURE 19.1 Wall-Hung Kitchen Cabinets

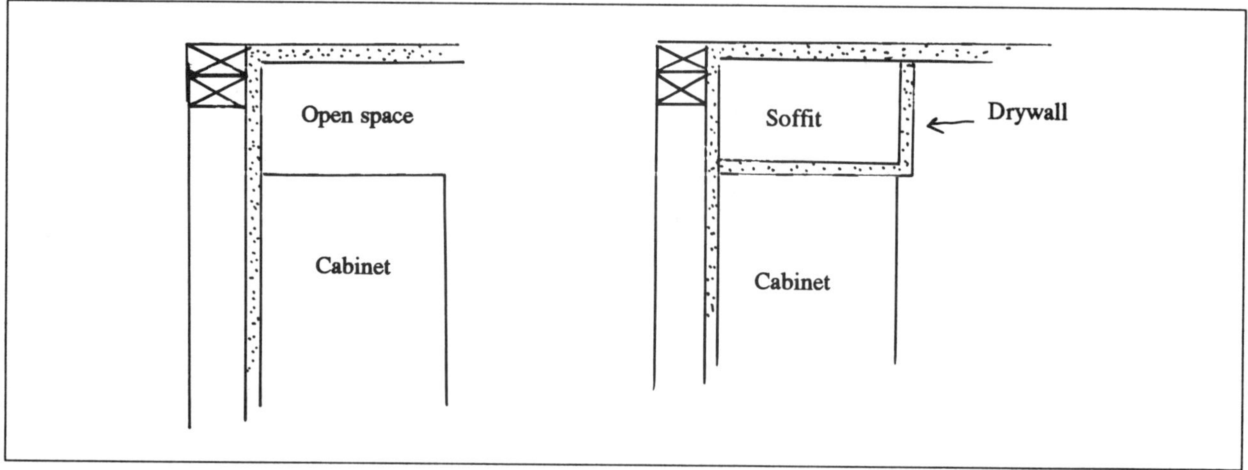

If you have selected the factory-made cabinet, you may not have any choice in wall cabinet height because most of them are made only at the size that requires a 1-foot soffit down from the ceiling. The space also may be left open.

The decision about the soffit for kitchen cabinets must be made before the completion of the framing so that the carpenters can install the 2×4s needed to hang the drywall and secure the wall cabinets if soffits are required.

Bathroom Vanities Present One Problem

Bath vanities are usually supplied by the same source as the kitchen cabinets. The finish, material and color is simply a matter of personal choice and need not be the same as the kitchen cabinets.

The normal height of an installed vanity with top is about 30 inches to 32 inches. This is low for a tall person. Consider ordering your vanities so that the height fits the user. If your vanities are factory built with only one choice of height, the trim carpenter can build a platform to mount the vanity to give the desired height.

Cabinet Countertops Require More Choices

Plastic laminate tops are available in two choices—custom and postformed (see Figure 19.2).

The custom-made top has the advantage of greater flexibility in shape and form. It has a seam (between the back splash and the top) that is difficult to keep clean. It has a seam in front that is exposed to

FIGURE 19.2 Countertops

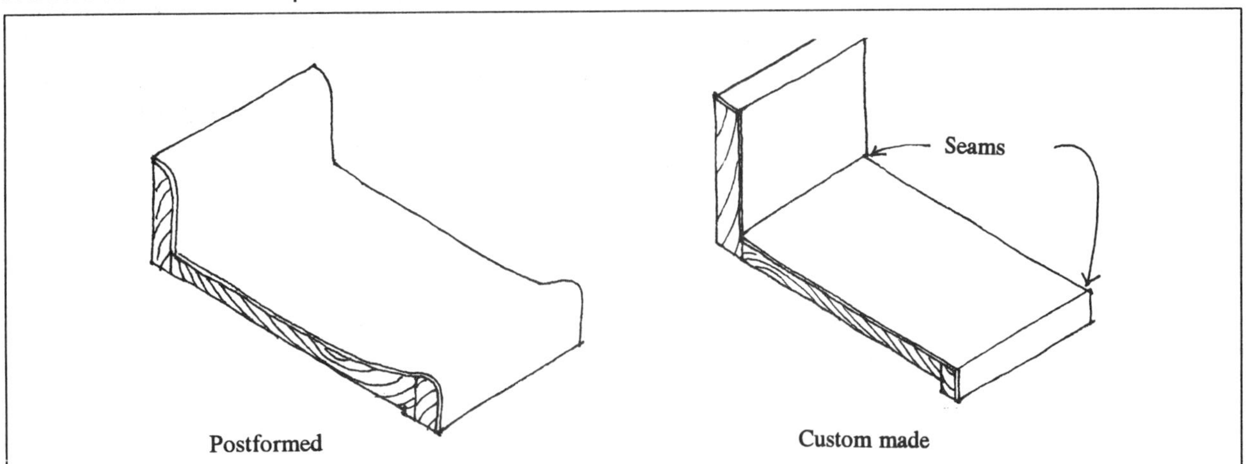

wear and, like all laminate seams, may part when the cement fails. A well-made top with proper care, however, should last 20 or more years.

The postformed top is molded under high pressure by machinery especially designed for this process. The result is a rounded-back joint with no seam that is easy to clean and has a lip on the front, also without seam, that will prevent liquid spills from falling on the floor. The laminate used in the manufacture of this top is usually thinner than that used for the custom top so that it will bend and adhere properly to the base.

Solid surfacing material tops such as Corian, Nevamar, Surrell®, Fountain Head®, and Avonite®, with or without integrated sinks, make excellent kitchen and vanity countertops. They are long wearing, easy to install and go well with almost any cabinet. They are more expensive than the laminate top, and the choice of color is limited.

Ceramic-tile countertops used to be very popular some time ago. In recent years they were largely replaced by the plastic laminate that offered a smoother top without the problem of cleaning the grouted joints. Lately, the ceramic top is regaining popularity. Many more choices of color, texture and shape of tile are available today than 20 or 30 years ago.

Other Cabinet Work

If your house plans contain other cabinet work, such as bookcases, you can have this work done by the same source as your kitchen cabinets and bath vanities, or you can have it done on the job by the trim carpenters and finished by the painter. Your choice should depend on the complexity of this additional cabinet work. Most trim carpenters are perfectly capable of building good-looking bookcases and most painters are capable of a good finishing job. Question the trim carpenters about what type of wood they prefer to work with. Inquire about their experience and ask to see some of their work. Generally, this approach to cabinets is less expensive than the custom-made or the factory cabinet.

Costing

If you select cabinets through a custom-cabinetmaker or a cabinet store, either should furnish a complete bid including cabinets, tops and the labor to install them.

If you are buying your cabinets from a building supply store or some other source that does not provide installation, the cost of the materials is provided by the supplier and the labor cost by an installer such as the trim crew.

Management

Remember the following:

- Order your cabinets early. Some suppliers take two months or more to deliver them. When you decide on your cabinet source, ask how long it will take and then add another month. Schedule your order based on this figure.
- Cabinets with the countertops must be installed before the plumbing, electrical and trim work can be completed.
- Vinyl floor covering should be installed after the kitchen cabinets and the bath vanities are in place. See Chapter 20, Looking at Flooring Options, for further details.
- One of the most prevalent problems with cabinet work is warpage of the doors. To lessen the chances of this occurring, avoid selecting cabinets whose doors are made with thin plywood (¼ inch or less) let into a ¾-inch wood frame.

■ CHAPTER 20 ■

Looking at Flooring Options

■ WOOD IS A NATURAL FOR FLOORING

The most popular wood flooring is white or red oak. These are hard woods with excellent wearing qualities. The standard type comes in widths of 2¼ inch and in random lengths. To achieve a more custom look, oak flooring can also be supplied in random widths with or without a distinct V-groove between the planks. If exposed large-headed nails are driven at the ends (either two or three depending on the width of the particular plank), a very colonial look can be obtained (see Figure 20.1).

FIGURE 20.1 Random-Width Wood Flooring with V-Groove and Boat Nails

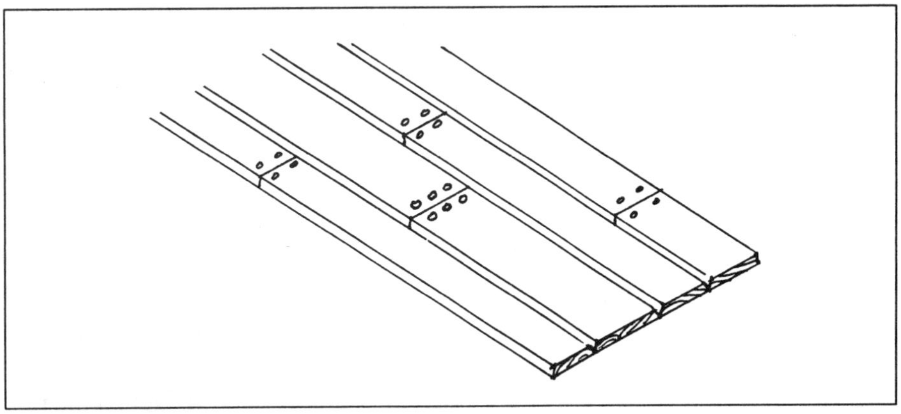

FIGURE 20.2 Wood Parquet Flooring

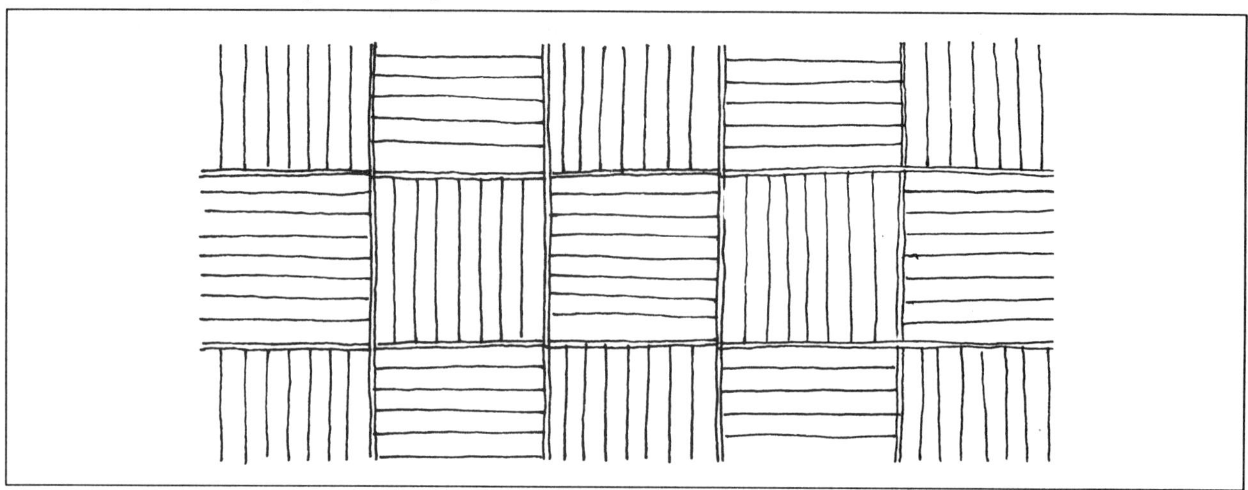

One of the best nails to use for this purpose is the large-headed heavily galvanized nail used by boat yards. When applied to the flooring, this nail gives the appearance of being old and handmade. When driven flush with the top of the flooring, the soft galvanizing permits the use of sanding machines to finish the floor without ripping the sandpaper. In addition to the exposed nailing at the end of each plank, the usual blind nailing along the tongue side into each floor joist should be done.

Pine can also be used for flooring material in standard or random widths. It is a softer wood than oak and will show wear before the oak. It has a beautiful grain and takes staining well.

All the above wood flooring is normally applied over the plywood subfloor and nailed to the floor joists.

Parquet flooring consists of small pieces of wood combined into a square tile (see Figure 20.2). Some parquet flooring is very thin and requires an underlayment of particleboard over the subfloor. Parquet is more difficult to finish because all sanding must be done with fine paper in order not to make large scratches across the grain.

Prefinished Wood Flooring Simplifies Installation

There are many different kinds and styles of prefinished wood, flooring from plank to parquet. The finishes are excellent and generally long lasting. Follow the manufacturer's instructions for installing.

New Wood Floor Finishing Eases Care

The most widespread finishing system for wood floors consists of filling (if required by the type of wood), sanding and applying a hard coating such as polyurethane. If staining is desired, it is applied before the polyurethane. Polyurethane is made with either a matte (soft shine) or hard shiny finish. Both do an excellent job; the choice is one of personal preference.

In addition to giving floors a pleasing look, polyurethane requires no waxing, but the finish will eventually have to be renewed.

Another type of floor finish is the use of commercial penetrating resins or oils that are soaked up by the wood. This finish does not cover the wood with a hard film. Its principal advantage is that you can refinish the floor by merely adding additional penetrating resin without removing the original coating.

■ CARPETING OFFERS MANY CHOICES

Carpet Construction Virtually all residential carpets are tufted. Yarn loops are inserted into a backing material forming the carpet pile. If the carpet is to be cut pile (the most popular), the tips of the loops are sheared off to produce a smooth finish. If the carpet is to be loop pile, the loops are not sheared.

Quality and Performance The carpet should be warranted against stains, dirt, static and wear.

A dense, thick pile wears longer, resists crushing and matting better, and retains texture longer in heavy use. Compare density by bending two carpet samples as they would be bent over a stair tread. The higher-density carpet will show more pile fiber and less backing material. In carpets of equal density, the one with the higher or the heavier pile will perform best. *In general, the deeper and denser the pile, the better the carpet will perform.*

Carpet Cushion Properly installed, it will add 17 percent to 50 percent to the carpet's useful life. A medium-thick pad is the best place to start. Thin pads can tear, wear or disintegrate too quickly. Ultra-thick pads can be too soft for comfortable walking and balance.

Carpet Styles Are Bountiful

- *Velvets,* most elegant, give an ultra-smooth sweep of rich color.

- *Saxonies* or *Plushes* are not as formal as velvets but are easier to live with.
- *Textured Saxonies* are the most casual and rugged of pile carpets.
- *Level loops* have loops that are easily visible; the style blends with any decor.
- *Multilevel loops* have a carved pattern and more random effect.
- *Cut-and-loop styles* or *traceries* have a cut pile and loop pile combination that offers an infinite variety of effects.

Carpet Color Selection Can Create a Specific Mood

- Light color carpets will make the room seem larger, particularly if the walls are white or a light tint of the carpet color.
- In cold, snowy climates red, yellow and brown carpets can warm up north-facing rooms.
- In warm climates, blue, green or violet carpets can be used to "cool off" south-facing rooms.
- Warm reds and oranges create an active atmosphere that is great for family rooms.
- Cooler blues and greens generate a tranquil setting for bedrooms and other quiet areas.

Installation Can Influence Carpet Life

Carpeting should be installed over underlayment nailed to the subfloor, with at least one layer of building paper in between the underlayment and the subfloor. If the room has little moisture, the underlayment can be ⅝-inch-thick particleboard, an inexpensive material. If the carpeting is installed in a bathroom or kitchen, however, the underlayment should be ⅝-inch thick plywood underlayment. This material is more expensive than the particleboard but will usually not be affected by normal amounts of moisture found in kitchens and baths. Particleboard, on the other hand, tends to absorb moisture, swell and disintegrate.

If carpet is to be installed over a concrete floor, first lay down a cover of high-density fiberboard (usually ½ inch thick), followed by the carpet padding, then the carpet. This system will provide a warmer, softer floor with better personal comfort.

VINYL TILE IS VERSATILE

Vinyl tile and sheet material make a fine floor covering for baths, kitchens, sun rooms or any other room for that matter. The choices in pattern, color and quality are many.

This material should be installed over plywood underlayment. Most manufacturers will void their warranty if it is laid over particleboard.

CONSIDER CERAMIC TILE, EARTHSTONE, SLATE AND STONE

All of these materials make excellent flooring. They will show practically no wear and require little maintenance. For the best results, they should be laid in cement mortar and, with the exception of bathroom floors, they should be laid over a dropped subfloor (see Chapter 6, Foundations).

Slate and stone can be very heavy depending on the size and thickness selected. For these heavier materials, the floor joists in the area should be installed 12 inches OC to give more strength.

BRICK IS OFTEN OVERLOOKED

Brick makes an excellent floor and can be laid over concrete or a wood subfloor with mortared or unmortared joints. Use the special brick made for this purpose.

Remember that brick is a heavy material, so install the floor joists 12 inches OC in that area.

Most brick is porous and should be sealed. Use a phenolic-type concrete sealer and apply at least two coats. If the brick has been installed with mortared joints, be sure that the material is completely dry before applying the sealer. Drying time can be as long as eight weeks.

COSTING

In the bidding process for wood flooring, it is best to ask the contractor to provide all material and labor. Although many building supply houses sell wood flooring material, you will simplify the management task if you have the contractor supply all material. If you feel that you can get the job done at less cost by buying your own flooring, then ask for bids with two prices, one with the contractor supplying all materials and labor, and the other with the owner providing the flooring and the contractor all other material and labor. Then select the method that is more advantageous to you.

The entire cost of carpeting is provided by the contractor in his bid. It is best if the bid is based on actual measurements from the blueprint rather than a statement of the required number of square yards of area to be covered.

The entire cost of the vinyl floor covering should also be provided in the bid from the contractor, who will need an exact drawing of the area, particularly if the specifications call for sheet material rather than square tiles. Most vinyl sheet material is manufactured in rolls 6 feet and 12 feet wide. The bidding contractors will select the widths that best fit your plan.

Unlike carpeting, vinyl sheet material cannot be cut and patched without creating undesirable seams and pattern mismatches. Therefore in most cases, there will be waste that the owner must expect to pay for. For example, in a room that is 12 feet × 16 feet, a piece of vinyl 12 feet by 16 feet will do the job nicely with practically no waste. In a room 10 feet wide × 16 feet long the contractor must still supply a piece of sheet vinyl 12 feet × 16 feet and charge the owner for the full amount, even though the room is not that big.

The cost of all labor and material for ceramic tile, slate, earthstone, stone and brick should be provided in the contractor's bid.

With your ceramic-tile floors, specify whether or not you want tile or wood baseboards. Either can be used. It is a matter of personal choice, with the tile having the advantage of low maintenance. The wood base gives a more traditional touch and, because painting or staining is required, offers the option of changing the color from time to time. The ceramic tile contractor will furnish all material and labor but will expect you to furnish and have installed any wood base.

■ MANAGEMENT

Because flooring plays such an important part in the enjoyment and ease of maintenance of a house, pay attention to the following when installing it:

- Unfinished wood flooring can be installed before or after the drywall or plaster. Trim work, plumbing, heating and cabinet work cannot be completed until the wood flooring has been installed.
- Protect prefinished flooring immediately after it has been laid. Heavy canvas does a good job.
- Wood floors should be finished only after all other interior work has been completed (with the exception of laying carpeting).

During the finishing process and for three or four days thereafter, only the floor finishers should be permitted inside the house. Activity stirs up dust and other particles in the air that may settle in the wet finish and ruin it.

- After the floor finish has completely dried, protect it by laying flint paper or some similar material on those areas where people will walk.
- The laying of the carpeting is usually the last job to be done. It is the owner/general contractor's responsibility to have the underlayment down (by the carpentry crew) before the carpeting is installed.
- In all areas where a wood baseboard with wood shoe molding is part of the trim, it is best to lay the flooring first, then apply the trim. One exception to this rule is carpeting. The carpet is laid after the baseboard is installed, and the carpet layer draws it up to the baseboard with special equipment. Shoe molding is generally not used with carpet.
- If baseboard heating units, such as baseboard electric heat or baseboard radiators for hot water heating systems, are in those rooms in which carpeting is to be installed, the radiator element should be raised higher on the wall so that the carpet material does not interfere with the free flow of air up under the element and out through the top.
- Floor underlayment and wood flooring (unfinished) should be installed before the base cabinets.

CHAPTER 21

Painting and Decorating

EMPHASIZE QUALITY—BOTH MATERIALS AND LABOR

Because painting and decorating produce results that you will be looking at for many years, it is most important that these results be good ones. Pick quality materials and the best labor. The paint will last longer and look better throughout its life.

To make sure you use quality materials, visit one of your local paint suppliers and pick out the top of the line for each painting task. Use this paint designation in your specifications, indicating that either this paint or its equal must be used. The brand of paint need not be a national one, because many excellent paints are made at local factories. But if you do use a local paint, be sure that it is fine quality. The major cost of the total paint job is the labor. It just doesn't make any sense to pay for good labor and use a mediocre paint.

EXTERIOR PAINTING PROTECTS AND BEAUTIFIES

Your choices of paint are:

- Alkyd oil-base paint has been the standard house paint for many years. It is now being strongly challenged by the water-based paints. Alkyd paint will do an excellent job on wood and metal and offers unlimited choices of color.

- Acrylic latex or water-based paints are available in an unlimited range of colors.
- Stain is available as water- and oil-based and as semitransparent or acrylic-latex solid formulas.

In making your selection, consider the following:

- Acrylic latex paint is less costly than oil-based paint, lasts almost as long, is easier to apply and clean up and its labor costs should be lower.
- Both alkyd-oil and acrylic-latex paint require a primer over bare wood. Although an oil-based primer is best, an acrylic-latex primer is a good second choice.
- If you live in a mildew-prone area, antimildew additives can be put in both acrylic-latex and alkyd-oil paint. Most quality paints have some mildew fighter already mixed in.
- A three-coat system (primer plus two additional coats) will last almost twice as long as a two-coat system (primer and one additional coat).
- From the standpoint of cost alone, the three-coat system is the logical choice the first time the material is painted.
- If poor-quality paint is used on areas above brick or other non-painted material, chalking of the paint down over the brick may occur and spoil its appearance. Select a top-quality paint to prevent chalking. Some quality paints are purposely formulated to scale off some of the top layer so that the remaining paint maintains its bright color. These paints should also not be used above unpainted brick and similar surfaces.
- If exposure of the wood grain is important, use a semitransparent stain. The number of coats of the stain depends on the desired color.
- Exterior stains do not last as long as paint and should never be clear coated because the sun will erode the clear material that cannot block the sun's ultraviolet rays.

Back Priming Is Worth the Effort

All wood exposed to the weather should be back primed to reduce warping and cupping of the wood and to prolong its life. The painter should apply on the *nonexposed side of the wood* one coat of the same primer to be used on the exposed side. Don't forget the exposed ends of butt joints in the siding and trim.

Caulking Is Mandatory

Caulking, a job normally done by the painting contractor, is required regardless of which paint or stain is used. Caulking is applied at all joints in the exterior painted wood surface to seal around the trim of windows and doors, the joints where the lap siding abuts the corner boards and so forth. Latex caulking is one of the best choices for house painting considering cost, durability and ease of application. While caulking with silicone added lasts longer, it is more expensive.

How To Fight Mildew

Mildew lives in the environment and will normally flourish in areas that are warm, humid and shady, areas encompassing a large part of the country. No paint or stain can be made completely mildew proof, but additives can be put into the paint to retard the development of mildew. For this reason, it is important to prime and paint the exterior of the house as soon as possible so that mildew cannot form on the bare wood or between the coats of paint or stain.

■ CHOOSE INTERIOR PAINTS WISELY

Select a flat or satin finish latex paint for walls and ceilings, except in baths and kitchens, where a gloss or semigloss enamel paint should be used for easier cleaning. The enamel paint also gives better protection to the drywall or plaster.

Use an oil-based paint to prime wood trim. For first-time painting, use a good-quality primer for both plaster and gypsum board walls and wood trim.

For the interior penetrating stains, only one coat is usually necessary. Additional coats may be applied, however, to get the desired depth of color. Apply a clear sealer over the last coat for easier cleaning.

Bare wood trim should be painted with an enamel paint or stained. Acrylic latex is a good second choice if the wood is primed with an oil-based primer.

In selecting colors for the interior, consider the following:

- Dark colors make a room seem smaller but give a more dramatic appearance.
- To create a more restful room, use pastels.
- A white or light-colored ceiling gives the impression of height, whereas a dark color appears to lower the ceiling.

SPECIAL CEILING FINISHES

Two methods for finishing ceilings (or walls, too) are popular. One is for the drywall finisher to cover the entire ceiling with a coat of joint compound and then go over it with a broom or similar device putting a swirling pattern into the still-wet compound. The other method is for the painter to spray the ceiling with heavily textured paint material.

TIPS FOR LOVERS OF WALLPAPER AND WALLCOVERING

If you select wallpaper or wallcovering for the final finish on some of your walls, here are some tips:

- For baths or kitchens, choose a vinyl or vinyl-coated wallcovering that can be scrubbed.
- Behind the stove, use a fabric-backed-vinyl paper, the toughest kind.
- Using strippable wallpaper will facilitate its removal if you redecorate in the future.
- If you want to make the room seem taller, select a vertical stripe for the wallpaper pattern.
- If you want to make the room seem larger, select a pattern with small figures and light colors with large amounts of clear space.
- Some wallpapers are water or moisture resistant. If you select one that is not, however, you can use a wallpaper sealer on it after it has been installed and the paste has dried. Sealers can change the color of the wallpaper, so test a sample before sealing the entire wall.
- Leftover wallpaper can be cut to the proper size and used to cover switch plates or line drawers and cabinet shelves.
- For walls that are untreated drywall, plaster or plaster veneer, sizing should be applied before hanging the wallcovering. Without this sizing, the paper may not adhere properly to the wall. In addition, without sizing, when redecorating in the future, the paper will be difficult to remove and the drywall or plaster may be damaged.

COSTING

The cost of the painting, both labor and material, should be included in the bid of the painting contractor.

Cost of the wallpaper and mounting material is provided by the supplier. Have the supplier compute the amount of paper needed so you are assured of not running short because you forgot to allow for pattern matching and other waste. The labor for installation may be provided by the supplier or it may be part of the painter's bid. Many painters hang wallpaper.

MANAGEMENT

Even if you are planning to do some of the painting and decorating yourself, remember the following:

- Schedule the painter to back prime all exterior wood before it is applied to the framing.
- Apply the paint to the exterior of the house as soon as the job can be done, particularly if you live in a mildew-prone area.
- Make certain that the top and bottom edge of all doors, particularly the exterior doors, are painted as fully as other areas. Most door manufacturers will void their warranty if this is not done.
- If your windows require painting, check to see that the seam between the glass pane and the wood frame has been sealed with paint. There should be a small strip of paint actually on the glass. The same procedure applies to wood doors that have glass inserts.
- Your paint contractor may want to spray the interior walls and ceilings with the prime coat before the wood trim is installed and after the drywall has been finished and dried. This is a normal and efficient practice and should save on labor costs.
- Complete the interior painting or staining of a room before hanging the wallpaper or wallcovering.
- Before accepting the color selection for exterior paint or stain, have the painter show you samples on scraps of the exterior wood material. For interior walls, have him show you samples on a small section of the wall or on pieces of drywall scrap.
- If you select some wallpaper or wallcovering, be sure to order more than you will need for the initial hanging. This will give you some extra to make repairs to the wallpaper later should the need arise. Many wallpaper designs are often taken out of production without notice and are not available later.

■ ═ CHAPTER 22 ═ ■

The Finishing Touches

Landscaping Not Only Beautifies, It Protects

Landscaping serves two purposes: it drains water away from the foundation and beautifies the lot. As a minimum, landscaping should include the final grading so that the drainage is accomplished, and then the grade should be stabilized by planting grass or other ground cover that will prevent water and wind erosion. Usually, a layer of straw spread over the area will minimize erosion until the ground cover has grown enough to do the job. If the grading and grass planting is performed by a contractor, there should be a clear understanding of his responsibility for repairs of damage due to washout.

The completion of the landscaping is a matter of personal choice. You may elect to have the job done by a professional nursery, most of whom will provide you with a recommended plan. This is the most expensive option, but if you need professional help, it is usually worth the additional cost. Most nurseries will guarantee the survival of their plants. You may also decide to do your own planting by buying plants and providing the labor. Under these circumstances, however, the plant suppliers will probably not guarantee their products.

Garage Doors Need Special Attention

Because garage doors are a complex part of your house requiring a special skill for proper installation, you should have a contractor who specializes in this work provide both the labor and the material. If your

FIGURE 22.1 Deck Construction

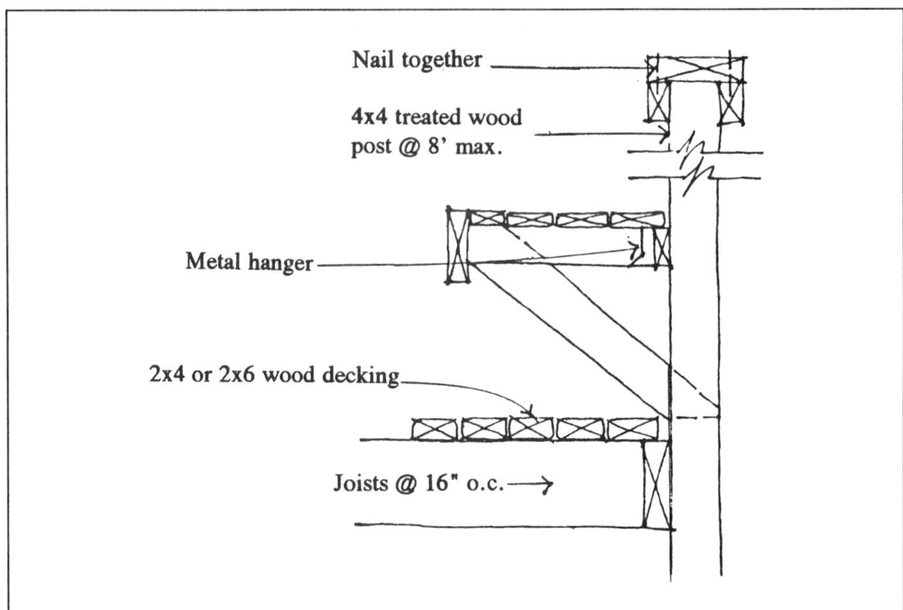

plans include radio-controlled doors, the professional approach becomes even more important.

The overhead garage door is the most popular primarily because it is readily adaptable to radio-controlled electric-door openers. If your plans include two single doors (each about 8 feet wide), an electronic door control system with two frequencies is preferable so that each door can be controlled separately.

Build Decks To Last

Wood decks should be built with lumber that can withstand the rigors of constant exposure to the weather. Redwood, cypress and cedar are all excellent selections but are expensive. Salt-treated southern yellow pine is also an excellent lumber for decks and is less expensive. Be sure to order grades of salt treatment labeled .25CCA for lumber to be used above the finished ground level and .40CCA if it is to be used in contact with the ground.

Southern yellow pine has a greater tendency than most other lumber to warp when exposed to the sun. To compensate for this tendency, design your horizontal railings as indicated in Figure 22.1. Nailing the two pieces perpendicular as shown will reduce warping. In addition, warping will be reduced if the railing spans are less than 8 feet. Benches add to the stability of the structure and improve the usefulness of the deck.

FIGURE 22.2 Railing Installation

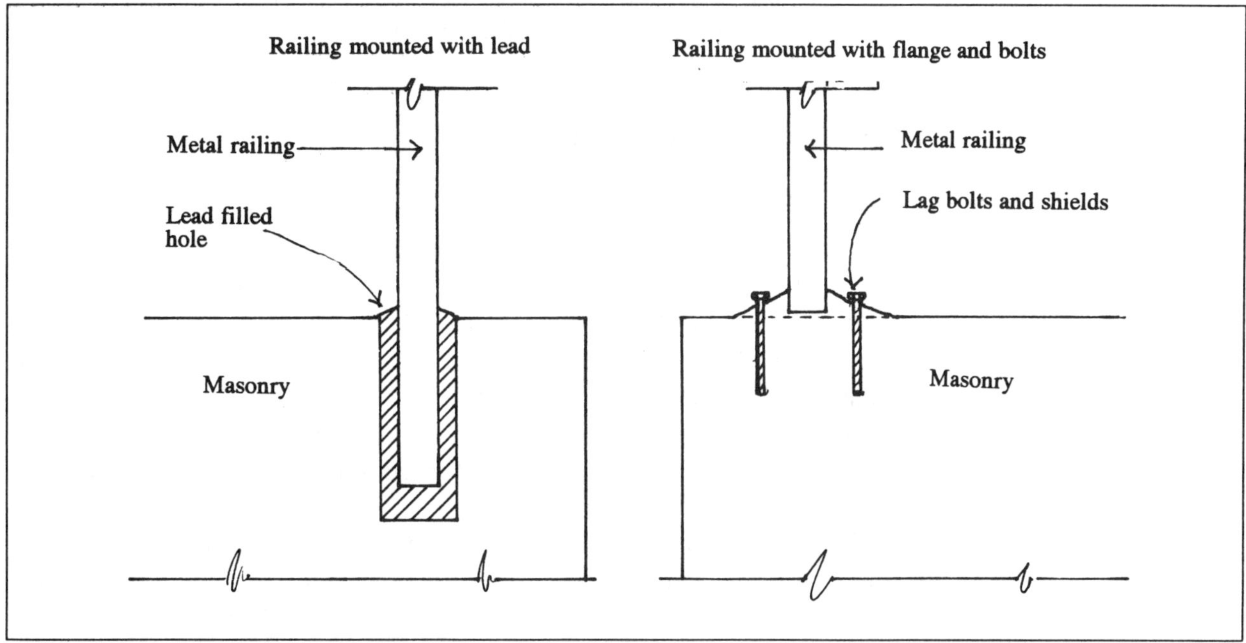

Use *hot-dipped* galvanized nails or aluminum nails for the deck construction. Other types will begin rusting soon after the structure has been completed.

Local Code May Require Metal Railing

If your plans include metal (usually steel or aluminum) railing on the front steps or elsewhere, you can buy the railing already built and have it installed or you can contract with a firm specializing in this work and have them design and install the railing.

Check your local building code for the railing requirement. Even though your plans may not include a railing, the code may require it, especially if the grade of your lot has created higher outdoor steps than the original plan indicated. This situation often occurs if the plans were not specifically designed for your lot.

The main problem with metal railing is proper installation. Two methods are illustrated in Figure 22.2. The best method installs the vertical pieces of railing down into the brick or concrete in a large hole that is filled with molten lead. This method gives the railing the strength to withstand the pushing and pulling it will have to undergo in normal use.

A second method is to install the railing with bolts especially made for masonry and concrete (there are several varieties). They should extend into the masonry at least 2½ inches.

Plan for Three Major Cleanups

There will be occasions during the construction period when you will have to do major cleanups of the area. Plan for at least three. The first will be needed after the framing, exterior trim and siding have been completed and the shingles installed. The second will be after the drywall or plaster has been finished. And the third is when the house is basically completed but before the final grading is done. Many of the wood scraps will be useful to you in the future for fireplace kindling or wood working. If you can find a storage space that does not interfere with the progress of the construction, save the wood scraps. *Do not use scraps of treated lumber in your fireplace or stove.* The chromate copper arsenate (CCA) preservative gives off poisonous fumes when burned, possibly causing cramps, headaches, earaches, diarrhea, rashes and other disease.

To get these cleanup jobs done, find a worker with a truck to do the work and haul the debris to the nearest dump. Remember to avoid paying wages and getting involved in a lot of extra paperwork. Have a contract for a fixed price for each cleanup.

Crews can also be found to clean the inside of the house including bathrooms and kitchen, to scrape off windows, and to do other chores that should be done before moving in.

Costing

Costs for the finishing touches can get out of hand surprisingly fast so watch them all carefully, including these:

- The costs of labor and materials for landscaping are provided by the contractor plus whatever plants you buy yourself.
- Labor and materials for the garage door are in the contractor's bid.
- The cost of the material for wood decking should be given by the lumber supplier; the labor cost should be included in the carpentry bid.
- Metal railing costs are provided by the contractor. Or, if you buy the railing, the material costs are given to you by the supplier, with the labor by whomever is to install them.

- Cleanup costs should be provided by the person with whom you have made arrangements to do the job.

Management

Management of the final touches includes at least the following:

- Final grading and landscaping may reveal construction debris such as pieces of masonry and wood that should be removed from the lot. Make sure that all loose wood has been removed from the crawl space, particularly if you are located in a termite-prone area.
- Contact the garage door installer to determine what framing features he would like to have completed before he installs the door. Have this job done by the carpentry crew before they leave.
- Have the garage door installed early to help secure the structure and to give you protected space to temporarily store other building materials such as interior trim and cabinets. The garage floor should be poured before the door is installed.
- Before the garage floor is poured, check the forms to ensure that the floor is exactly level at the line where the bottom of the garage door will rest so there will be a good seal at this point.
- Final grading should be completed before the deck is installed, particularly if the deck is large. If this is not done, it will force the landscaper to use hand methods under the deck and thus increase your costs.

■ ═ CHAPTER 23 ═ ■

House Expansion Possibilities

This chapter discusses construction techniques used when expanding an existing house, not when building an all-new one. The reader is assumed to be familiar with all of the chapters that came before and the appendixes that follow.

Before going ahead with plans for house expansion:

- Determine whether or not your lot can accommodate the size of the expansion and remain within the setback lines established by the local government.
- If your present plumbing system uses a septic tank and drain field and your expansion includes additional plumbing with an increase in the sewage, have a professional contractor check your system to make sure it can handle the additional load. In some cases, a larger tank and/or drain field may be necessary, requiring additional space on the lot.
- Make sure your plans have been approved by local architectural review boards, if required.

In many cases of house expansion, it is more difficult to arrive at a practical, well-done plan than in a completely new construction. For this reason, during the planning phase, it is usually wise and less expensive in the long run to get professional help, such as an architect, at least on an hourly consultant basis.

FIGURE 23.1 Expanding Right or Left

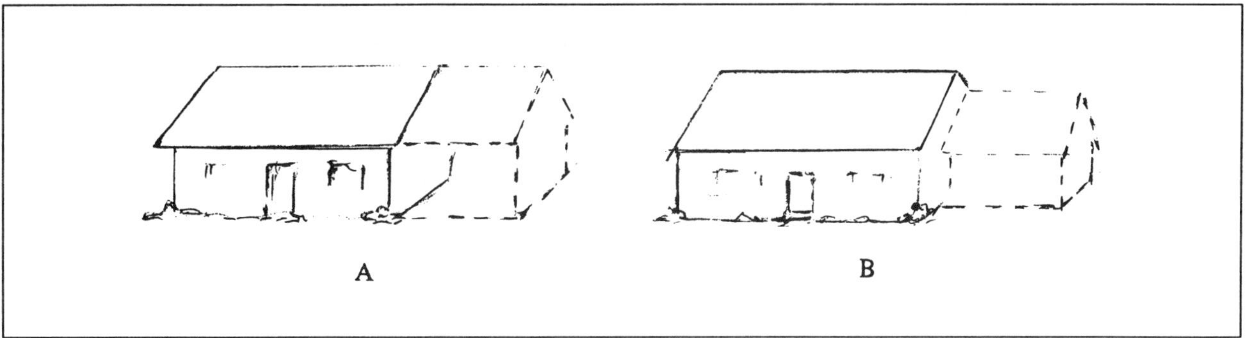

Compared to new-house construction, in many house-expansion cases it is difficult for the contractor to determine his exact costs. For this reason, many contractors will not offer a fixed price for the job.

■ EXPANSION CHOICES: GO UP, DOWN, ALL AROUND

There are many ways additional room can be added to a house. Several of these choices are:

Expand Right or Left

You can add room by extending the existing roof (see Figure 23.1). "A" is a simple solution, but the overall look of the house will be more attractive if the wing or wings are narrower than the main house so that the roof line is different as in "B." In addition, "B" is a better choice because it minimizes the problem of matching the shingles between the old and new sections, making any differences in shingles less conspicuous.

Expand to the Rear

You may like a wing that is perpendicular to the main line of the existing house (see Figure 23.2).

Turn Existing Garage into a Room

Convert the existing garage to living space and add a new garage. Most houses are built with the living area over a crawl space (2 feet to

FIGURE 23.2 Expanding to the Rear

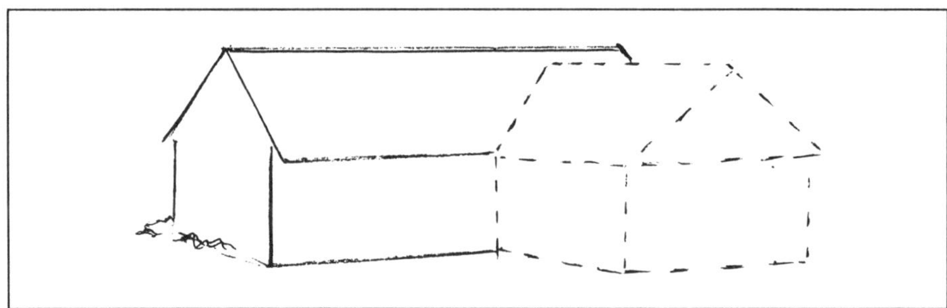

3 feet above the lot level) with the concrete garage floor poured at the level of the lot. If this difference can be spanned by one or two steps (about 8 inches each), this choice has merit. With differences of more than two or three steps, however, other expansion choices may be preferred.

With a garage conversion, much of the construction already exists and, with the exception of the garage door area, the design features of the original house are retained.

Add a Second Story

Add another story, full or partial, to an existing house. The footings and foundation should be checked by an engineer, architect or qualified contractor to see if they can safely carry the additional weight of a second floor. In addition, the ceiling joists of the first floor, usually 2×8s, now become the floor joists for the second floor and may have to be replaced or reinforced with stronger material, such as 2×10s or 2×12s. Several styles of second-floor additions are illustrated in Figure 23.3.

With the conventional colonial second floor additions, the first and second floors have equal floor space.

The salt-box design uses the rear of the roof to provide both roofing and exterior walls for the rear part of the second story. Dormer windows can be used for additional light and ventilation.

The second floor of both the story-and-a-half and the salt box have less floor space than the first floor.

The existing roof of the story-and-a-half provides both the roof and the exterior walls of the second floor. Additional light and ventilation are gained through front and rear dormers, and with shed dormers usually in the rear only.

In the garrison colonial style, the second floor projects about 2 feet beyond the first floor, offering additional floor space and a different but

FIGURE 23.3 Two-Story Houses

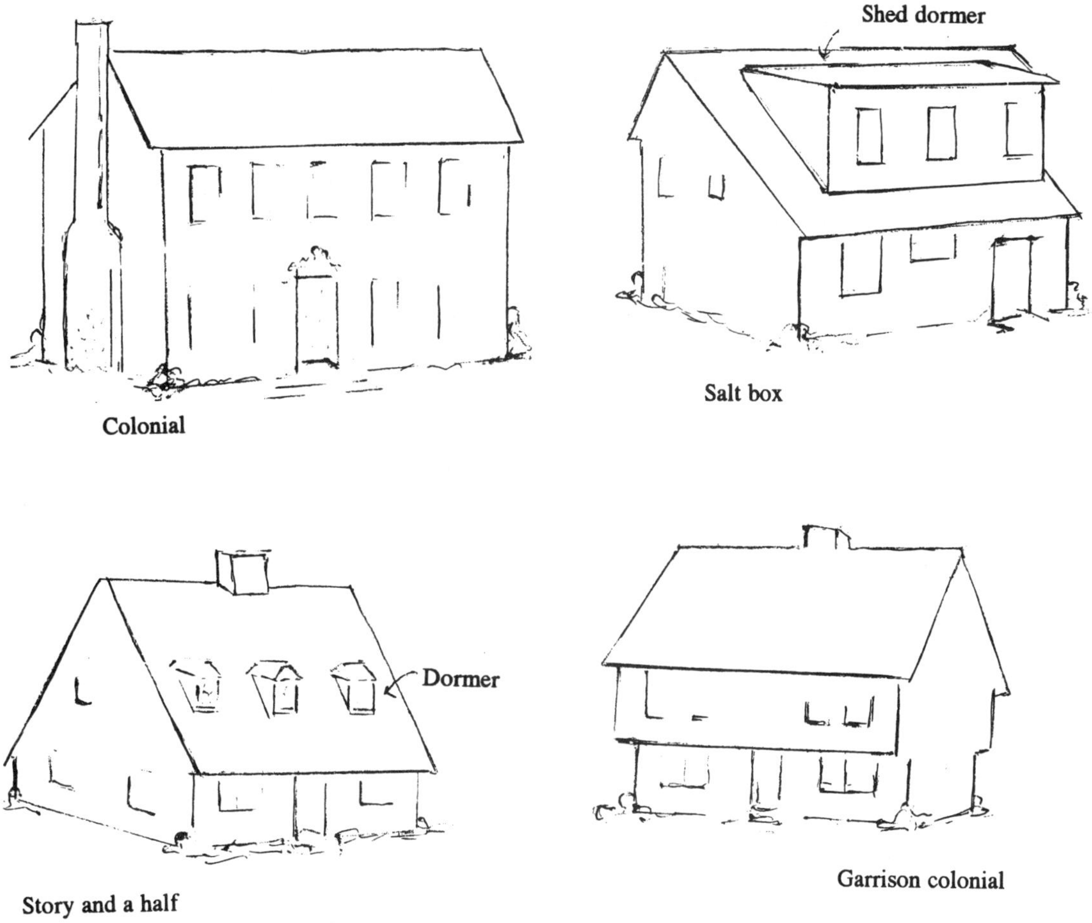

Shed dormer
Colonial
Salt box
Dormer
Story and a half
Garrison colonial

attractive front view of the house (see Figure 23.4). To achieve this additional floor space, the floor joists of the second floor are placed perpendicular to the front of the house and cantilevered beyond the first floor. For projections beyond 2 feet, check your design with an architect or engineer. Most framing crews are familiar with this technique.

Choosing the type of two-story house to build is a matter of personal taste. Architects can be most helpful in making this choice.

How about Adding Rooms in the Basement?

If you have one, why not convert the basement to comfortable living space? The outer walls and floors are already built.

FIGURE 23.4 Cantilevered Floor Joists

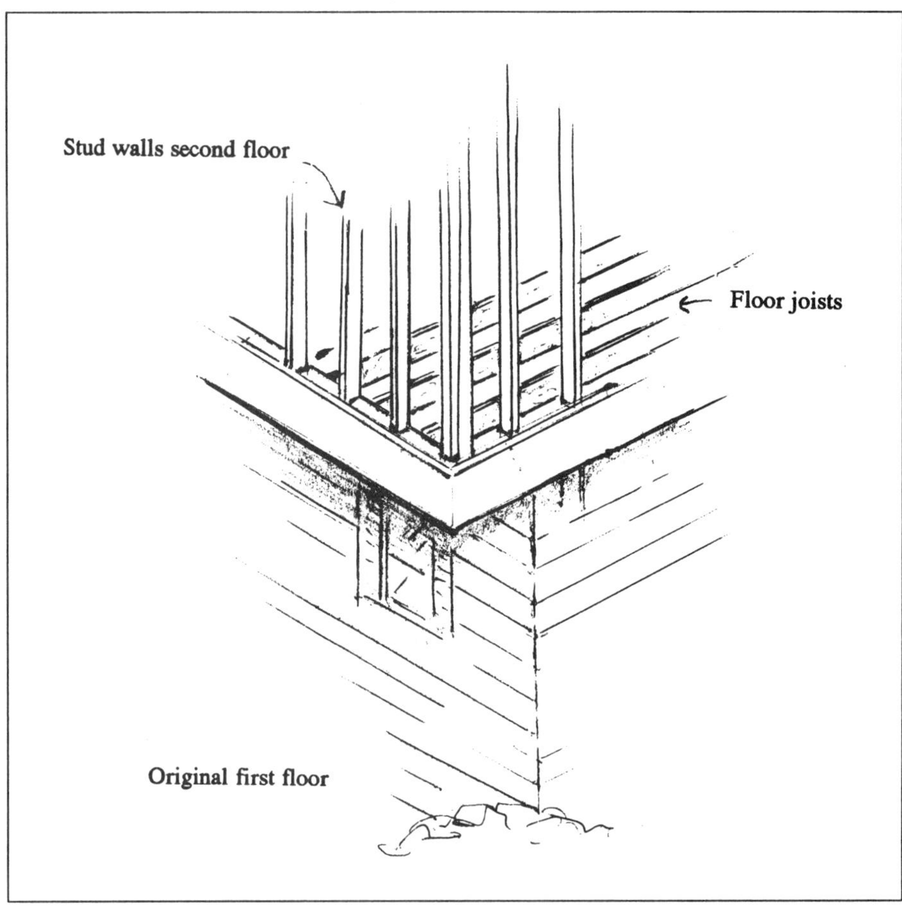

Is your basement damp? There are methods for correcting this fault:

- First try to get rid of the dampness by applying masonry waterproofing material to the *interior* of the exterior walls (see Figure 6.4). Several kinds are on the market. After the job is complete, plug in an electric dehumidifier to remove all of the dampness and then wait about two weeks to see if the problem has been solved.
- If the above solution does not do a complete job, consider this more expensive but more effective method. Cover the interior of the wall with rubber-like membrane (described on page 47), install a drain trough in the concrete floor inside the basement next to the wall, and drain this ditch into a sump equipped with a sump pump. This work should be done by a professional waterproofing contractor. With this system, the rubber membrane will normally stop moisture coming through the wall. Moisture may come through the juncture of the wall and the

floor, however, but the ditch collects this moisture, moves it to the sump, where it is pumped out of the house.

- The most effective solution is the proper preparation of the exterior of the basement walls. These walls, of course, must be exposed by excavation to permit the application of the rubber-like waterproofing membrane. In addition, a drain along side the footings as shown in Figure 6.4 is installed. Again, this work should be done by a professional waterproofing contractor.

Basement living spaces have an additional advantage over above-ground space in that the temperature of the ground in the winter is usually much warmer than the air above, and the temperature of the ground lower than outside air in the summer. Thus it takes significantly less energy to heat and cool the basement.

Because concrete and concrete block provide little insulation, the finished basement will be made much more comfortable by building a stud wall of 2×4s or 2×2s on the inside so that fiberglass or similar insulation can be installed between the studs. These stud walls also provide space to run concealed electric cables, pipes, and heating and cooling ducts.

Like the garage modification, this choice also generally retains the original design of the house.

Enlarge Your Detached Garage

The addition of a second story to a detached garage offers space with a great deal of privacy from the main house. Water, sewer and electrical power can usually be brought from the main house. Review the construction problems discussed in "Add a Second Story" on page 224.

An exterior stairway to the new second floor that avoids going through the garage is desirable.

Avoid Expansion-Plan Uglies

Some expansion plans may distort the original house to such an extent that its appearance becomes objectionable to neighbors and to review boards (subdivision, county or city) who must approve the plans. The primary legal basis for these objections may be that the unattractiveness of the expanded plan may lower the market value of neighboring houses.

FIGURE 23.5 An Unattractive Expansion Plan

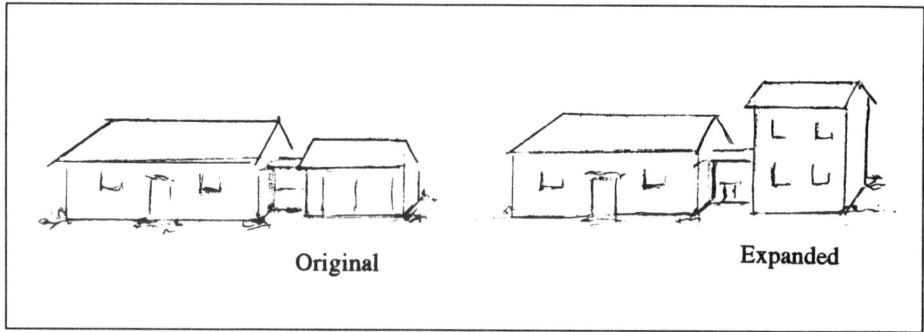

Note in Figure 23.5 how the addition of a second story on the garage of a one-story house results in an awkward design.

A second floor over a garage for a rancher is more practical if it can be built within the existing roof, perhaps with dormer windows.

SOME SPECIAL CONSTRUCTION TECHNIQUES FOR ADDITIONS

How To Join Footings and Foundations

Review Chapter 5, The Importance of Footings, and Chapter 6, Foundations. To minimize separations between the old and the new structure, the footings and foundations walls of each must be connected. If both old and new footings and foundations are concrete, steel reinforcing bars should be installed. Generally two rebars of ½-inch diameter are adequate for the footings, with an additional two in foundations walls that are not over 3 feet high. For higher walls (if you are connecting old and new full-basement walls, for example), add one additional ½-inch rebar for each 2 feet of additional height. When building the new concrete foundation wall, include a concrete pilaster as shown in Figure 23.6.

Install the rebar in the existing footings and foundation *before any new concrete is poured.* Drill the horizontal holes at least 1 inch in diameter and 1 foot deep for each rebar. The large hole diameter is necessary to allow the newly poured concrete to move into the hole and bind the rebar to the old concrete.

In addition to the rebar, the existing footings should be undercut. The length of this undercut should be double the width of the footing, and the depth of the footing in the undercut should be at least 10 inches. When the new footings are poured, make sure that the new concrete completely fills this excavation to tie the old and new footings together.

FIGURE 23.6 All-Concrete Footings and Foundation

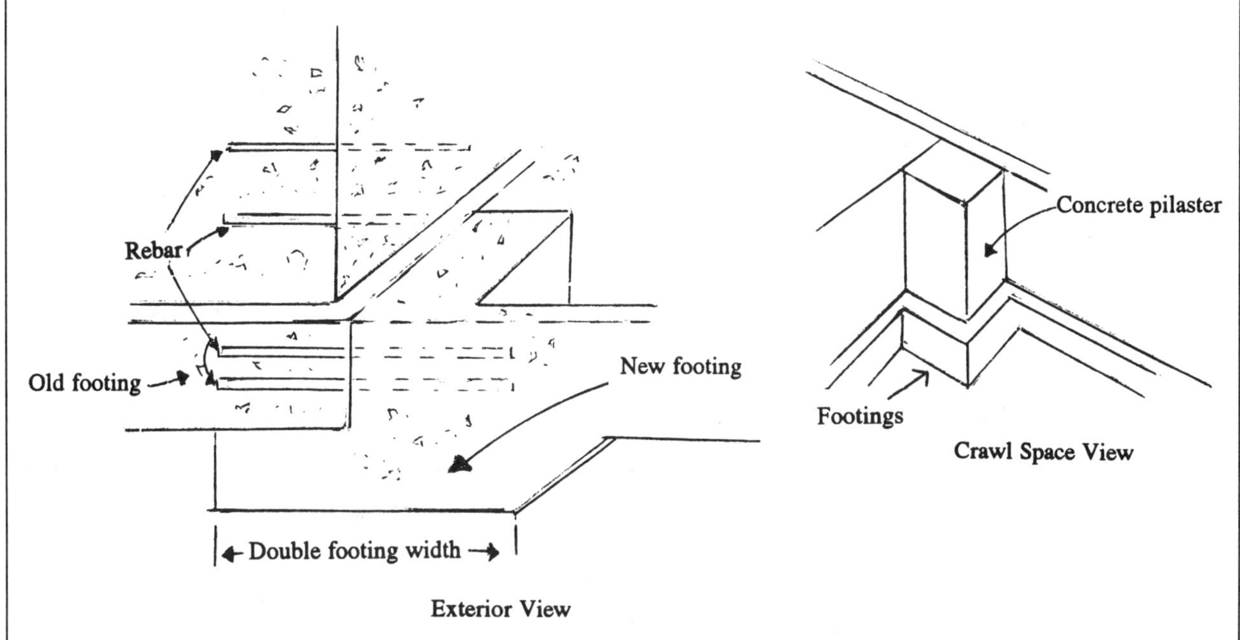

If the existing foundation wall is concrete block, rather than use rebar to connect the new and the old, use horizontal truss reinforcing (see page 44). In every other course that does not already have truss reinforcing, install an additional truss by cleaning out the mortar of the existing foundation wall back about 1 foot. Then install the new truss reinforcing into this joint and run the truss completely around that course of block in the new foundation wall. Replace the mortar in the old wall. Install the concrete block pilaster with the new block wall for additional strength (see Figure 23.7).

Don't forget the vertical reinforcing in the new foundation wall, if required.

What To Do with Siding on the Existing Wall

On that portion of the existing exterior wall where an addition is applied so that it becomes an interior wall, should the masonry, wood, vinyl or aluminum siding be removed to expose the wood framing beneath? This is the owner's choice. If, in the new addition, you want an interior wall of the same material as the existing siding, then go ahead without removing it. The new framing can be readily attached to the existing wall by using the proper bolts or nails.

FIGURE 23.7 Concrete Footings with Block Foundation

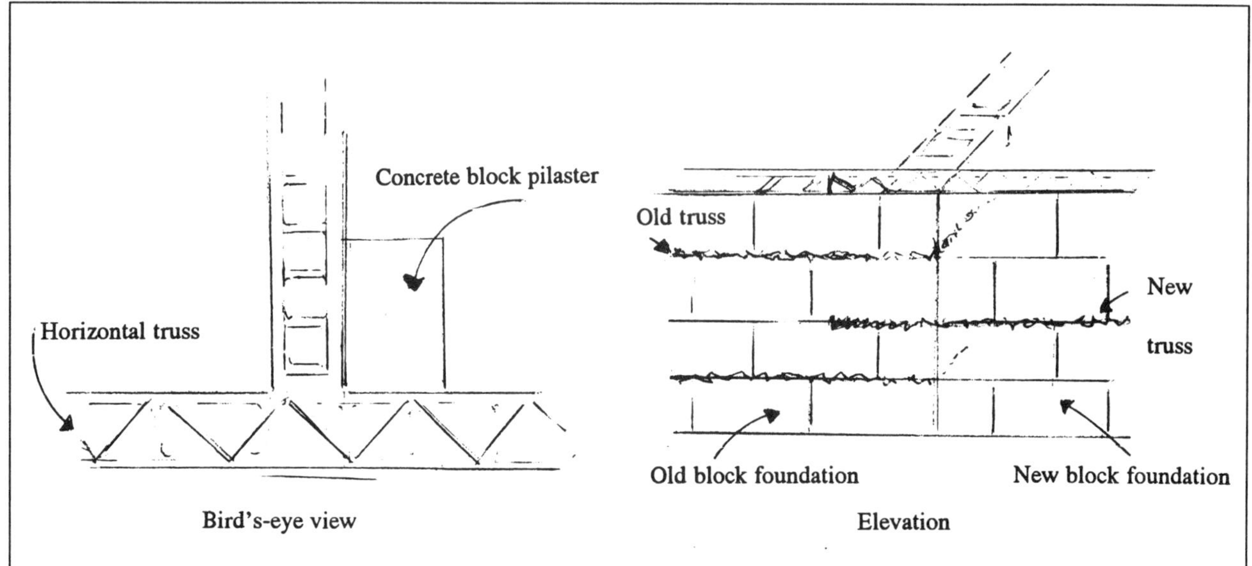

On the other hand, if you want a plaster, Sheetrock or a paneled interior wall, you can remove the old siding or masonry revealing the original stud wall to which the plaster, Sheetrock or paneling can be attached. Another solution to providing a base for the plaster, Sheetrock or paneling is to leave the existing siding and masonry in place and install a new stud wall in front of it on the new room side. In either case, you have the space to run electric cables, pipes and heating duct work concealed behind the interior wall finish.

How To Match New and Old Exterior Wall Coverings

It is difficult to get a good match between an old brick wall and a new one even if you are able to find the source of the original brick. Time weathers practically all construction materials, including brick, stone (to a lesser degree), vinyl and factory-painted aluminum. About the only exception is painted wood, and the new will differ from the old unless both are newly painted with the same type of paint.

One solution to this problem is to make your expansion design somewhat smaller than the original house. That will usually establish a break between the old and new exterior walls so different siding can be used on the new addition. For example, if the original house is brick or brick veneer, change to vinyl, aluminum or wood for the exterior of the new section (see Figure 23.8).

FIGURE 23.8 Different Siding

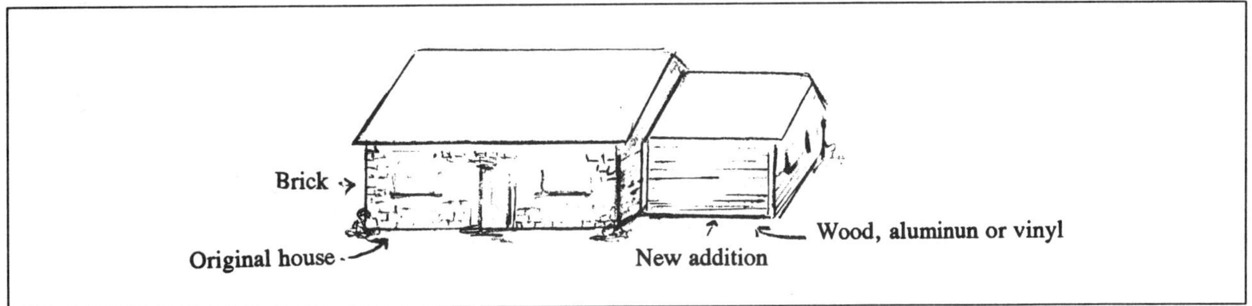

This design will also result in a break in the roof lines of the old and new sections of the house and de-emphasize a difference in the color of the old and the new shingles.

Home Expansion Window Tips

Review Chapter 8, Selecting Your Windows and Doors, to help you select the type of window and glass you want in your addition. If your existing house has single-glazed windows, you should consider replacing them as well as part of your home improvement project.

If the design of your new addition permits, place as much glass (windows and doors) facing south or near south to take advantage of passive solar heat. See Chapter 14, Heating with Sunshine (Solar Energy).

■ SOLVING HEATING AND AIR-CONDITIONING PROBLEMS

Forced-Air System Problems

The duct system for an existing house (seen in Figure 23.9) was designed to move warm and/or air-conditioned air to the rooms of just that house. Extending that system to take on additional room(s) will badly unbalance the duct design and produce an unsatisfactory air flow for the entire house, both old and new sections, even if the furnace or heat pump can take on the additional load.

A more efficient solution is to install a through-the-wall heat pump for the new addition. The modern versions of these systems are very efficient and can be fitted neatly anywhere in the exterior wall.

If air-conditioning is not required, you can install electric-resistant heating coils in the ceiling or along the baseboard. Because heat tends

FIGURE 23.9 Typical Supply Duct System

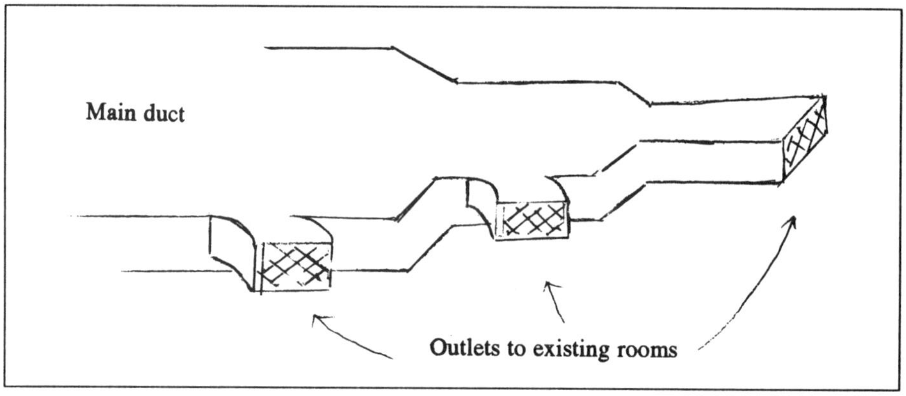

to rise, the baseboard coils will most likely produce the more comfortable system.

With this form of additional heat, a thermostat is installed in each new room to control the temperature of that room alone. If the new room is to be used only occasionally, the temperature for that room can be lowered when not in use. In addition to insulation in the exterior walls, however, insulation should also be installed in the wall that separates the added room from the original house to prevent unnecessary leakage of heat from the original house to the new room when the temperature in the new room is lowered. Also, adding weather stripping to the door between the new and the old will improve the overall system.

Steam and Hot Water Heating Problems

If the current heating system is steam or hot water, you might consider extending it into the new addition. Have a professional heating contractor examine the boiler to determine whether or not it can take on the additional capacity. In addition, have the pipes delivering the hot water or steam checked to see if they can be extended. If the original system is very old, the pipes may be clogged and unable to support the original house let alone any additional system. Under these circumstances, you should consider replacing the whole system with a new one.

Electric-Resistance Heat

If the original heating system is nonducted electric-resistance heat, it probably can easily be extended. Additional circuits may be required and perhaps an increase in the capacity of the service panel may be necessary. Neither of these changes are difficult to make.

Fireplaces

Adding a fireplace to the new addition is another choice, particularly if wood is readily available. Choose an energy-efficient system. Also consider a gas-fired fireplace or stove. If gas is not available at your lot, you can provide it by using a gas storage tank.

Depending on the weather in your area, a fireplace may do the job by itself or work in conjunction with another system such as electric resistance heat.

■ SOLVING PLUMBING PROBLEMS

First review Chapter 16, Planning for Your Plumbing. Usually, your current house water supply can meet the additional demand, but the system within your house may need to be checked, particularly if you are adding a bathroom or kitchen. Have a plumbing contractor inspect the water supply pipes to make sure they can take the additional load. If they are too small or internally corroded, they should be replaced.

The sewer capacity should also be checked. Usually there is no problem if your house is connected to a public system. If you are hooked up to a septic tank system, however, additional sewage disposal may create a problem if your present tank is too small or the drain field inadequate to take on an additional load. A larger or supplementary septic tank can be installed, however, and drain fields can be expanded if your lot has the additional room with proper soil for these fields.

If you are adding plumbing to a basement addition, you may have to install a grinder pump to draw the sewage from the basement level to the sewer line if this line is above the floor level of the basement.

■ ELECTRICAL PROBLEMS ARE USUALLY MINOR

Usually there are no major problems installing electrical circuits and equipment. Installing additional circuits and increasing the capacity of the service panel are routine electrical tasks. Original wiring in your present house should be checked for any defects, such as bad aluminum wire connection and capacity of main system to take on additional loads.

FINANCING YOUR HOME EXPANSION IS USUALLY EASY

Review Chapter 3, Arranging Contracts, Financing and Insurance. In addition to the usual first mortgage on a home, home improvement costs can be financed by the "equity loan" or second mortgage. If you have lived in your home for some time, you have increased the equity in your ownership. For example, assume you bought your home a few years ago for $100,000. You made a down payment of $10,000 and financed the payment of the remaining $90,000 by a first mortgage. Several years later, the market value of your house had probably increased to, for instance, $115,000.

You now have the $10,000 down payment plus the reduction (assume $2,000) of the principal over the last few years plus the $15,000 increase in market value, for a total of $27,000 in equity. Many banks will loan you up to 80 percent to 90 percent with the collateral being your equity. This equity loan or second mortgage is paid off in monthly installments along with the monthly payment of your first mortgage.

APPENDIX A

Sample Specifications

Appendix A contains a sample of the specifications for a typical rancher built on crawl space with attached garage. The quality of the materials is above average, and energy conservation is emphasized.

The specifications contain information that usually does not appear on the blueprints. For example, the blueprints may show the location of a stove or heating system, but the specifications must indicate the type of stove or heating system, its size, the manufacturer and the model number.

The most important point to understand is that the owner must provide sufficient detail in the specifications to ensure getting exactly what is wanted and to provide an accurate base for real competitive bidding. If specifications are vague or contain too little information, the owner will not be able to properly compare the prices of the different bidders with any assurance of accuracy.

Although products of certain manufacturers have been used in developing these specifications, this use should not be construed as a recommendation for this certain product instead of any other. By specifying model numbers and manufacturers, the homeowner informs the bidders of exactly what is wanted in the house. The term *or equal* indicates that bidders may substitute products of other manufacturers of the same or better quality and performance.

In certain cases the owner may need assistance in preparing the technical details. Most suppliers and contractors offer their assistance without charge in this task.

The paragraphs in italics are not part of the specifications. They are notes explaining to the reader the importance of the preceding specification.

■ SPECIFICATIONS

Home of Mr. and Mrs. J. L. Brentwood to be built on Lot #29 Jasmine Hills Subdivision, Center City, North Carolina. The owner has the final determination of acceptable materials, equipment and quality of workmanship.

1. **EXCAVATION:** Bearing soil for footings to be undisturbed soil.

   Designates the soil conditions for the footings. Important that the soil not be loose fill.

2. **FOUNDATION:**

   a. Footings: Per plan. Concrete mix 3,000 psi. Reinforcing bar #4. Top of footings to be not less than 8″ below grade.

      The blueprint will show size of the footings. It's necessary to designate type of concrete for strength and to indicate the size of the rebar. The blueprint should show the amount of the rebar. If it does not, that information should be indicated here. In cold areas, specify that the top of the footings should be not less than 8″ below the frost line.

   b. Foundation wall: Exterior walls to be 8″ concrete block per plan with brick veneer. Interior walls to be 8″ concrete block per plan. Girders and sill plates to be #2 grade SYP salt pressure treated to .25 CCA. Anchor bolts ½″ × 12″—6′ OC. Brick to be Triangle Brick Co. 3700 Castletone laid with V-joint and standard mortar.

      These are important details of the foundation construction. The wall description reinforces data that should be part of the blueprint and is repeated for emphasis. The type of lumber and the salt treatment ensures the use of strong, long-lasting lumber for that part of the framing that may be exposed to more than the normal amount of moisture. The .25 CCA specification designates a degree of impregnation normally used for salt-treated lumber installed above the ground. The sizes of the girders and sill plates are shown on the blueprint.

   c. All concrete slab on grade to be 4,000 psi.

      Tougher concrete should be used on floors to prevent cracking.

   d. Termite Protection: Soil poisoning by treatment along exterior and interior walls and piers with 1% chlorodane solution.

      The chemical treatment is the most effective against termites and other wood-boring insects.

3. **FIREPLACE:**

a. Wood-burning Heatilator Model FP36 with FK15 fan kit, AK20 outside air kit and CD10 heat-circulator ducts and outlet boxes, or equal.

This equipment will provide an energy-efficient fireplace as described in Chapter 15, Heating and Cooling Considerations. By selecting a specific model with attachments, you express exactly what you want and provide a specific base for bidders.

b. Chimney, per plan, zero-clearance Heatilator. Exterior section framed and covered with redwood lap siding to match the exterior of the house. Top of framing covered with galvanized sheet metal cap to prevent moisture entrance into the framing.

Tells the carpentry crew that they must furnish the labor and tells the supplier to provide the material for finishing off the chimney exterior. Also tells the Heatilator supplier to include the metal chimney sections in the bid.

c. Facing: Colonial wood mantel with ceramic tile per plan.

Detail of fireplace finish to show the carpentry crew, the supplier and the tile contractor the work and material required.

4. **EXTERIOR WALLS:**

a. Studs and plates, SPF KD #2 grade, 2×6—24″ OC.

Indicates the grade and type of lumber to be used. SPF is a more stable wood than SYP and will provide a straighter wall. KD indicates that the lumber must be kiln dried rather than air dried. The latter may have an unusually high moisture content with more shrinkage after the house has been built. And, #2 grade is well suited for framing.

b. Metal bracing at all exterior corners and at all intersections of exterior and interior walls.

Sheathing to be used is polyurethane or polystyrene that has little strength. Diagonal corner bracing is the only practical method to use with this sheathing. Metal bracing is better than wood.

c. Sheathing to be polyurethane or polystyrene 1″ thick 4′×8′ sheets to be applied by hand nailing only. Sheathing to be covered with plastic house wrap.

This material will give much better insulation than either plywood or asphalt-impregnated sheathing. Hand nailing will minimize damage to the sheathing. The plastic house wrap will reduce air infiltration through the walls and eliminate the need for some of the other sealing measures. See paragraph 25, Sealing, on page 245.

d. Siding to be colonial beaded 1×6 redwood lap with ⅝″ butt and 4″ exposure. Corner boards, same material, to be 4″ × ¼″.

Designates the type, form and size of the siding. The ⅝″ butt is important because it will minimize splitting problems that would be more prevalent with a ½″ butt. The size of the corner boards was selected for appearance and to provide enough thickness so that the caulking between the corner board and the siding will have a good base.

e. Gable-wall construction to be the same with wood gable vents per plan.

The attic space behind the gable wall is not heated. Therefore, some saving might have been realized by substituting impregnated sheathing in lieu of the poly sheathing. Because impregnated sheathing is usually available in only ½″ thickness, the poly was used to retain the 1″ depth and to eliminate problems in siding installation because of the different thicknesses of the sheathing. A double layer of the ½″ impregnated sheathing could have been used, but the increase in material and labor costs would have negated any savings.

f. Exterior painting: All exterior wood to be back primed with one coat of SWP Promar® exterior wood undercoat or equal. All exposed surfaces to be painted with one coat Promar undercoat and two coats SWP A-100 latex gloss or equal. Rate of coverage to be not more than 400 square feet per gallon for both the undercoat and the A-100. All paint to be delivered to site in its original containers. Colors to be selected.

Both the quality of the paint and the number of coats is designated to provide a basis for painting bids. The original containers statement minimizes the possible switch to cheaper material. The rate of coverage ensures that the paint is not overly thinned.

5. **FLOOR FRAMING:** Joists to be #2 grade KD SYP with blocking not greater than 8′ OC.

Designates the grade and type of lumber to be used. SYP was selected because of its strength. Blocking is necessary to prevent undue warping of the lumber. Blocking is more rigid than bridging. It also pulls the joists into alignment before the subfloor is installed.

6. **SUBFLOORING:**

   a. ½″ × 4′ × 8′ flake board glued and nailed or stapled to joists. Glue to be Weldwood Subfloor and Construction Adhesive or equal.

   Specifies type and size of material. Should be not less than ½″ and need not be thicker than ⅝″. Gluing increases the strength of the structure and helps to eliminate squeaks in the floor. Stapling has been included to permit the use of powered nailing and stapling systems. Flake board resists moisture much better than exterior plywood and will generally eliminate delamination caused by rain and snow before the house is weathertight.

   b. Attic space: 10 ½″ × 4′ × 8′ sheets of CDX plywood or flake board to be laid near pulldown stairs. Installed only after the ceiling insulation has been put in. Pulldown stair to be Besseler Model 100 size #2 or equal.

   Provides some storage space in the attic. Depending upon the roof construction, it is very difficult or even impossible to move full sheets of plywood up the opening of a pulldown stair. This plywood should be placed in the attic space during the framing but not nailed down until after the insulation has been installed.

7. **INTERIOR PARTITION FRAMING:** #2 grade KD SPF studs and plates. Studs 16″ OC. Interior walls of both baths to be staggered 2×4 studs with 2×6 plates and double plaster lathing on one side. 3½″ batt insulation without vapor barrier woven between studs horizontally.

   Staggering the studs and installing insulation provides sound insulation for the bathroom.

8. **CEILING AND ROOF FRAMING:** Joists and rafters #2 grade KD SYP.

9. **ROOFING:** Sheathing ½″ × 4′ × 8′ CDX plywood. Shingles 215# fiberglass self-sealing Certainteed Glasstex or equal. Underlayment to be single-layer 15# asphalt-felt building paper.

   The ½″ plywood is preferred because thinner material may sag between roof rafters giving the roof a wavy appearance. Heavier plywood is not necessary for this type of shingle. Designating a specific shingle determines the quality and type. Flake board could be used for roof sheathing, but it is more slippery than plywood and may increase roof labor costs. Because roof sheathing is usually covered with waterproof building paper right after being installed, the plywood is normally dry and not subject to delamination from rain and snow.

10. **GUTTERS AND DOWNSPOUTS:** Per plan. Material to be Raingo All-Vinyl Rainwater Handling System or equal. Concrete splash blocks at the bottom of each downspout.

Blueprints usually show the gutter and downspout detail. If they do not, the lengths and number of downspouts and length of gutter should be determined. If needed, get some help from a supplier. A particular brand is specified to establish quality, in this case a tough vinyl type. The splash blocks (usually formed concrete) reduce the erosion of the newly graded yard.

11. **INSULATION:**

   a. Ceiling R-30 with vapor barrier of 6-mil polyurethane under plaster lathing.

   b. Walls R-19 with vapor barrier or 6-mil polyurethane under plaster lathing.

   c. Floor R-13 with vapor barrier of kraft paper.

   d. Interior walls of each bath 3½″ batts without vapor barrier for sound insulation.

   The polyurethane vapor barrier is more effective than the integrated barrier in the batt. The sheathing and plaster will raise the total R-value of the walls to about R-19.

12. **LATH AND PLASTER:** All walls and ceilings to be two-coat plaster veneer with gypsum lath base including the interior of all closets and the garage. Lathing applied to studs and joists with adhesive and screws except for exterior walls where screws only are to be used.

Method of installing lathing is detailed to eliminate the use of lath nails and reduce the use of screws. Nails have the tendency to pop out from the studs. Adhesive cannot be used on exterior walls because of the polyurethane vapor barrier.

13. **DECORATING:**

   a. All walls and ceilings except kitchen and baths to be painted with one coat of oil-based primer and one coat of SWP Classic 99 latex or equal.

   Quality of paint and number of coats specified.

   b. Walls and ceilings of kitchen and baths and all the wood trim (including doors and windows), one coat of oil base primer and two coats of SWP Classic 99 latex enamel semigloss or equal.

Use enamel paint in rooms where a higher-than-normal moisture content is expected and on all the wood trim.

c. Rate of coverage of all painting to be not more than 400 square feet for each gallon.

14. INTERIOR DOORS AND TRIM:

a. Doors to be six-panel colonial, wood, paint grade, Morgan F-66 or equal.

b. Door and window trim to be colonial 3¼". Window trim to be installed "picture frame" without stool and apron.

c. Base trim to be colonial bead 4¼" with shoe molding where vinyl, earthstone and hard-wood flooring are laid.

Type and quality of doors has been established. Size and style of trim and method of trimming windows is specified.

15. WINDOWS: Size per plan. Pella, clad, casement windows dual glazed, dark bronze with removable colonial muntins and complete operating hardware. Slim Shades installed in all windows in rear of house in lieu of muntins.

The style, color and type of window is established, as is the quality. "Slim Shades" in the Pella line are venetian blinds installed between the two glass panes. Muntins are removable strips that give the appearance the window is made of small glass panes—the traditional look. Because both Slim Shades and muntins fit between the panes of glass, only one or the other can be used in the same window. The interior pane of the Pella is removable giving access to the muntins and the Slim Shades.

16. ENTRANCE DOORS:

a. Front entrance door to be Benchmark insulated steel door and frame, Williamsburg model, six panel, or equal. Size 3'-0" × 6'-8". Hardware to be Weiser E360DL Troy, finish 12.

b. Kitchen to garage door to be Benchmark insulated steel door and frame, Williamsburg model, six panel, or equal. Size 2'-8" × 6'-8". Hardware to be Weiser E360DL Troy, finish 12.

c. Sliding door in family room to be Pella, clad, dark bronze XO 34-8 dual glazed with sliding screen door or equal.

The above specifications establish the size, quality, finishes and style of all exterior doors and door hardware.

17. **CABINETS:**

a. Kitchen cabinets to be Wheaton Oak by American Woodmark or equal. Countertops to be plastic laminate, postformed.

b. Bath vanities to be Nutone Savannah or equal.

The range of type and quality, both of which reflect price, seems to be endless in the cabinet line. Select a specific line you like and use it as the requirement in your specifications. The blueprints will show size and arrangement of cabinets. Designate the type of countertops as they differ in price. For countertops for vanities, see paragraph 21.

18. **FINISH HARDWARE** (medicine cabinets, towel racks, door locks, etc.): Allowance for material—$300.

By using an allowance, the owner provides the cost of material with the contractors bidding for labor only. This method permits the owner to postpone the actual selection of the items until construction is under way. Do not delay too long, however, because the framing crew must know the rough opening for the medicine cabinets and the location of other hardware so any required framing back-up can be installed.

19. **FLOORS:**

a. Entry hall to be earthstone set in cement over dropped subfloor per plan.

b. Kitchen and laundry to be Congoleum Prestige Cushioned vinyl or equal installed over ⅝″ plywood underlayment.

c. Bath floors to be ceramic tile American Olean® C1 crystaline face, or equal, installed over cement on plywood subfloor. Base to be matching ceramic material.

Be specific in your selection of tile. Prices of tile vary. Detail the method of installation. The one used here is good and trouble free.

d. Wood flooring in living and dining rooms. To be select white oak random width 3″, 4″, 6″ with V-groove. Finish to include sanding, one coat of stain and two coats of polyurethane, matte.

Typical example of the detail needed in wood flooring.

e. All other flooring to be carpet installed over ⅝″ particleboard. Allowance of $14 per square yard installed for the carpet.

20. **WAINSCOTING:** Tubs in each bath to have ceramic tile laid over tub on metal lathing and cement to height of 6′ from floor. Tile to be American Olean A-1 matte glace or equal.

21. **PLUMBING:**

 a. Water supply: hookup to public system.

 b. Sewage disposal: hookup to public system.

 c. House drain inside and outside to be PVC. All vent pipe will exit through the roof on the rear side of the house.

 The house will look better from the front if vents are installed on the rear side of the roof where they cannot be seen from the street.

 d. Water supply pipe, both hot and cold, to be polybutylene. All hot water pipes run through exterior walls and in unheated spaces will be wrapped with 1″ pipe insulation.

 e. Sill cocks: Two per plan.

 f. Water heaters: Two Ruud #PE40-2 40-gallon energy miser or equal. Installed per plan, one vicinity bath area and one vicinity kitchen/laundry area as shown in plan. Both hot water heaters to be wrapped with additional insulation of not less than 2″ of fiberglass.

 Denotes the quality and capacity of the hot water heaters. Illustrates the use of two heaters for more efficient distribution of hot water. Extra insulation is specified because both hot water heaters will be installed in unheated attic space.

 g. Fixtures:

  (1) Bath #1: American Standard water closet 2109395 in blue. American Standard 14″ cast-iron tub 2265379 in blue with Moen 2434 tub/shower combination controls. Mount controls halfway between shower head and tub supply outlet. Corian double, integrated-bowl lavatory with two Moen 4220 faucets. Shower rod. Or equal.

  (2) Bath #2: American Standard water closet 209395 in yellow. American Standard 14″ cast-iron tub 2265379 in yellow with Moen 2435 tub/shower combination controls mounted halfway between shower head and tub outlet. Corian double, integrated-bowl lavatory with two Moen 4220 Faucets. Shower rod. Or equal.

  (3) Kitchen: Elkay CR 3322 stainless steel sink with Moen 73-10 faucet with spray. Or equal.

(4) Laundry: Fiat F-1 laundry tub with Sterling 31-200 faucet, or equal.

Because there are many grades and styles of bath fixtures, you should indicate manufacturer, model and color. The mounting of the tub/shower controls is spelled out because this is the most convenient position for the user. Otherwise the plumber may mount the control too low for convenient showering.

h. Hookup for garbage disposal and dishwasher.

i. Install Water Tite washer box in laundry for clothes washer.

"Water Tite" is an in-the-wall box that provides an efficient, nice-looking recess for the hot and cold water valves and the drain.

22. **HEATING VENTILATING AND AIR-CONDITIONING (HVAC):**

a. Carrier 38Q046—4 ton heat pump and matching fan coil with 15KW auxiliary strips. Thermostat with separate outdoor thermostat to stage electric heat strips. Minimum HSPF 6.5, SEER 10.

Specify the manufacturer, model number, capacity and additional features to ensure getting the proper system. Because these specifications are somewhat technical, contact a contractor and get some help. The separate outdoor thermostat is important because it will bring on the auxiliary heat in time to avoid a temporary drop in the inside temperature.

b. Humidifier integrated into system to be Aprilaire Model #440 bypass type.

Forced-warm-air heating systems will dry out the air inside the house. The humidifier will put moisture back into the air and provide greater comfort for occupants at lower temperatures and reduce damage to furniture caused by excessive dryness.

c. Electrostatic air cleaner to be Carrier unit 31MP220 integrated into the forced-warm-air heating system.

Provides cleaner air inside the house, and this is particularly important in a well-sealed house.

d. Ducts to be galvanized sheet metal with complete coated sound insulation lining throughout. In addition to the sound insulation, one layer of 2" duct insulation applied to the exterior of all ducts passing through unheated areas.

The lined ducts will provide a quiet system. The lining also offers additional thermal insulation. As indicated, add insulation to those ducts that pass through unheated spaces.

e. All duct openings, both supply and return, will be covered temporarily after rough-in to prevent debris, dust and other materials getting into the duct system. Covers to be removed when grilles are installed during final finishing.

23. ELECTRICAL WIRING:

a. Underground service with 200-ampere circuit breaker panel with 24 circuits.

Underground service eliminates the unsightly wires coming into the house from the power company's transformer. The size of the panel and the number of circuits control the power your house can handle.

b. Wiring to be nonmetallic copper cable except that aluminum-stranded cable may be used for #8 and larger.

Standard for house wiring. The "nonmetallic" refers to the cable cover and not the copper itself.

c. Special outlets for range, water heaters, oven, clothes dryer and heat pump.

Highlights the special 220-volt circuits needed for this equipment.

d. Door chimes with buttons at front, back and patio doors.

24. LIGHTING FIXTURES: Allowance of $600.00 to include electric wall heaters for the bathrooms and ceiling fans in the family room and master bedroom.

The allowance method permits the owner to select his fixtures at a later date.

25. SEALING:

a. Door frames in exterior walls and all window frames shall be sealed to rough openings.

b. All electrical, plumbing, telephone and heating penetrations of exterior walls, floor and ceiling of heated space shall be sealed.

c. All sheathing construction damage including nail holes, breaks and utility openings shall be sealed.

d. All cracks in framing members where daylight is visible from the inside shall be sealed.

26. **SPECIAL EQUIPMENT:** Allowance of $2,500 for appliances.

27. **SIDEWALKS:** Per plan 4″ thick exposed aggregate 3,000 psi with wire-mesh reinforcing; 3′ wide.

28. **DRIVEWAY:** Per plan; 6″ compacted clay base with top coat of 2″ of gravel. Culvert to be 24″ flared-end concrete pipe.

29. **GARAGE DOOR:** Wayne overhead 16′ × 7′ model 54 with Genie Model #880 by Alliance Mfg. Company; radio-controlled operation with two transmitters, or equal.

    Specify the type of garage door. Because this is a double garage, two transmitters have been specified for the two cars that will use the garage.

30. **LANDSCAPING:** Final grade with slope away from house foundation. Grade, fertilize and grass seed all of the area of the lot that has been cleared for construction. Lay cover of straw over the seeded lawn.

Cost Table

Appendix B illustrates a form for you, as your own general contractor, to determine the cost of your house based on the specifications in Appendix A and your blueprints. All costing data are bids from suppliers and contractors.

The "material" column should contain only those items on which you must pay a sales tax if required in your locality. Usually these are items you buy directly from a supplier.

Where the contractors provide both materials and labor, the total bid figure is recorded in the "labor" column as well as the "total" column because the contractors pay the sales tax on materials that they buy for you.

Figures shown in this Cost Table are representative and should not in any way be used in costing your home.

For safe financial planning, add a few thousand dollars over your computed cost to cover omissions (there always seem to be some) and changes that most people make as the construction progresses.

Item	Material	Contractor	Labor	Contractor	Total	Remarks
Preliminaries	$145	Acme Plans	—	—	145	9 sets
Building Permit	—	—	$132	Center City	132	
Survey, Layout	46	Colonial Bldg. Supply	100	A.J. White	146	
Culvert Pipe	120	August Concrete	—	—	120	
Driveway			350	E. Norris	350	Labor and Materials
Other (Clearing)			650	E. Norris	650	Includes labor for culvert pipe
Masonry						
Footings	450	August Concrete	300	Joe Gallager	750	
Block	830	"	610	Brown Masonry	1,440	Includes mortar brick ties
Durwall						
Slab						
Waterproof						
Backfill						
Vents	48	August Concrete	—	—	48	Labor in block col.
Access Door	17	"			17	" "
Page Total	$1,656		$2,142		$3,789	

Item	Material	Contractor	Labor	Contractor	Total	Remarks
Brick Veneer	$670	August Concrete	$825	Brown Masonry	$1,495	
Soil Poisoning	—	—	65	Jones Pest Control	65	
Lintels						
Rebar	36	August Concrete	—	—	36	Labor in footings
Fireplace	834	Taylor Fireplace Co.	—	A.J. White	834	Labor in framing
Patio	270	August Concrete	100	Joe Gallager	370	Form materials in framing
Sidewalk	75	"	30	"	105	" "
Garage Floor	388	"	130	"	518	Includes wire mesh expansion joint & poly
Steps	Included in block and brick veneer					
Stoop						
Headwalls	55	August Concrete	75	Brown Masonry	130	Brick walk & culvert openings
Other						
Carpentry						
Framing	7,635	Colonial Bldg. Supply	3,280	A.J. White	10,915	
Steel						
Page Total	$9,963		$4,505		$14,468	

Item	Material	Contractor	Labor	Contractor	Total	Remarks
Rough Hardware	Included in framing materials					
Doors		"	"	"		
Windows	$2,650	Pella Co.	—	—	$2,650	Labor in framing
Siding	3,800	Colonial Bldg. Supply	410	A.J. White	4,210	
Interior Trim	—	—	375	"	375	Materials in framing
Finish Hardware	300	(Allowance)	—	—	300	Labor in interior trim
Other						
Roof						
Shingles	884	Colonial Bldg. Supply	312	Neal Roofing	1,196	
Gutters, Downspouts			328	"	328	Includes labor & materials
Flashing			52		52	" "
Other						
Cabinets						
Kitchen		}				
Vanities		}	2,265	Morris Cabinet	2,265	Includes material & installation
Page Total	$7,634		$3,742		$11,376	

Item	Material	Contractor	Labor	Contractor	Total	Remarks
Built-ins						
Other						
Wall Finish						
Drywall						
Plaster	$1,185	August Concrete	$2,660	Miller Plaster	$3,845	August supplies lathing, Miller all other materials
Other						
Plumbing						
Pipe, Fixtures			2,875	Lyons Plumbing	2,875	Material and labor
Well/Water			350	Center City	350	Water hook-up fee
Septic/Sewer			1,200	"	1,200	Sewer hook-up fee
Other						
Electrical						
Wiring			2,245	Stuart Electric	2,245	Material and labor
Baseboard Heat						
Fixtures			600	"	600	Allowance
Page Total	$1,185		$9,930		$11,115	

Item	Material	Contractor	Labor	Contractor	Total	Remarks
HVAC			$3,863	Shaw Heating	$3,863	Materials and labor
Flooring						
Hardwood			384	Morgan Floors	384	Material and labor
Vinyl			210	Acme Carpet	210	" "
Ceramic			1,268	Lucas Tile	1,268	Includes tub & shower, earthstone foyer
Carpet			2,253	Acme Carpet	2,253	Material and labor
Other						
Painting						
Paint/Stain			4,100	Eubank Painting	4,100	
Papering						
Other						
Insulation			2,408	Atlantic Insulation	2,408	Includes sealing against air infil.
Appliances	$2,500	allowance			2,500	
Landscape						
Final Grade						See next items
Page Total	$2,500		$14,486		$16,986	

Item	Material	Contractor	Labor	Contractor	Total	Remarks
Seed/Fertilize			$240	Capitol Nurseries	240	Includes final grade
Haul Excess Dirt						
Shrubbery						
Other						
Miscellaneous						
Ornamental Iron			220	Wythe Iron Works	220	Material and labor
Cleaning/ Hauling			150	Dick Nash	150	Three trips
Garage Door						
Special Equipment						
Interior Clean			95	Smythes Cleaning	95	
Total This Page			705		705	
Total All Pages	22,938		35,510		58,448	
Taxes @% 4%	917.52				917.52	
Grand Total					$59,365.52	

■ — APPENDIX C — ■

Construction Schedule

Appendix C contains a composite construction schedule that includes tasks for houses built on a crawl space, concrete slab, with basement, and so forth. Using this schedule as a guide, make up one to fit your own plan by eliminating those tasks not called for in your case and perhaps adding a few special ones not included in this general guide.

The use of the word "owner" indicates what you must do when acting as your own general contractor.

This schedule is designed to assist you in determining what tasks should be done in the general order of the whole construction project. Because no schedule can be rigid, common sense will dictate changes as you get into the job.

The amount of time indicated for the accomplishment of the various tasks is only a guide. Actual timing will vary according to many local factors, of which the weather and the response of the trade contractors are the two most important.

Contractors sometimes do not show up on the job when promised for valid and not-so-valid reasons. You should keep the pressure on and insist that they inform you when changes occur and give you their best estimate of the new schedule.

Time	Task	Materials	Labor	Remarks
1st Week	Building permit		Owner	From local office.
	Temporary electrical power	Electrician	Electrician	Installs post & box; notifies power co.
	Culvert and driveway OK		Owner	From Highway Department.
	Sewer & water permits		Owner	From local government office.
	Initial house layout	Owner or contractor	Owner or contractor	If no clearing required, can be complete house layout.
	Clear lot	Contractor	Contractor	Include all site work that can be done before final house layout.
2nd Week	House layout	Owner or contractor	Owner or contractor	If excavation required, this is partial layout.
	Excavation	Contractor	Contractor	If required; usually done by site contractor.
	Complete house layout		Owner or contractor	After excavation.
	Driveway base & culvert	Contractor	Contractor	Usually by site contractor.
	Septic system	Contractor	Contractor	If required to install, before foundation.
3rd Week	Fill, compact and grade house site	Contractor	Contractor	If house built on concrete slab.
	Under-slab HVAC plumbing and electric	Contractors	Contractors	Install rough-in that goes under slab.
	Footings	Owner	Contractor	*Inspection* before pouring concrete.
	Temporary water	Plumber	Plumber	
	Temporary electric	Electrician, Power Co.	Electrician, Power Co.	Hookup *inspected*—power company installs cable.
4th Week	Foundation & basement	Owner	Mason	
	Soil poisoning	Contractor	Contractor	Check timing with contractor.
5th Week	Basement slab	Owner	Concrete contractor	
	1st floor slab	Owner	Concrete contractor	
	Waterproofing, drain pipe	Owner	Contractor	Exterior wall of underground living area.

NOTE: If house is built on crawl space, none of the above tasks for the fifth week are required. The following sixth week becomes the fifth week, and subsequent weeks are changed as well.

<table>
<tr><th>Time</th><th>Task</th><th>Materials</th><th>Labor</th><th>Remarks</th></tr>
<tr><td>6th Week</td><td>Framing</td><td>Owner</td><td>Carpenters</td><td>For stick-built house.</td></tr>
<tr><td></td><td>Framing</td><td>Supplier</td><td>Carpenters</td><td>For panelized house.</td></tr>
<tr><td colspan="5">Note: The schedule that follows is based on the stick-built house. The panelized house will usually require the same tasks but less time.</td></tr>
<tr><td></td><td>Backfill</td><td>Contractor</td><td>Contractor</td><td>If excavation has been done; backfill only after floor system of first floor has been installed.</td></tr>
<tr><td>7th Week</td><td>Framing continues</td><td>Owner</td><td>Carpenters</td><td>Coordinate delivery of supplies with the crew chief throughout the framing period.</td></tr>
<tr><td></td><td>Roofing</td><td>Owner for shingles</td><td>Roofer</td><td>Get shingles on as soon as framing permits; roofer provides all other materials.</td></tr>
<tr><td></td><td>1st cleanup</td><td>Contractor</td><td>Contractor</td><td>Remove lumber and shingle scrap and other debris. Save useful material.</td></tr>
<tr><td>8th Week</td><td>Framing continues</td><td>Owner</td><td>Contractor</td><td>Exterior trim; don't forget to back-prime all exposed wood.</td></tr>
<tr><td></td><td>Siding</td><td>Owner</td><td>Carpenters</td><td></td></tr>
<tr><td></td><td>Plumbing rough-in</td><td>Plumber</td><td>Plumber</td><td>Inspection required.</td></tr>
<tr><td></td><td>HVAC rough-in</td><td>Contractor</td><td>Contractor</td><td></td></tr>
<tr><td></td><td>Measure for cabinets</td><td>Contractor</td><td>Contractor</td><td>Cabinetmaker will make allowances for drywall not yet installed.</td></tr>
<tr><td></td><td>Masonry</td><td>Owner</td><td>Mason</td><td>Brick veneer, fireplace, etc.</td></tr>
<tr><td></td><td>Concrete garage floor</td><td>Owner</td><td>Contractor</td><td>Need garage for storage.</td></tr>
<tr><td colspan="5">Note: The amount of time to complete the framing, exterior trim and siding and install all of the exterior doors and windows will vary with the size and complexity of the house.</td></tr>
<tr><td>9th Week</td><td>Electrical rough-in</td><td>Electrician</td><td>Electrician</td><td>Inspection required.</td></tr>
<tr><td></td><td>Sealing</td><td>Contractor</td><td>Contractor</td><td>All inspections must have been completed.</td></tr>
<tr><td></td><td>Wall insulation</td><td>Contractor</td><td>Contractor</td><td>Includes vapor barrier.</td></tr>
<tr><td></td><td>Garage door</td><td>Contractor</td><td>Contractor</td><td>Secure garage for storage of building materials.</td></tr>
<tr><td></td><td>Masonry</td><td>Owner</td><td>Mason</td><td>Complete masonry, steps, porches, etc.</td></tr>
<tr><td>10th Week</td><td>Drywall or plaster</td><td>Drywall by owner</td><td>Contractor</td><td>Hang and finish after insulation is installed.</td></tr>
<tr><td></td><td>Exterior paint</td><td>Painter</td><td>Painter</td><td>Get paint on exposed wood as soon as possible.</td></tr>
<tr><td></td><td>Second cleanup</td><td>Contractor</td><td>Contractor</td><td>Remove drywall scrap and other debris.</td></tr>
<tr><td></td><td>Finish drywall or plaster</td><td>Contractor</td><td>Contractor</td><td></td></tr>
</table>

Time	Task	Materials	Labor	Remarks
	Complete exterior painting	Painter	Painter	
	Install gutters and downspouts	Contractor	Contractor	After completion of painting. Paint galvanized gutters before installation.
11th Week	Prime interior walls and ceiling	Painter	Painter	Before trim installed—usually sprayed.
	Install wood flooring	Contractor	Contractor	Install but do not finish.
Note: The total time for interior trim depends upon the size and complexity of the house.				
12th Week	Interior trim	Owner	Carpenters	Install underlayment first, then trim.
13th Week	Install cabinets	Contractor	Contractor	Baseboard trim cannot be completed until cabinets are in.
	Ceramic tile	Contractor	Contractor	
14th Week	Appliances	Owner	Contractor	Installed by plumber and electrician.
	Plumbing final	Plumber	Plumber	Include sewer and water hookup. *Inspection required.*
	HVAC final	Contractor	Contractor	*Inspection required.*
	Electrical final	Electrician	Electrician	*Inspection required.*
	Electrical hookup to house	Power co.	Power co.	Must have completed inspections.
15th Week	Interior painting	Painter	Painter	Select colors ahead of time.
	Ceiling, floor insulation	Contractor	Contractor	After plumbing, HVAC, electrical completed and final inspection.
	Final cleanup	Contractor	Contractor	Cleanup of exterior before final grading.
	Final grade	Contractor	Contractor	Ensure that dust does not interfere with interior painting.
	Sidewalks and patios	Owner	Contractor	After final grading.
16th Week	Railing	Contractor	Contractor	
	Driveway	Contractor	Contractor	Install final surface, gravel, concrete or asphalt.
	Landscape	Contractor	Contractor	
	Finish wood floors	Contractor	Contractor	Allow about a week; keep all others out of house.
17th Week	Install flint paper	Owner	Owner	Protect floor finish.
	Lay vinyl floor	Contractor	Contractor	
	Lay carpet	Contractor	Contractor	
	Occupancy permit	Building official		

■ — APPENDIX D — ■

Contractors' Tasks

This listing provides assistance to the homeowner/general contractor by showing what work contractors in the various trades normally perform.

Local customs, however, may differ from this list, so check with the contractors in your area to verify in detail what work to expect from each trade.

Item	Who Does	Remarks
Building permit	Owner	May include payment of sewer and water hookup fees.
Site work Clearing Grading Excavation Driveway Culverts Backfill	Site contractor	Materials needed: Fill dirt, culvert pipe. Determine who furnishes. Include final grading here or with landscape contractor.
House layout	Contractor/Owner	Determine who furnishes material.
Concrete Footings Slabs Sidewalks Patio Exterior steps Driveway	Concrete contractor	Most small contractors prefer that owner provide the material, which consists of concrete, rebar, mesh, and poly.
Soil poisoning	Contractor specialist in termite control	Should include five-year warranty.
Framing Exterior doors All windows Roofing paper Exterior trim	Framing crew*	Owner furnishes all materials through building supplier. Exception may be nails if crew uses powered nail gun system.
Siding	Siding crew*	Owner furnishes all material. If siding is vinyl or aluminum, crew should have experience and equipment for this material. Crew may want to furnish material.
Interior wood trim	Trim crew*	Crew completes all interior wood trim. Usually can install cabinets and countertops. Use if cabinet supplier does not install. Includes hanging all interior doors.
*All of these functions may be performed by the same crew.		
Masonry	Masonry contractor	Owner usually furnishes all materials; block, brick, horizontal reinforcing, rebar, masonry sand, steel and concrete lintels, foundation vents and doors, anchor bolts.
Waterproofing	Mason, roofer or other—depends on type of waterproofing	Determine who furnishes materials. Usually mason will do parging and roofer will do tar or elastomeric roofing material. Waterproofing specialist can handle whole job.
Shingles Flashing Gutters Downspouts	Roofer	Owner furnishes shingles. Roofer furnishes nails and flashing material. Roofer may furnish gutters and downspouts.
Cabinets	Cabinet shop	If contractor is with supplier only, installation is usually by interior trim crew.

Item	Who Does	Remarks
Drywall, plaster, plaster veneer	Drywall or plaster contractor	Drywall paneling or plaster lathing usually furnished by owner. Verify all other materials with contractor.
Plumbing	Plumbing contractor	Contractor furnishes all materials and labor.
Electrical system	Electrical contractor	Contractor furnishes all materials and labor. Verify that contract includes hookup of electrical power to hot water heater, appliances and heating system. Also cook stove venting system.
Sewer or septic system	Contractor	Sewer work can be done by plumber. Septic system usually requires specialist. All materials and labor by contractor.
Well water hookup	Contractor	May be plumbing contractor for water hookup. Well digging usually requires specialist. All materials and labor by contractor.
Heating, ventilating, air-conditioning	HVAC contractor	Contractor furnishes all labor and material.
Sealing and insulating	Contractor	Contractor furnishes all materials and labor. Because sealing is relatively new in house construction, this job is better done by a contractor specializing in this work.
Ceramic	Contractor	Contractor furnishes all labor and material.
Floor		
Walls		
Flooring	Contractor	Contractor may furnish all labor and material.
Wood		
Carpet		
Vinyl		
Other		
Appliances	Electrician or Plumber	Equipment usually provided by supplier. Installation by plumber and/or electrician.
Garage door	Contractor	Usually the supplier will also do the installation. If not, carpentry crews are usually qualified for the job.
Cleanup		
Exterior	Contractor	One or two people with pickup truck.
Interior	Contractor	Specialists in interior cleaning.
Landscaping	Landscape contractor or owner	Depends on extent of the landscape job. Contractor usually furnishes all materials and labor. Contractor will normally guarantee plants.

Glossary

active solar heat Heating system using heat from the sun as its sole source of energy and using mechanical means for distributing the heat throughout the house.

air infiltration Movement of air into and out of the heated (or cooled) space of a house through cracks in floors, walls and ceilings (see Chapter 12, Air Infiltration).

amortization The repayment of the principal of a mortgage.

ampere An expression of the amount of electricity moving through a circuit. Also, an expression of the capacity of a cable or wire to carry electricity.

anchor bolts Large (usually ½ inch in diameter and 12 inches to 16 inches long) bolts set in the foundation wall or slab (when foundation is an integrated slab) that anchors the sole plate to the foundation (see Figure 6.7).

angle iron Steel bars shaped like an "L" with variable length. Used as lintels to support brick veneer over window and door openings (see Figure 6.6).

apron Piece of wood interior trim under the window stool (sill) (see Figure 18.2).

awning window Window that pivots on a horizontal hinge at the top (see Figure 8.1).

backfill Material, usually dirt, sand or gravel, used to change the level of the ground for specific purposes such as to fill in the voids around the house between the excavation for the basement and the basement wall.

back prime Primer paint applied to the back side (nonexposed side) of exterior wood to prevent warping of the wood.

balloon framing Framing system in a two-story house in which the studs of the outer walls are one continuous piece from the first floor to the roof system (see Figure 7.2).

baseboard Interior trim, usually wood, laid at the base of the wall to cover the gap at the wall/floor seam (see Figure 18.1 and Figure 18.2).

BATT Insulation in the form of rolls in various widths, lengths and thicknesses.

batten The outer board of board and batten siding (see Figure 9.4).

batter boards Wood boards that hold the strings used to mark the outer limits of the foundation. They are removed after the foundation is complete.

bay window A window composed of three or more flat sections that juts out from the exterior wall (see Figure 8.1).

beam Also called girder. A structural member, usually wood or steel, used to hold heavy loads over relatively long spans (see Figure 7.1).

bid An offer from a contractor or supplier to provide labor and/or material for a certain price.

bifold door A folding door normally used on closets (see Figure 8.5).

blocking A method of laying material between joists and rafters to prevent twisting and to increase strength of the framing (see Figure 7.6).

blueprints The drawings indicating the plans and elevations for a structure.

board foot Measurement unit for lumber. One board foot is the equivalent of a board 1 inch thick (nominal), 12 inches wide (nominal) and 12 inches long (actual).

bow window A curved window composed of several sections that juts out from the exterior wall (see Figure 8.1).

brick molding Molding used as exterior trim around doors and windows to finish the joint of the window or door and the siding, both brick and wood.

brick ties Galvanized corrugated steel straps about 1 inch wide and 4 inches long used by the mason to tie the brick to the wood framing.

brick veneer A single thickness of brick laid on the outside of a masonry or wood-framed wall as the exterior finish.

bridging A method of installing specially cut wood or steel bracing to prevent twisting of joists and rafters and to strengthen the overall framing (see Figure 7.6).

building code A set of building standards adopted by a local governing body to establish minimums for building houses.

building paper A heavy black paper used in the building trade to prevent moisture seepage.

building setback lines Lines that parallel the front, back and sides of the lot and establish the area in which the house must be built.

built-up roof A form of roof finish consisting of several layers of roofing paper with tar in between. Usually topped with gravel. This type of roofing is used primarily where the roof pitch is below 3/12 (see Figure 10.4).

cantilever A part of the house structure that extends out from the exterior wall, such as a bay or bow window; or, in some colonial plans, the second floor projects out over the first floor 2 feet or so.

casement window A window that swings on a vertical axis like a door (see Figure 8.1).

casing Wood interior trim applied around windows and doors (see Figure 18.2).

cathedral ceiling Framing structure that eliminates the ceiling joists and exposes the underside of the roof joists to the living area (see Figure 7.12).

caulking The process of applying latex or a similar material in order to seal exposed wood, aluminum and vinyl joints and seams.

cement A powdered binding element mixed with water, sand and aggregate (stone) to form concrete.

chair rail Wood interior trim applied to the wall at approximately chair back height to protect the wall and improve design (see Figure 18.2).

chase Usually refers to a "duct chase" that is part of the house framing in which heating and cooling ducts are installed. Separated from the room by drywall, plaster or paneling.

chimney cap A metal device applied over the top of the chimney to prevent rain and snow from falling down the flue.

circuit breaker An electrical safety device located in the service panel that automatically opens the circuit (stops the flow of electricity) when the capacity of the circuit is exceeded. Can be easily reset. Replaces the older fuse system.

clearing The process of removing trees and other growth from a lot so that construction can begin.

collar beam A brace between rafters in roof construction (see Figure 7.10).

colonial house By common usage, a style denoting a two-story house where both floors have about the same square footage. There is a true architectural colonial design, however, with distinctive features that are not included in the majority of two-story house designs.

concrete A mixture of cement, water, sand and an aggregate (stone) that hardens into a solid building material.

concrete block Building blocks formed of concrete with a height of 8 inches, length of 16 inches and widths varying from 4 inches to 12 inches. Used primarily for the construction of foundations and walls.

corbel Extending bricks out of pattern to provide a base for material installed on top, usually concrete (see Figure 11.4).

corner board Vertical pieces of wood installed at the corners of the house to trim lap and other wood siding (see Figure 7.16).

crawl space The space between the grade of the lot and the floor joists of houses with wood first floors (see Figure 6.3).

cricket A form of roof flashing applied between the upper side of a chimney and the roof, shaped to prevent water from settling at this point (see Figure 10.5).

crown molding Wood interior trim installed at the junction of the ceiling and wall (see Figure 18.2).

culvert A concrete or metal pipe that allows water to flow in a drain ditch underneath the driveway (see Figure 4.1).

cupping A form of distortion in thin lumber that results in the lumber curling around the long axis.

curing A process by which maximum strength in freshly poured and troweled slab concrete is attained by keeping it moist over a period of time (at least several days).

diffuser A metal cover on the room outlet of the air supply that directs the flow of air.

direct gain The acquisition of passive solar heat by collection through a window and storage in a wall or floor (see Figure 14.1).

direct hire Employment of labor directly in that the employer is responsible for payroll deductions, workers' compensation and so forth.

door stop Wood trim around the inside of the door frame (jamb) against which the door rests when closed.

dormer A window whose framing protrudes through the roof, usually found in a story-and-a-half house (see Figure 1.1).

double-hung window Window design in that both the upper and lower sashes move vertically within slots in the frame (see Figure 8.1).

dropped ceiling A ceiling, consisting of a light steel frame with rectangular composition board fillers, hung below the standard house ceiling.

drywall An interior wall finish material consisting of large boards of gypsum with paper finish.

dual glazing Also called insulating glass. Double panes of glass with air space between.

duct A large tubular or squared conduit made of fiberglass or galvanized sheet metal that carries heated or cooled air throughout the house.

earthstone Hand-molded clay tile floor covering.

elastomeric Synthetic rubber-like material used to waterproof flat built-up roofs as well as wood and masonry walls above and below grade. Has a high degree of elasticity even in very cold weather and resists the effects of the sun to a greater degree than the tar and paper built-up roof.

elevation A drawing of the vertical sides of a house. Also, the relative level of the ground at any particular point.

envelope house A house designed so that both cool and warm air are circulated around the house from crawl space to side wall to ceiling to side wall to crawl space.

equity The value of a house and lot (or any real estate) beyond the total amount owed on it in mortgages, liens and so forth.

exterior trim Trim material, wood or aluminum, applied to the exterior of a house (see Figure 7.16).

facia A trim board that runs parallel to the eaves of a roof.

fill Material, usually dirt, sand or gravel, applied to raise the elevation of the ground.

flashing Metal or vinyl material used to divert water from junctions in the roof (see Figure 10.5).

flint paper A special paper sold by building supply stores for use in covering finished floors to protect them until the construction is finished.

flitch plate A plate of steel or plywood bolted or nailed between 2-inch lumber to form a strong beam for relatively long spans.

folding door A door made of wood, plastic or other material that folds within the door frame (see Figure 8.7).

footing The concrete (or gravel in the case of the all-wood foundation) upon which the foundation rests (see Chapter 4, Starting the Construction).

forced-warm-air heating A heating system based on the principle of forcing heated air through a duct system (see Chapter 15, Heating and Cooling Considerations).

form Material, usually wood, built to hold concrete in place until solidified.

friction fit Usually refers to insulation batts that do not have an integrated vapor barrier. Held in place in the walls by the friction of the insulation material against the studs.

frieze board Wood trim board applied at the juncture of the siding and the soffit (see Figure 7.16).

grade stake A wood or metal peg placed so that the top of the peg indicates the final level of fill dirt, concrete or other material used to change the grade or elevation.

grading The task of using machinery or hand tools to change the level of the ground to conform to the construction requirements, such as the floor of a garage, a patio and so forth.

header A wood beam placed in the framing to span the opening of a door, window, pulldown stair, skylight, etc.

headwall A masonry wall built at each end of a culvert to prevent erosion of the driveway fill and to improve appearance.

hearth The part of the fireplace usually built of brick, slate or tile, extending into the room from the fireplace opening.

heat pump A heating system based on transferring heat rather than manufacturing it (see Figure 15.1).

house layout The establishment of the vertical and horizontal location of the foundation of a house by setting up the batter board system.

HVAC The Heating, Ventilating and Air-Conditioning system (see Chapter 15, Heating and Cooling Considerations).

index A term used in mortgages, particularly those with variable rates; an index establishes the base from which the interest rate of the mortgage may vary. If the index used in the mortgage increases, the interest rate of the mortgage also increases. Examples of these indexes are the Federal Home Loan Bank Board's national average mortgage rate, the U. S. Treasury bill rate and the prime rate. (See Chapter 2, Arranging Contracts, Financing and Insurance.)

insulating glass Two or more glass panes in a frame with insulating air space in between.

insulation The material used to establish a barrier to the movement of heat through the outer skin of a house living area.

job built Items, such as bookcases, that are built on the job site rather than in a factory or shop.

joist The load-bearing beam in a floor or ceiling (see Figure 7.1 and Figure 7.2).

let-in Relates to those structural members that are cut into other members, such as corner bracing (see Figure 7.7).

lintel Steel or concrete beams that span openings in the masonry wall of a house over doors and windows (see Figure 6.5 and Figure 6.6).

masonry Work consisting of the use of brick, stone or block.

mil A measurement, equal to 1/1000 inch, used to determine the size of wire and the thickness of a sheet of polyethylene.

mortar joint The joint between bricks, stone, block and tile and the finish treatment of the mortar.

mud A slang term referring to the setting of tile, brick, stone or similar material into a bed of mortar, usually in floor or wall finishing.

mullion The vertical member that separates the sections of a double, triple, quadruple, etc., window.

muntins The vertical and horizontal wood, plastic or metal members between the panes of glass in a window or door. For most insulating windows or doors, the muntin is normally a decorative device placed between the glass sheets covering the entire sash and does not separate panes of glass.

OC Means "on centers" and refers to the distance between the centers of parallel structural members such as studs—16 inches OC.

panelized Refers to a method of home construction in which sections of the wall are factory built in panels, transported to the site and assembled by the framing crew.

parging The placement of a coating of mortar over a masonry wall, generally for waterproofing purposes.

passive solar heat The use of heat from the sun to warm a house or its parts without any machinery with the exception of small fans to assist in circulation—see Chapter 14, Heating with Sunshine (Solar Energy).

permit An authorization by the local government to perform certain construction.

picture frame A method of trimming the interior of a window in that the stool and apron at the bottom of the window are replaced by the same type and size of trim used at the top and sides of the window, giving the appearance of a "picture frame."

pier Masonry or wood vertical member that supports floor beams or girders. Principally used in crawl space construction.

pilaster The thickening of a masonry, concrete block, brick or concrete wall at selected points to increase its strength (see Figure 6.2 and Figure 23.6).

plan A drawing, usually supplemented by written specifications, that indicates the details of construction of a house. Also, those particular drawings that show the horizontal views of the house compared to "elevations" that show the vertical views of the house.

plank-and-beam framing Method of framing in that heavier timbers with greater spans are used (see Figure 7.3).

plaster veneer An interior wall finish in which one or two thin coats of plaster are applied to a plaster lath base.

plastic housewrap A thin, about 6-mil, plastic, roll sheet material used to wrap exterior walls of the house over the sheathing. It prevents air from moving through the wall and reduces the cost of energy for cooling and heating.

plastic laminate Layered plastic material manufactured in a variety of colors and designs used for countertops and similar items in house construction.

plate Horizontal structural member in the wall. There are three types of platform framing: sill, sole and top plates (see Figure 7.1, Figure 7.2 and Figure 7.3).

platform framing A method of framing in which each floor has its own set of studs (see Figure 7.1).

pocket door A door that slides into a slot in the adjacent wall.

polyethylene A plastic sheet material used largely for vapor barriers in walls and in crawl spaces on the ground.

prehung door A door that is delivered to the job with frame and hinges attached. May also have the casing installed in part.

pulldown stairs Folding stairs used to provide access to the attic. Folds up into ceiling and attic.

R-value A number indicating the relative efficiency of a material to insulate from heat loss. The higher the R, the more efficient the material for insulation purposes.

radiant heating A heating system in which the heat is transferred principally by movement through the air as a wave similar to light.

rafter A structural member of the roof (see Figure 7.1).

rancher A house design on one floor.

rake molding Trim molding applied on top of the rake board (see Figure 7.16).

reinforcing bar (rebar) Steel bars with diameters of ¼ inch and greater used to increase the strength of masonry and concrete.

retaining wall A wall designed to prevent erosion and collapse of a dirt bank (see Figure 11.5).

ridge board A wood structural member at the peak of the roof against which the rafters are nailed (see Figure 7.2).

rough opening The size of the opening in the framing needed to accept a window, door or other item that is to be installed within the framing.

row lock A method of laying brick in a sloped horizontal position usually used on the exterior under windows and doors.

salt-treated lumber Lumber that has had a salt solution forced into it by high pressure to increase the ability of the lumber to withstand moisture and insects.

section A type of drawing that represents the details of part of the structure in a manner as though that part had been sliced vertically by a large knife (see Figure 6.4).

septic system A sewage disposal system that releases sewage to be absorbed into the ground (see Figure 4.3).

shake A wood shingle, usually cedar, that has been split by hand rather than machine.

sheathing Material, usually 4 feet x 8 feet or 2 feet x 8 feet, applied to exterior walls and roofs directly to the studs and rafters. May be plywood, impregnated composition board or rigid insulation material.

shingle molding Molding applied over the rake board just under the shingles (see Figure 7.16).

shoe molding The interior wood trim that is installed to fill the gap between the baseboard and the finished floor; it is usually not used with carpeting.

siding Material applied to the outside of the exterior walls.

sill cock Exterior water faucet.

sill plate The wood plate on top of the foundation that supports the floor joists (see Figure 7.1).

sizing Adhesive applied over bare plaster and drywall to provide better adhesion for wallpaper and other wallcovering.

skylight A window installed in the roof (see Figure 8.2).

soffit Underside of the roof overhang (see Figure 7.16).

soil pipe Waste (drain) pipe from a toilet.

specifications (specs) Written details of the overall plan that support and add to the blueprints (see Appendix A).

SPF Framing lumber consisting of a mix of spruce, western pine and fir.

splash block A preformed block of concrete or other material placed at the end of a downspout to prevent erosion of the yard.

spoil Material, usually dirt, removed from an excavation.

square A term pertaining to the area of the roof, meaning 100 square feet.

stick built A slang term denoting that method of framing in which the structure is job built from uncut lumber.

stool Another name for the interior window sill (see Figure 18.2).

stucco A cement type of siding that is applied over a masonry wall or a wood frame (on metal mesh lathing). (See Figure 9.5.)

SYP Southern Yellow Pine.

take-off The computation of the materials required for construction of a house such as lumber take-off or masonry take-off.

tempered glass Glass that has been given special treatment to minimize the danger of cutting when broken.

topsoil Dirt usually lying on top of the lot that is very fertile and suitable for supporting the growth of grasses and shrubs.

track The top and bottom plates over the steel studs in steel framing.

trowel finish A very smooth concrete finish suitable for interior floors and garages.

truss A plant-built structure used in roof and floor construction (see Figure 7.11).

U-value A numerical value assigned to different materials to indicate their relative efficiency in insulation. U is the reciprocal of R, hence the larger the U, the *less* the ability of the material to insulate.

vapor barrier A material, such as polyurethane, applied to walls, ceilings and floors on the inside of the house living space to prevent moisture from moving into the house's insulation and making it less effective.

vent Metal or wood piece that permits the ventilation of crawl spaces. The metal vents can be closed to reduce air flow during the winter.

volt An indication of the pressure pushing electricity through a conductor.

wainscot Wood, ceramic tile or other material applied to an interior wall to a height of about 3 to 4 feet (see Figure 18.2).

wallcovering A general term for material used to decorate walls, such as wallpaper, fabrics, vinyls and precovered paneling.

waste pipe Pipe that carries the waste from the fixture to the sewer.

water hammer Noise in pipes caused by the sudden stoppage of fast-running water when the valve is turned off. It may also be caused by turning off one valve when another valve in the house is partially open.

watt The power required to operate electric equipment. It is the product of the amperes multipled by the voltage.

whole-house exhaust fan A large fan installed in the ceiling or attic that will evacuate the air from the whole house in a reasonably short time.

Index

New

CD-ROM Money Maker Kits from Dearborn Multimedia

Features:

- *25 minute video help with the author*
- *12-28 interactive printable forms per CD-ROM*
- *On-Line glossary of terms*
- *Quick-start video tutorial*
- *Interactive printable book on CD-ROM*
  (Print out sections you like for closer reading or writing notes.)

Start Enjoying Greater Financial Freedom
Triple Your Investment Portfolio
SAVE Thousands on Real Estate as a Buyer or Seller

Personal Finance

The Budget Kit

Create a Smart Budget That Saves You Time and Money

With this multimedia kit:
- Automate your expenses and cash flow
- Save your money for the things that really matter to you.
- Spot your actual spending patterns.
- Stay organized at tax time.
- Start enjoying greater financial freedom

Order No. 1800-1301
$34.95

Judy Lawrence uses her years of experience as a personal financial counselor to show how to organize a personal budget.

Investing

How To Buy Mutual Funds the Smart Way

Find Out How Easily You Can Buy Mutual Funds and Earn Profits the Smart Way

With this multimedia kit:
- Set your own goals and build your lifetime investment program
- Discover an easy way to avoid brokers' fees and reduce your expenses
- Monitor your funds with fully interactive worksheets

Order No. 1800-0701
$34.95

Stephen Littauer has been involved in the sale and marketing of financial and investment products for over 30 years.

Real Estate

The Homebuyer's Kit

Find the Right House Fast

With this multimedia kit:
- Negotiate with confidence
- Prequalify using the automated formulas to determine your best mortgage terms
- Chart your progress using the interactive home comparison forms

Order No. 1800-0401
$34.95

More than 10 million readers watch for **Edith Lank's** award-winning real estate column, "*House Calls*".

The Mortgage Kit

Save Big $$$ When Financing Your Home

With this multimedia kit:
- Select the right loan
- Lock in the best interest rate
- Prequalify using the automated forms and checklists
- Determine how much money you will save when refinancing
- Organize your mortgage search using the interactive checklists

Order No. 1800-2201
$34.95

Thomas C. Steinmetz was a senior strategic planner with the Federal National Mortgage Association.
Phillip Whitt has worked 12 years in residential mortgage lending.

Real Estate

The Homeowner's Kit

The Homeowner's Kit Will Help You Protect Your Most Valuable Asset—Your Home!

With this multimedia kit:
- Save money and conserve energy
- Refinance for the lowest rates

Just point and click to discover:
- Hundreds of home safety and security tips
- How to inspect your home

Order No. 1800-1901
$34.95

Robert de Heer is a professional real estate author who simplifies home-owning with specific money-saving steps.

Small Business

The Business Planning Guide

Plan for Success in Your New Venture

With this multimedia kit:
- Just plug in your financials to plan your dream business
- Point and click to automate planning and financial forecasts
- Start, expand, or buy a business

Order No. 1800-0101
$34.95

David H. Bangs, Jr. is founder of Upstart Publishing Company, Inc.